CRITICAL ROLE

VOX MACHINA

ORIGINS

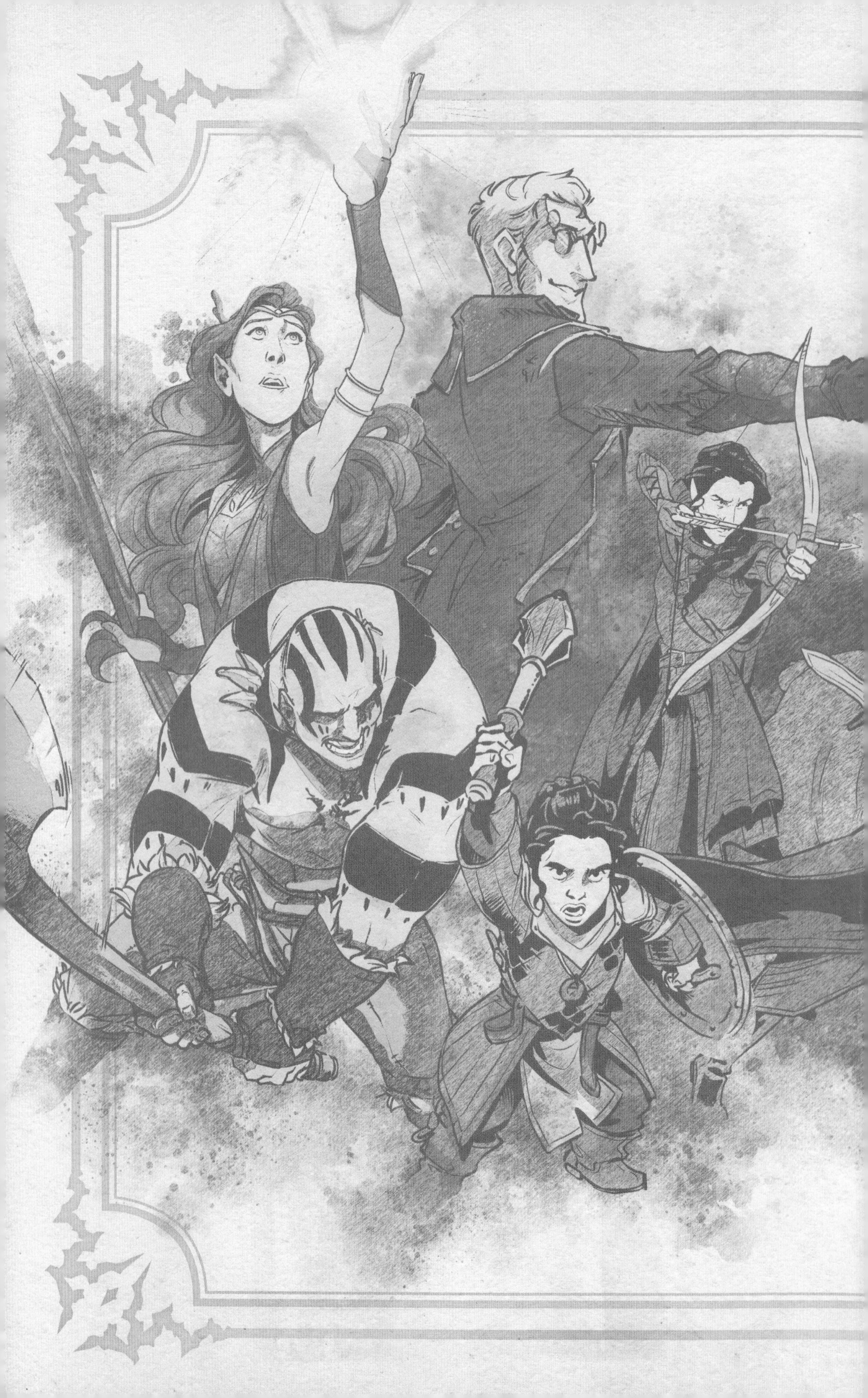

CRITICAL ROLE
Vox Machina™
ORIGINS

Story and Characters Created by the Cast of
CRITICAL ROLE

Script
JODY HOUSER

Art
OLIVIA SAMSON

Colors
MSASSYK

Letters
ARIANA MAHER

Cover Art
WILLIAM KIRKBY

Limited Edition Lithograph Art by
HUNTER SEVERN BONYUN
with **STEPHAN MCGOWAN**

DARK HORSE BOOKS

President and Publisher
MIKE RICHARDSON

Editor
RACHEL ROBERTS

Assistant Editor
JENNY BLENK

Designer
CINDY CACEREZ-SPRAGUE

Digital Art Technician
SAMANTHA HUMMER

⚜

Special thanks to **LAURA BAILEY, ADRIENNE CHO, TALIESIN JAFFE, ASHLEY
JOHNSON, MATTHEW MERCER, LIAM O'BRIEN, MARISHA RAY, SAM RIEGEL,
TRAVIS WILLINGHAM,** and **BEN VAN DER FLUIT** at Critical Role and to
KARI YADRO at Dark Horse Comics.

Facebook.com/DarkHorseComics
Twitter.com/DarkHorseComics

Comicshoplocator.com

CRITICAL ROLE: VOX MACHINA ORIGINS

This volume collects issues #1 through #6 of the Dark Horse comic-book series
Critical Role: Vox Machina Origins series II.

Published by Dark Horse Books
A division of Dark Horse Comics LLC
10956 SE Main Street
Milwaukie, OR 97222

DarkHorse.com

First paperback edition: June 2020
Limited edition: June 2020
eBook ISBN: 978-1-50671-450-9
ISBN: 978-1-50671-449-3
Limited edition ISBN: 978-1-50672-254-2

3 5 7 9 10 8 6 4 2
Printed in Canada

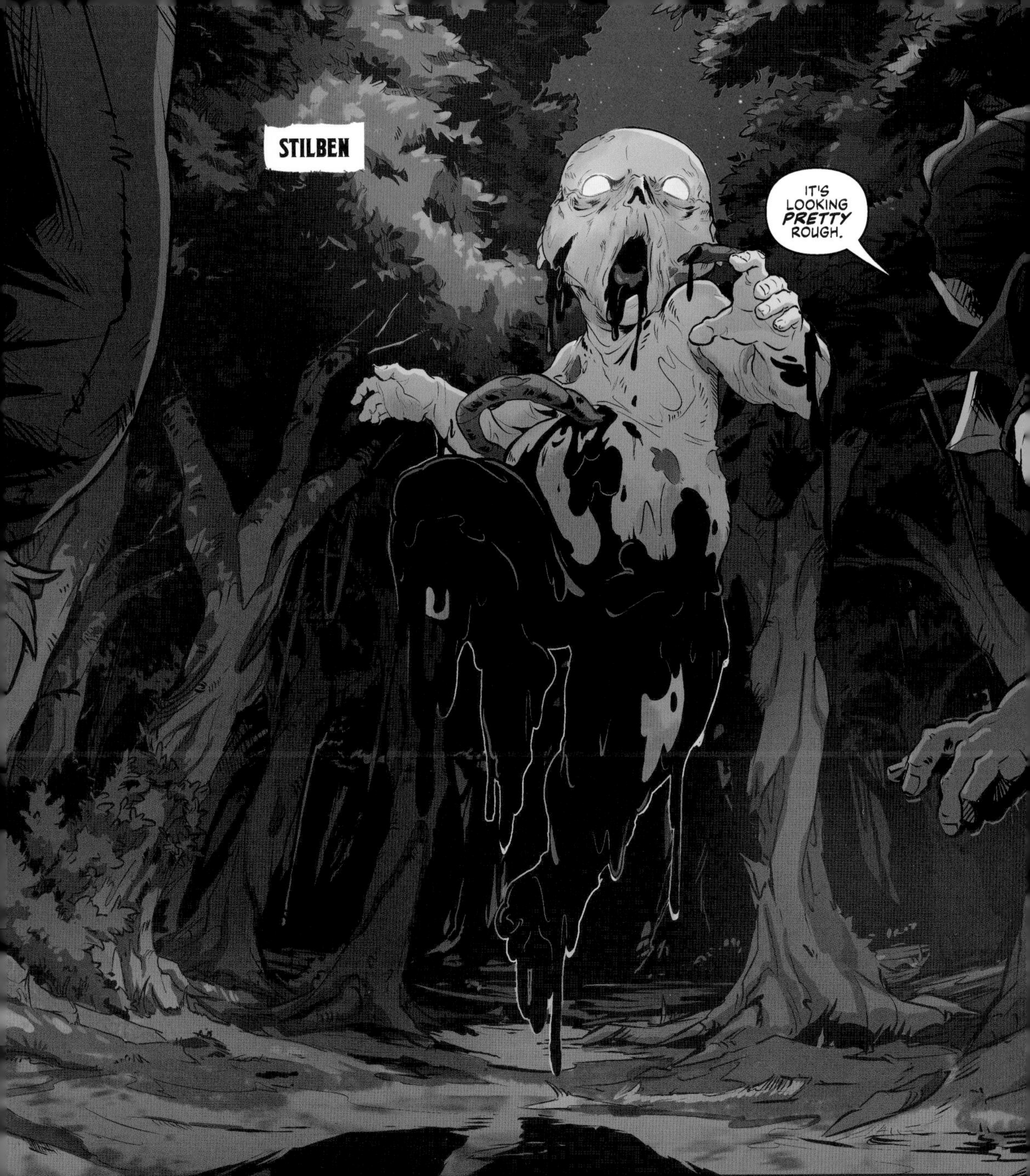
STILBEN
IT'S LOOKING PRETTY ROUGH.

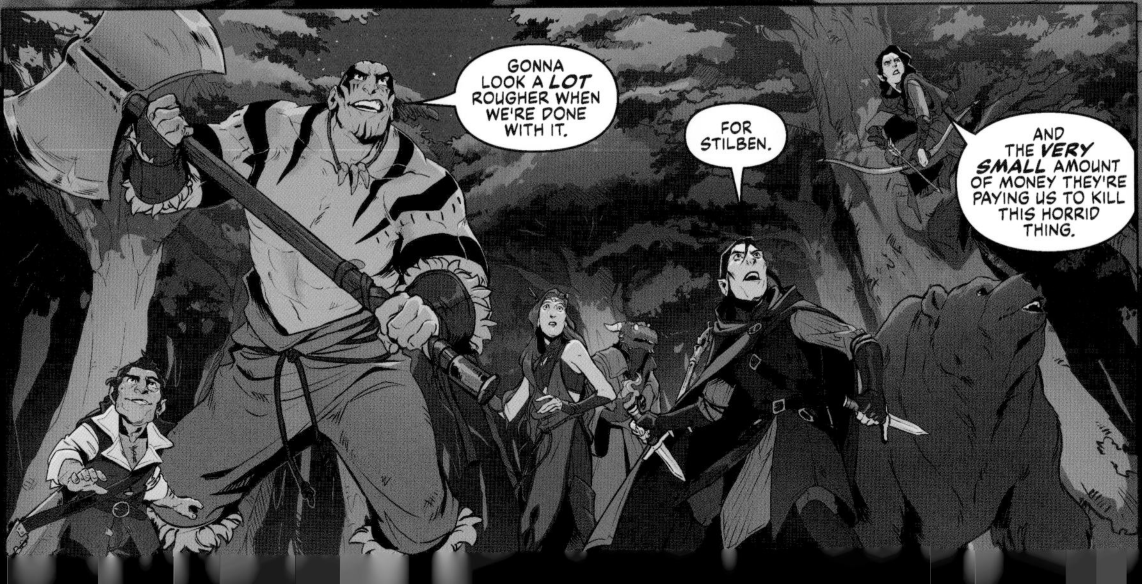
GONNA LOOK A LOT ROUGHER WHEN WE'RE DONE WITH IT.
FOR STILBEN.
AND THE VERY SMALL AMOUNT OF MONEY THEY'RE PAYING US TO KILL THIS HORRID THING.

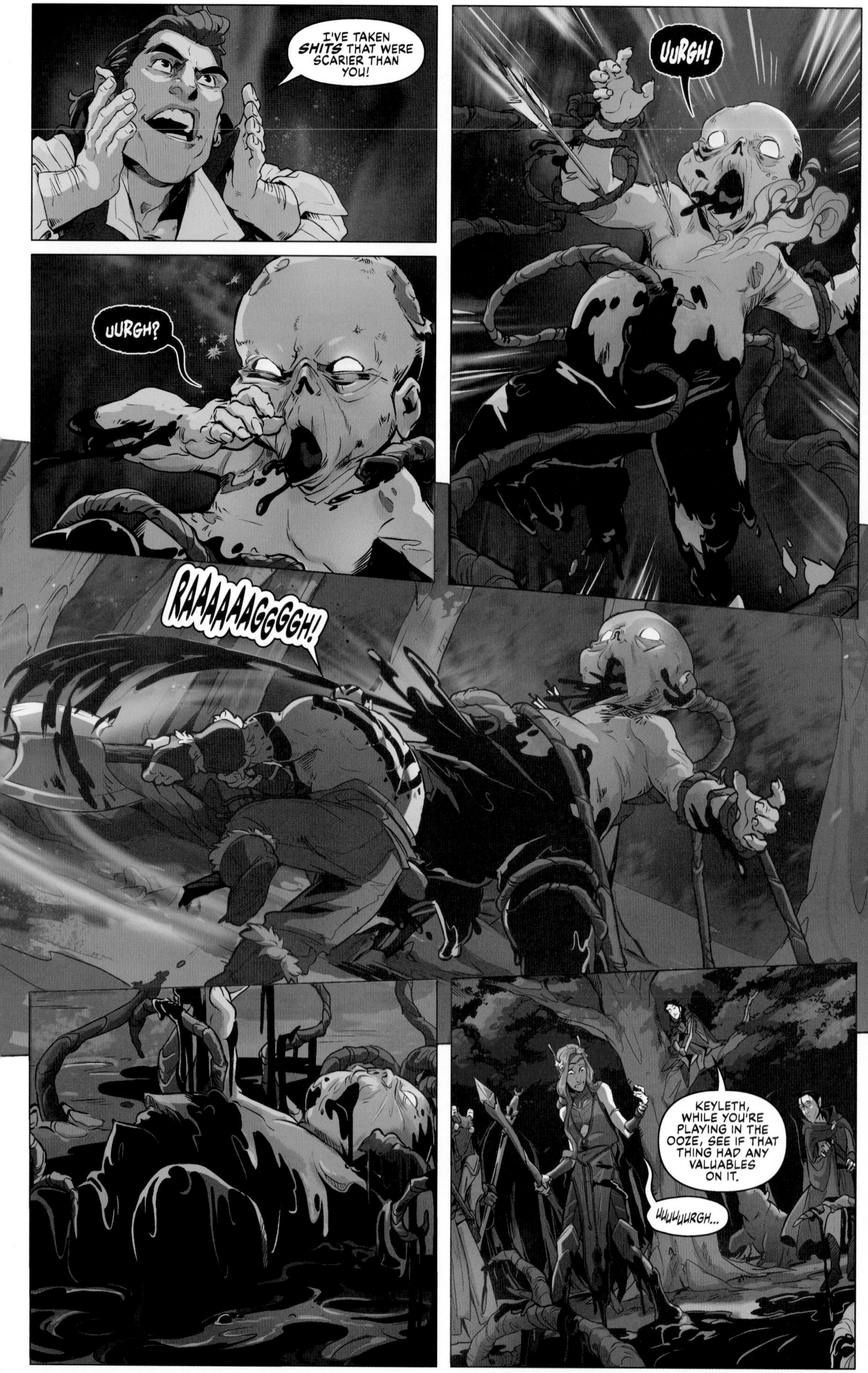
I'VE TAKEN SHITS THAT WERE SCARIER THAN YOU!
UURGH!
UURGH?
RAAAAAAGGGGH!
KEYLETH, WHILE YOU'RE PLAYING IN THE OOZE, SEE IF THAT THING HAD ANY VALUABLES ON IT.
UUUUUURGH...

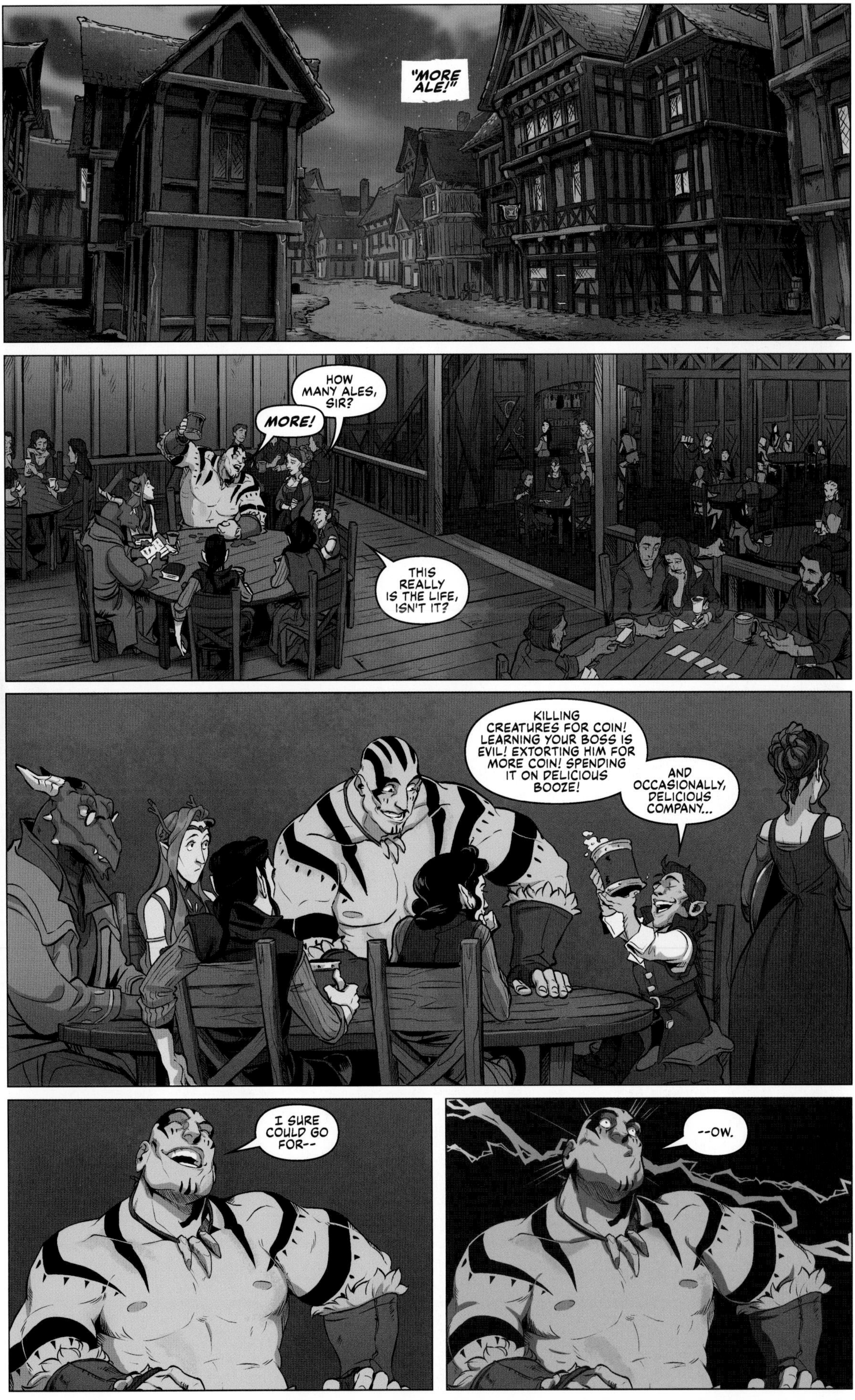
"MORE ALE!"
HOW MANY ALES, SIR?
MORE!
THIS REALLY IS THE LIFE, ISN'T IT?
KILLING CREATURES FOR COIN! LEARNING YOUR BOSS IS EVIL! EXTORTING HIM FOR MORE COIN! SPENDING IT ON DELICIOUS BOOZE!
AND OCCASIONALLY, DELICIOUS COMPANY...
I SURE COULD GO FOR--
--OW.

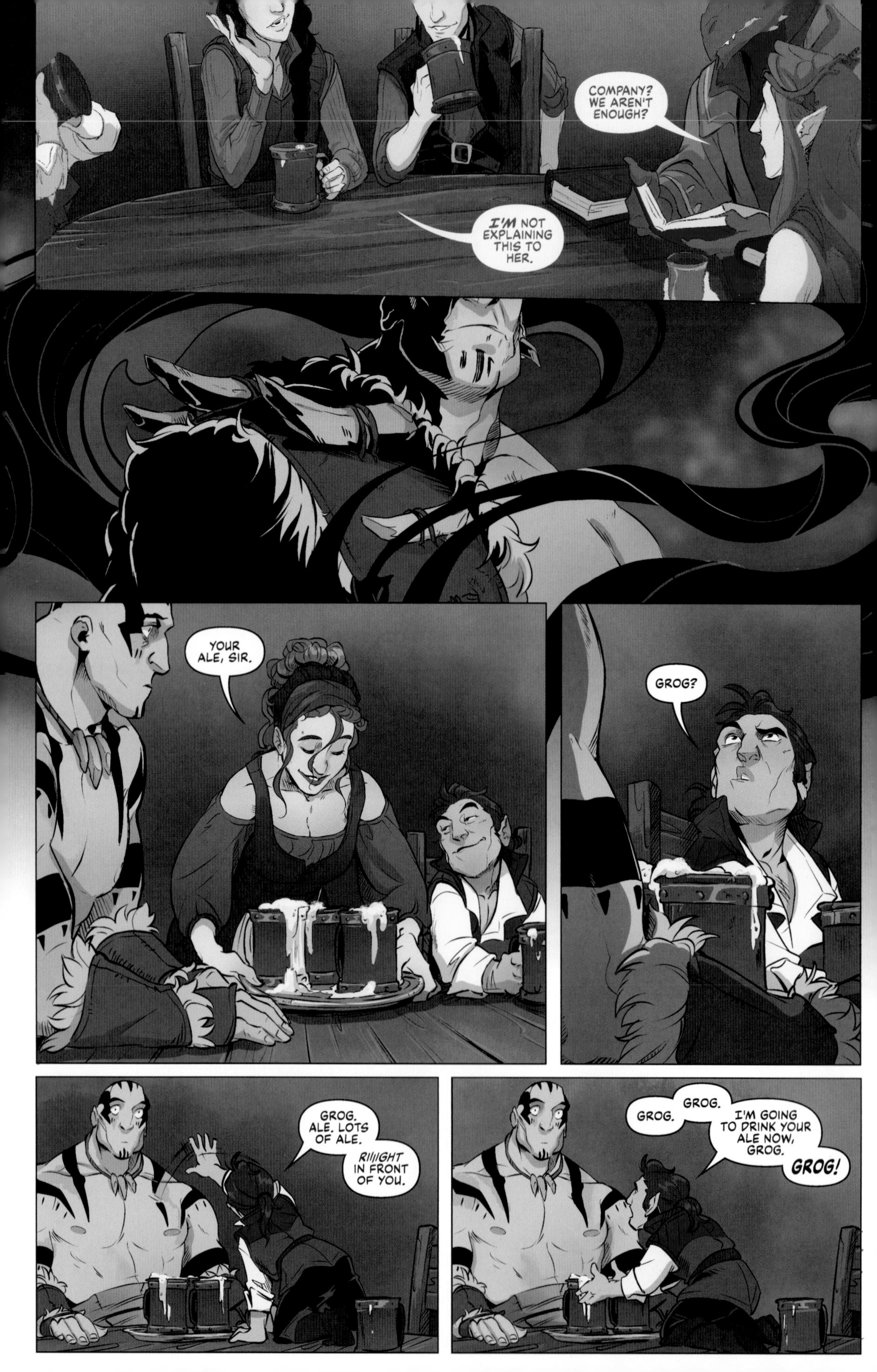
COMPANY? WE AREN'T ENOUGH?
I'M NOT EXPLAINING THIS TO HER.
YOUR ALE, SIR.
GROG?
GROG. ALE. LOTS OF ALE.
RIIIIGHT IN FRONT OF YOU.
GROG.
GROG.
I'M GOING TO DRINK YOUR ALE NOW, GROG.
GROG!

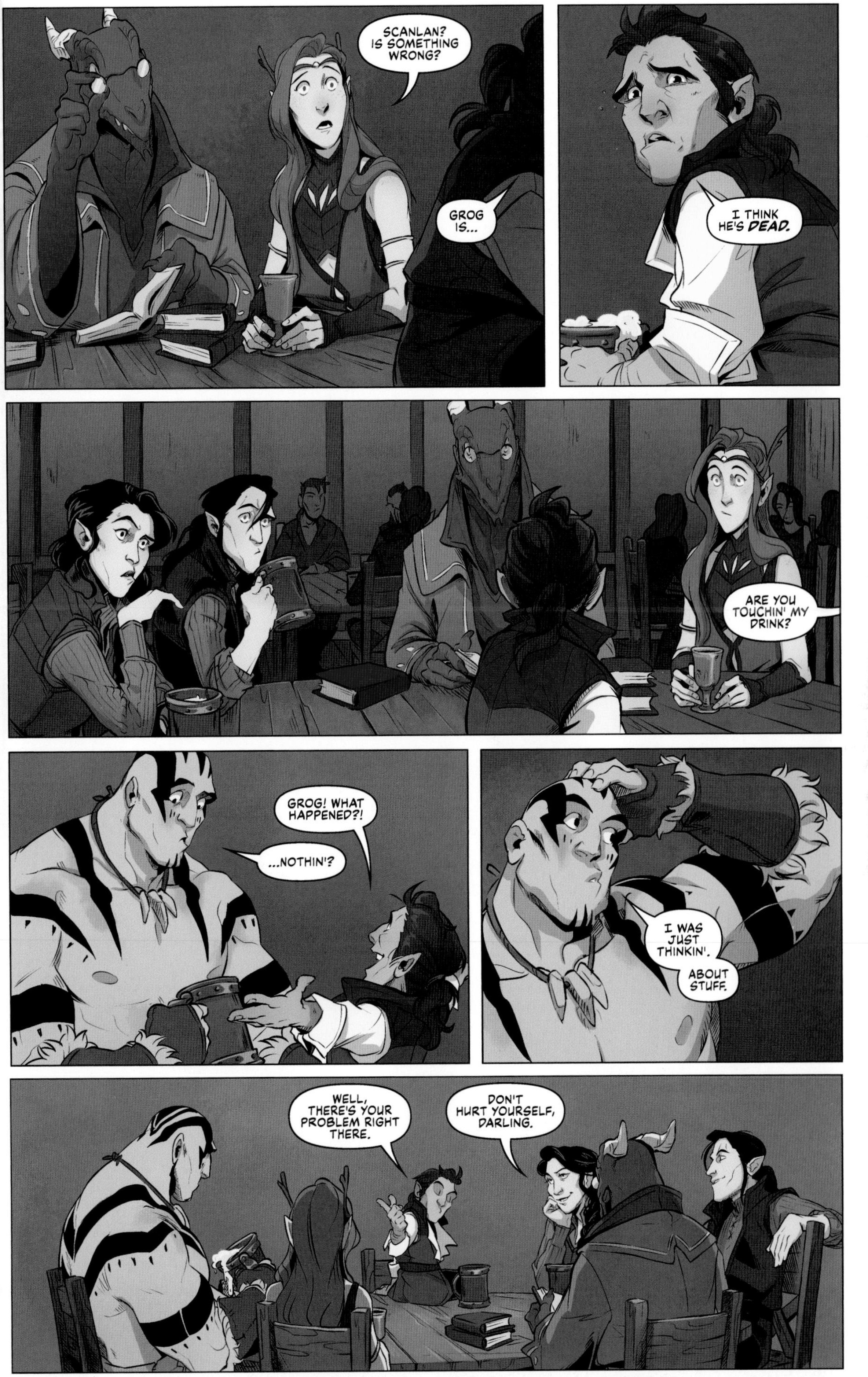
SCANLAN? IS SOMETHING WRONG?
GROG IS...
I THINK HE'S *DEAD.*
ARE YOU TOUCHIN' MY DRINK?
GROG! WHAT HAPPENED?!
...NOTHIN'?
I WAS JUST THINKIN'.
ABOUT STUFF.
WELL, THERE'S YOUR PROBLEM RIGHT THERE.
DON'T HURT YOURSELF, DARLING.

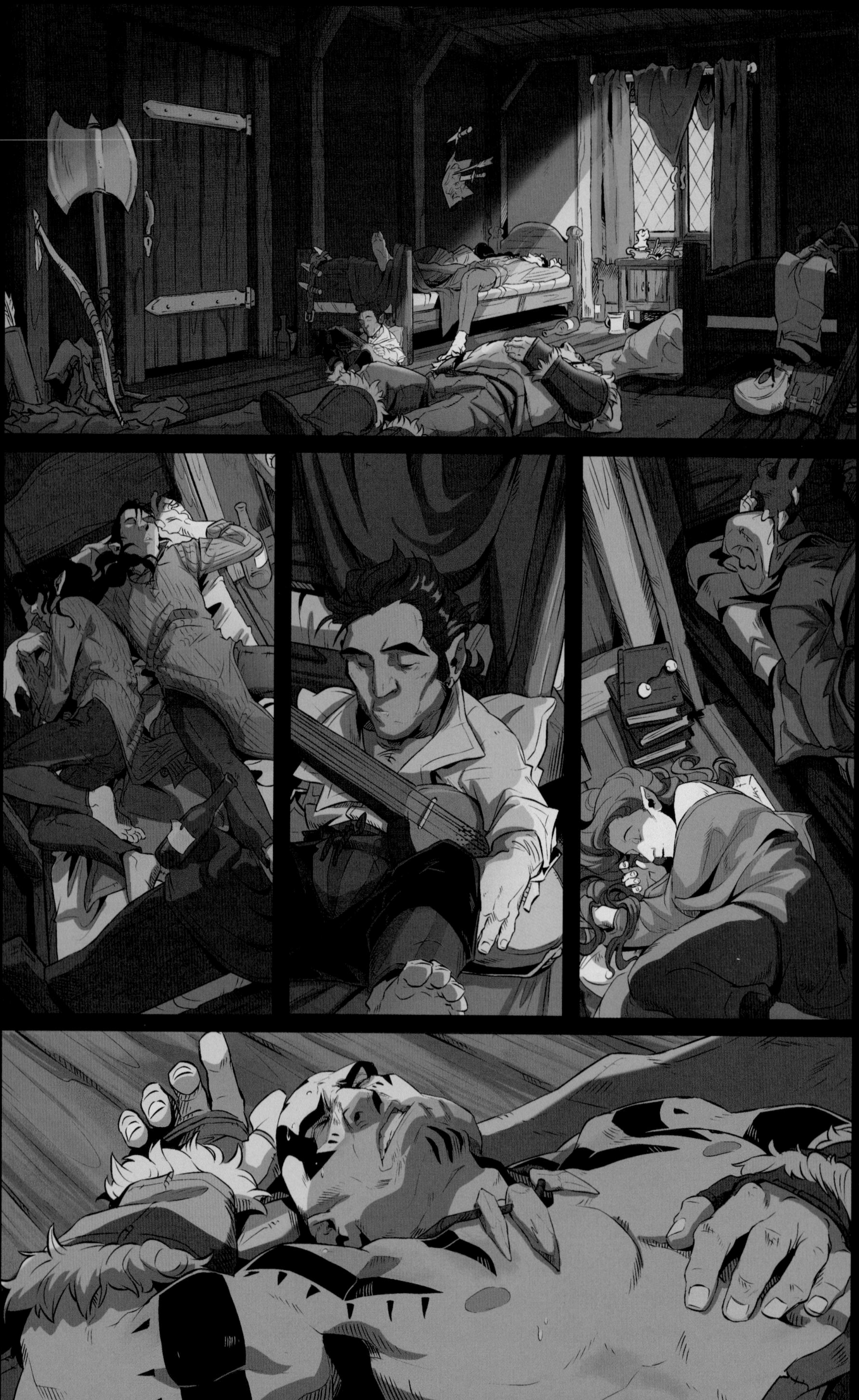

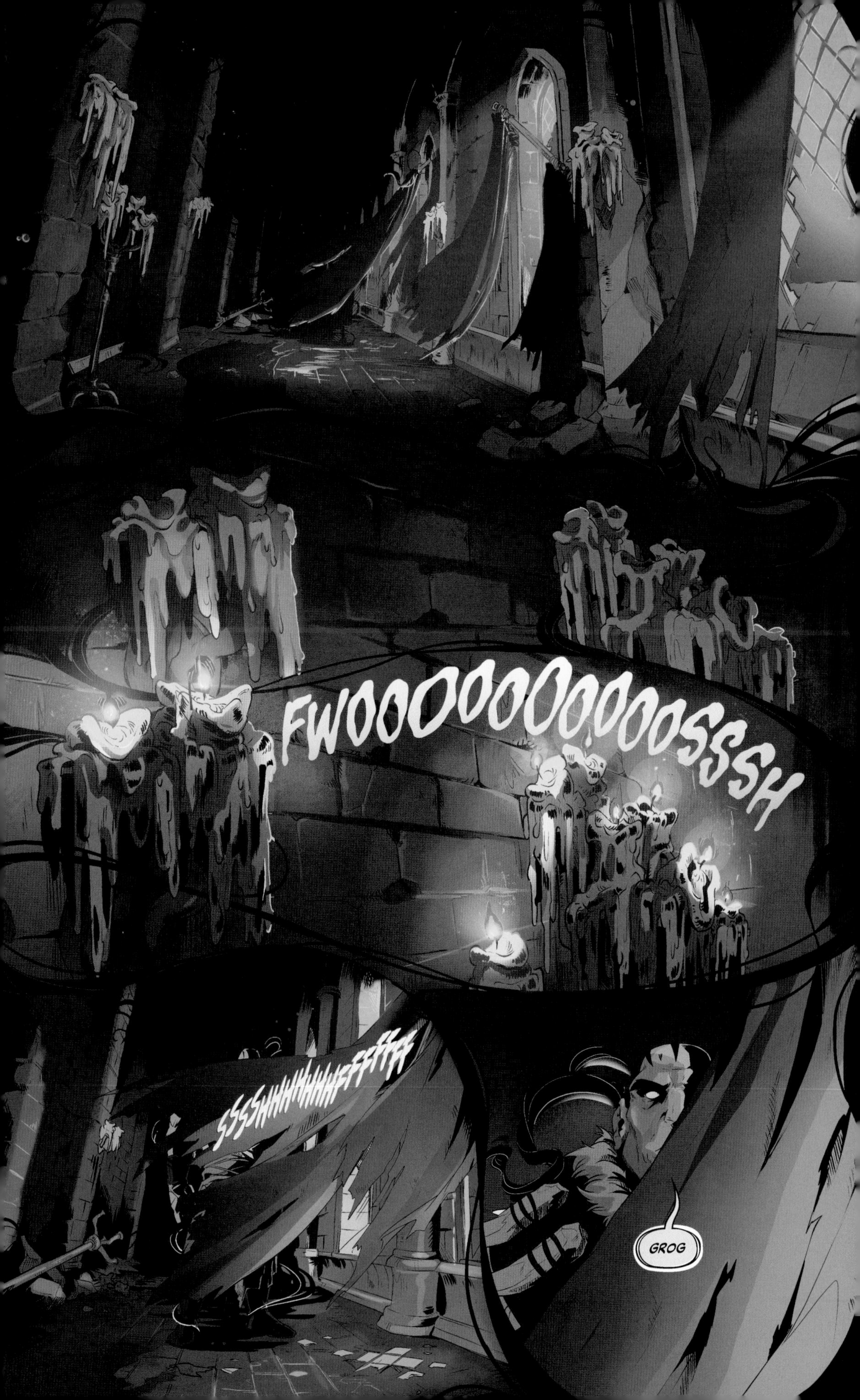
FWOOOOOOOOOOOSSSH
SSSHHHHHHHHHFFFFFF
GROG

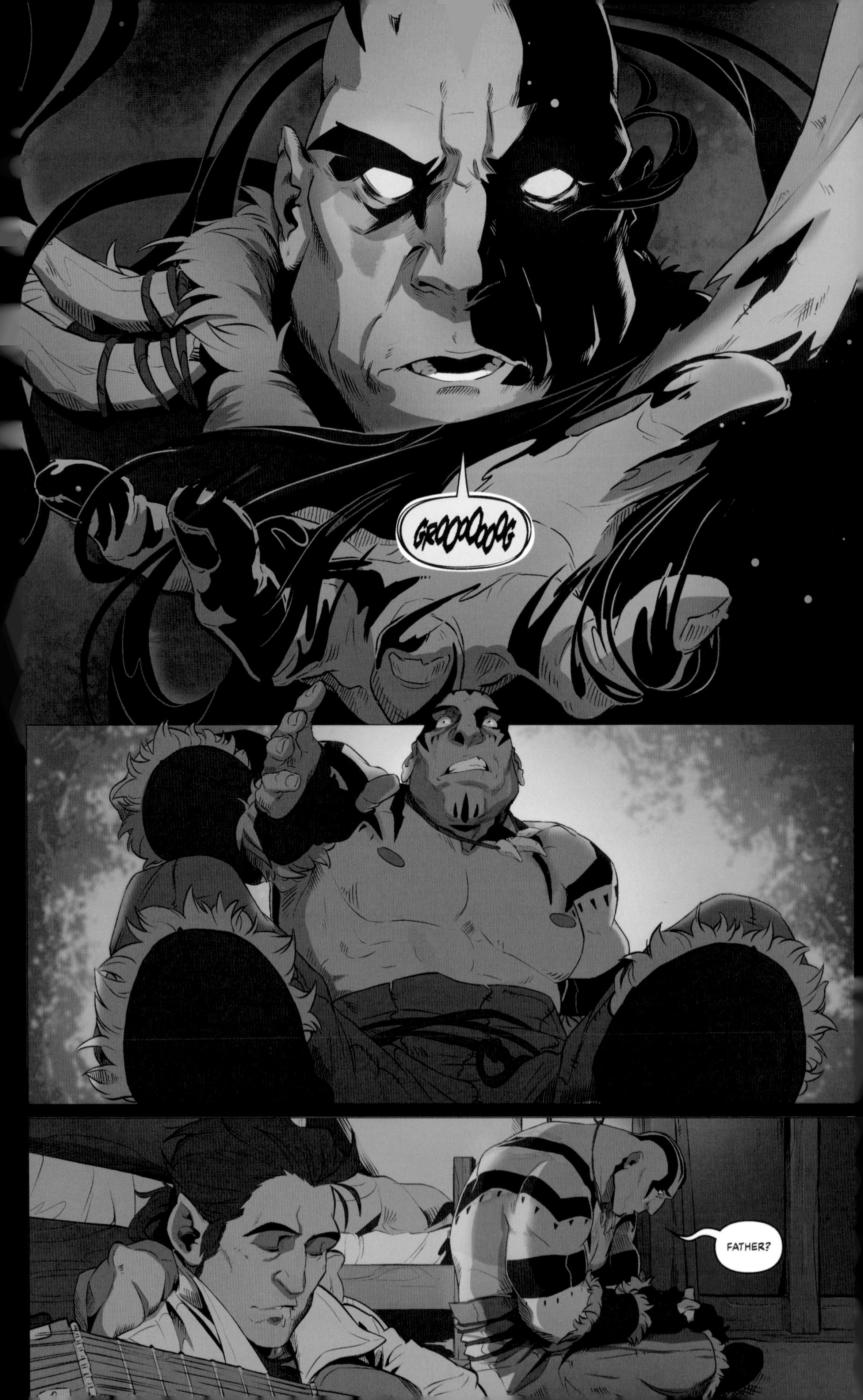
GROOOOOOOG
FATHER?

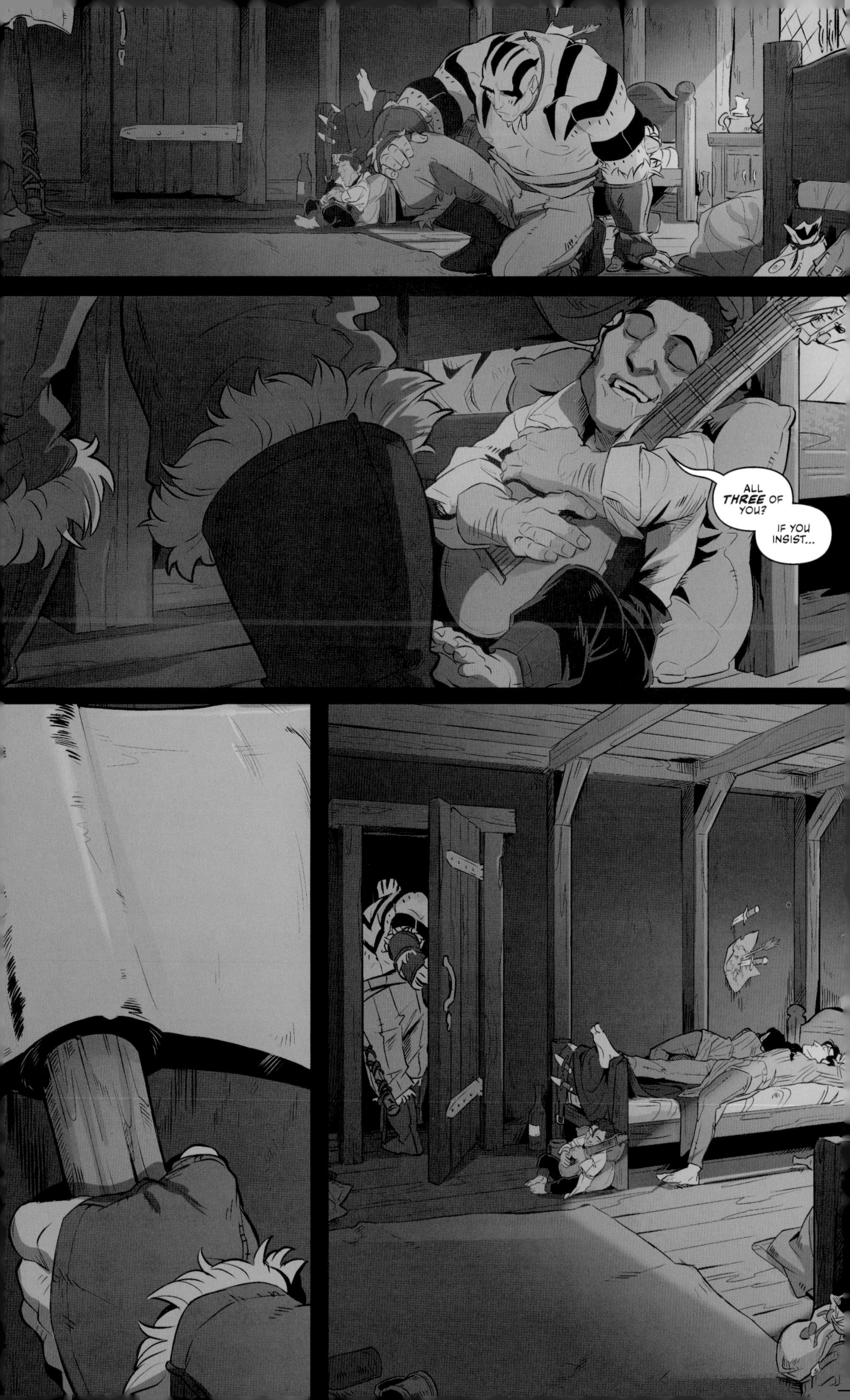
ALL THREE OF YOU?
IF YOU INSIST...

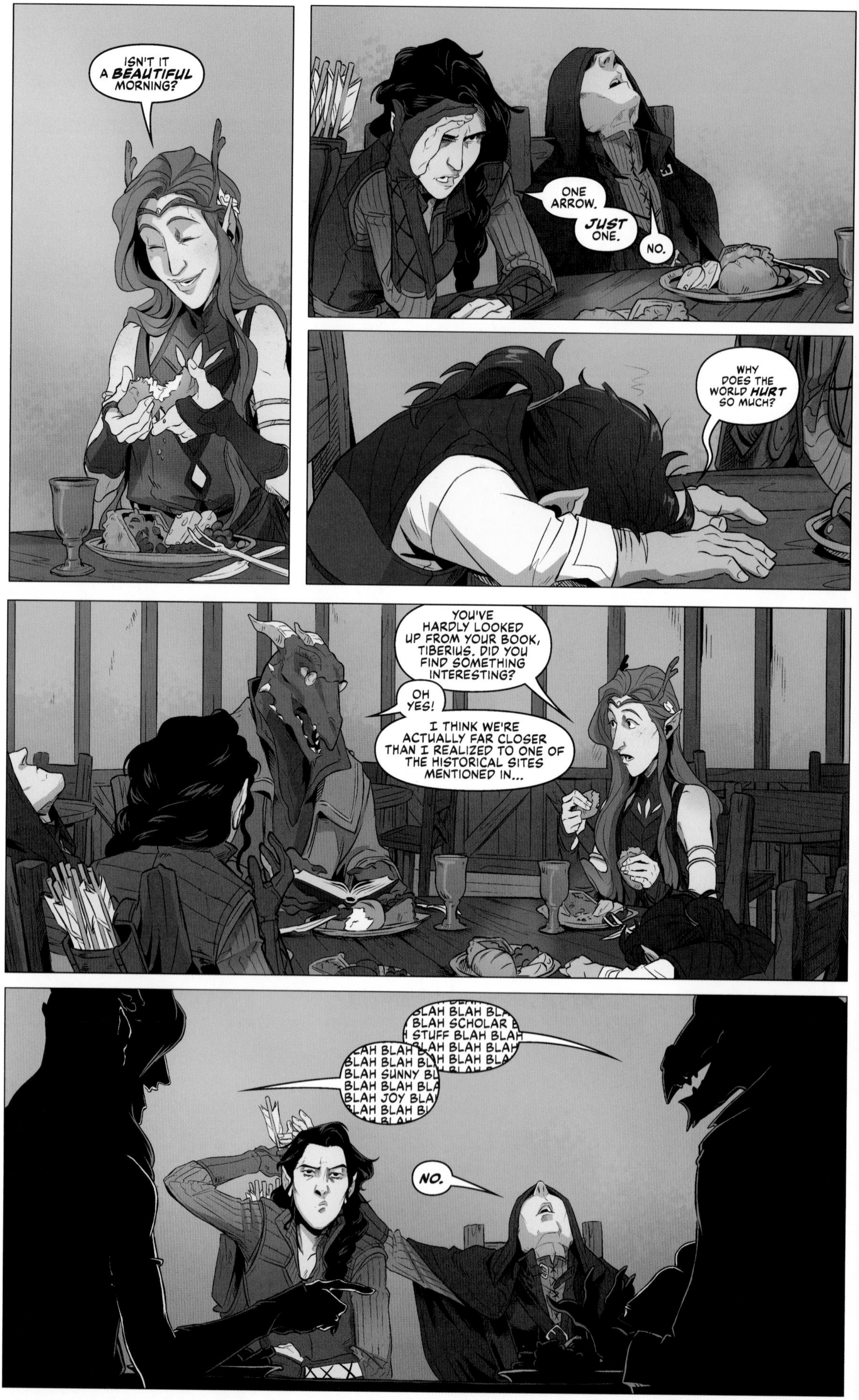
ISN'T IT A BEAUTIFUL MORNING?
ONE ARROW.
JUST ONE.
NO.
WHY DOES THE WORLD HURT SO MUCH?
YOU'VE HARDLY LOOKED UP FROM YOUR BOOK, TIBERIUS. DID YOU FIND SOMETHING INTERESTING?
OH YES!
I THINK WE'RE ACTUALLY FAR CLOSER THAN I REALIZED TO ONE OF THE HISTORICAL SITES MENTIONED IN...
BLAH BLAH BLAH SCHOLAR STUFF BLAH BLAH BLAH BLAH BLAH BLAH
BLAH BLAH BLAH BLAH SUNNY BLAH BLAH BLAH BLAH JOY BLAH BLAH BLAH
NO.

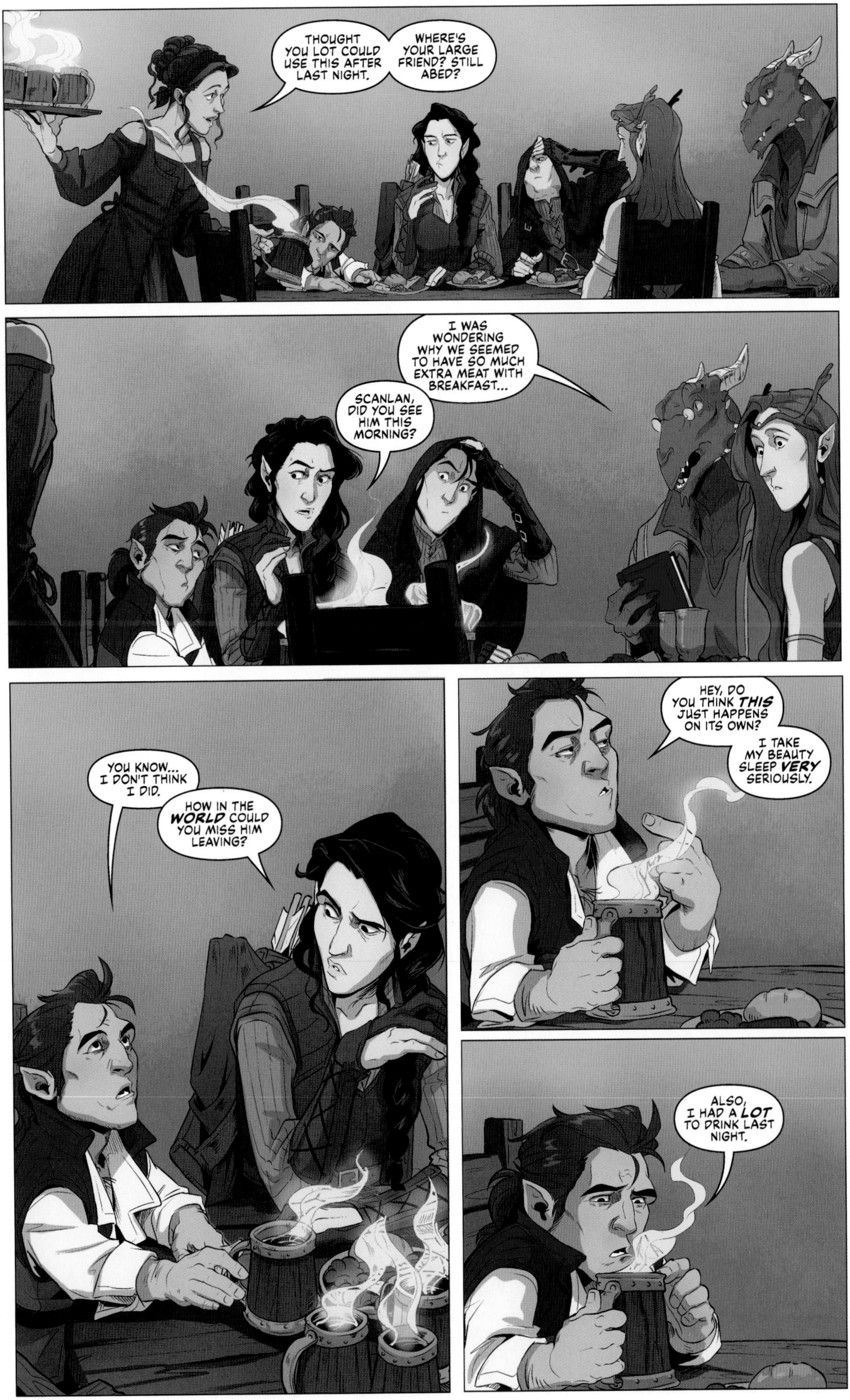
THOUGHT YOU LOT COULD USE THIS AFTER LAST NIGHT.
WHERE'S YOUR LARGE FRIEND? STILL ABED?
I WAS WONDERING WHY WE SEEMED TO HAVE SO MUCH EXTRA MEAT WITH BREAKFAST...
SCANLAN, DID YOU SEE HIM THIS MORNING?
YOU KNOW... I DON'T THINK I DID.
HOW IN THE **WORLD** COULD YOU MISS HIM LEAVING?
HEY, DO YOU THINK **THIS** JUST HAPPENS ON ITS OWN?
I TAKE MY BEAUTY SLEEP **VERY** SERIOUSLY.
ALSO, I HAD A **LOT** TO DRINK LAST NIGHT.

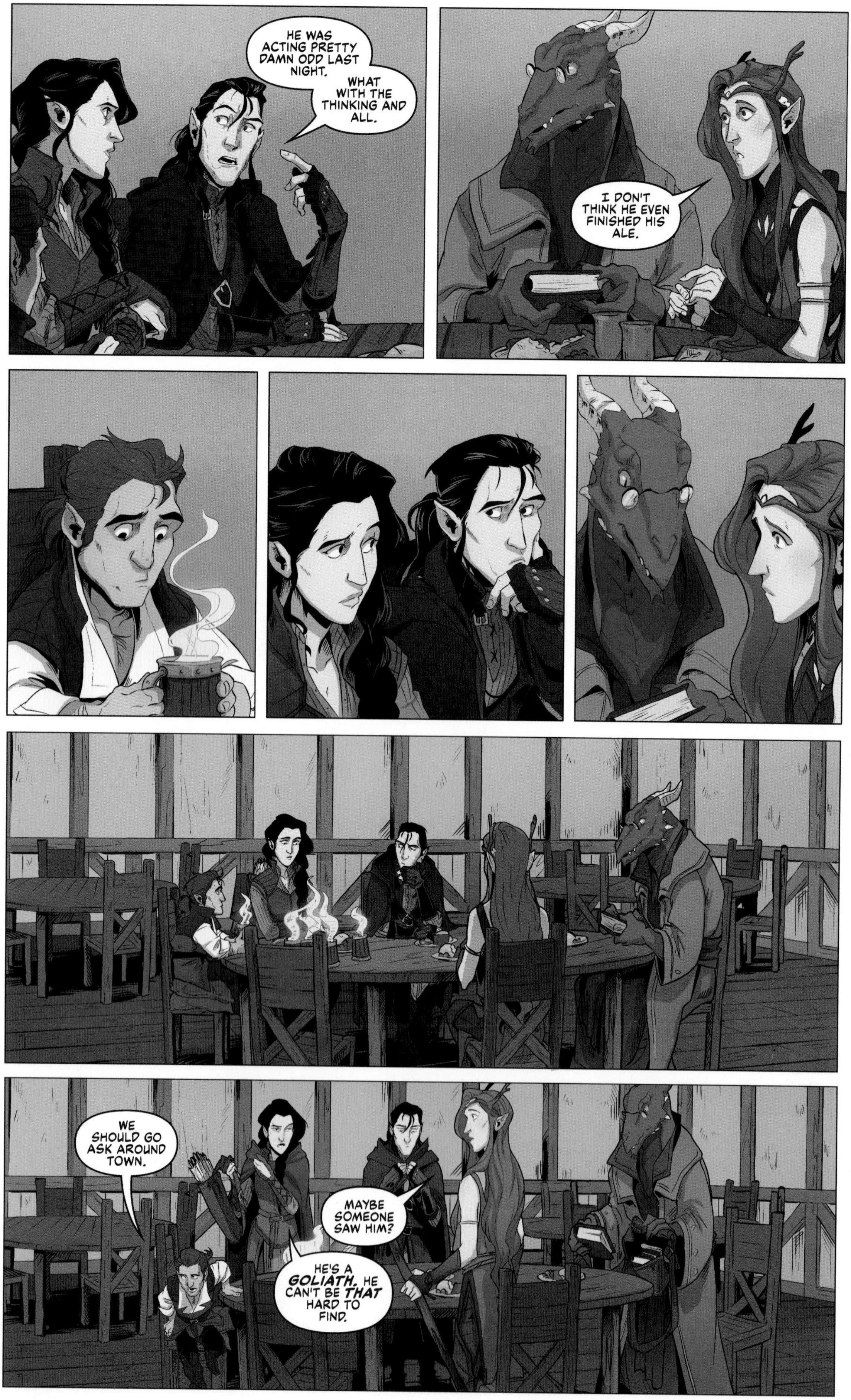

HE WAS ACTING PRETTY DAMN ODD LAST NIGHT.
WHAT WITH THE THINKING AND ALL.
I DON'T THINK HE EVEN FINISHED HIS ALE.
WE SHOULD GO ASK AROUND TOWN.
MAYBE SOMEONE SAW HIM?
HE'S A GOLIATH. HE CAN'T BE THAT HARD TO FIND.

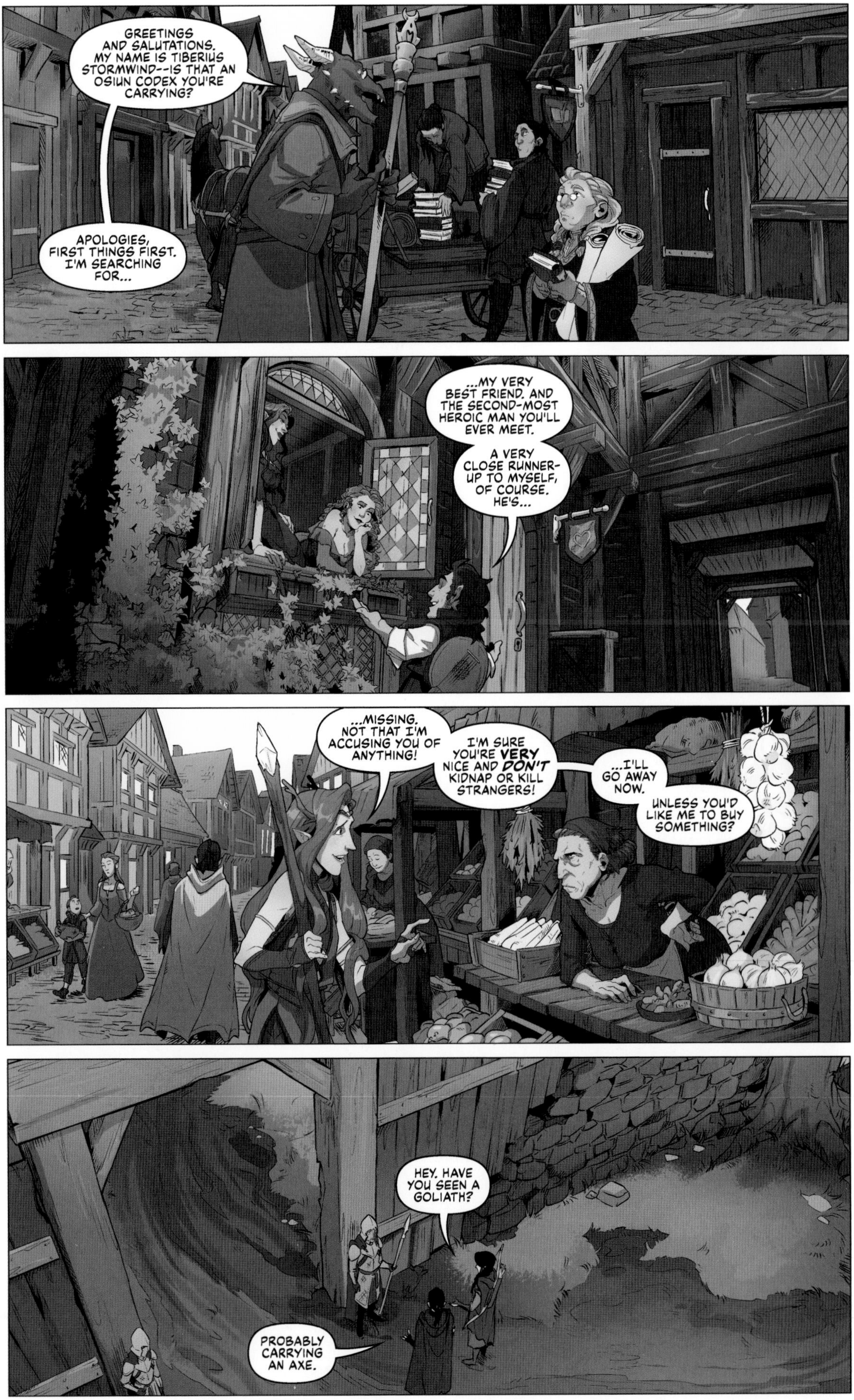
GREETINGS AND SALUTATIONS. MY NAME IS TIBERIUS STORMWIND--IS THAT AN OSIUN CODEX YOU'RE CARRYING?
APOLOGIES, FIRST THINGS FIRST. I'M SEARCHING FOR...
...MY VERY BEST FRIEND. AND THE SECOND-MOST HEROIC MAN YOU'LL EVER MEET.
A VERY CLOSE RUNNER-UP TO MYSELF, OF COURSE. HE'S...
...MISSING. NOT THAT I'M ACCUSING YOU OF ANYTHING!
I'M SURE YOU'RE **VERY** NICE AND ***DON'T*** KIDNAP OR KILL STRANGERS!
...I'LL GO AWAY NOW.
UNLESS YOU'D LIKE ME TO BUY SOMETHING?
HEY. HAVE YOU SEEN A GOLIATH?
PROBABLY CARRYING AN AXE.

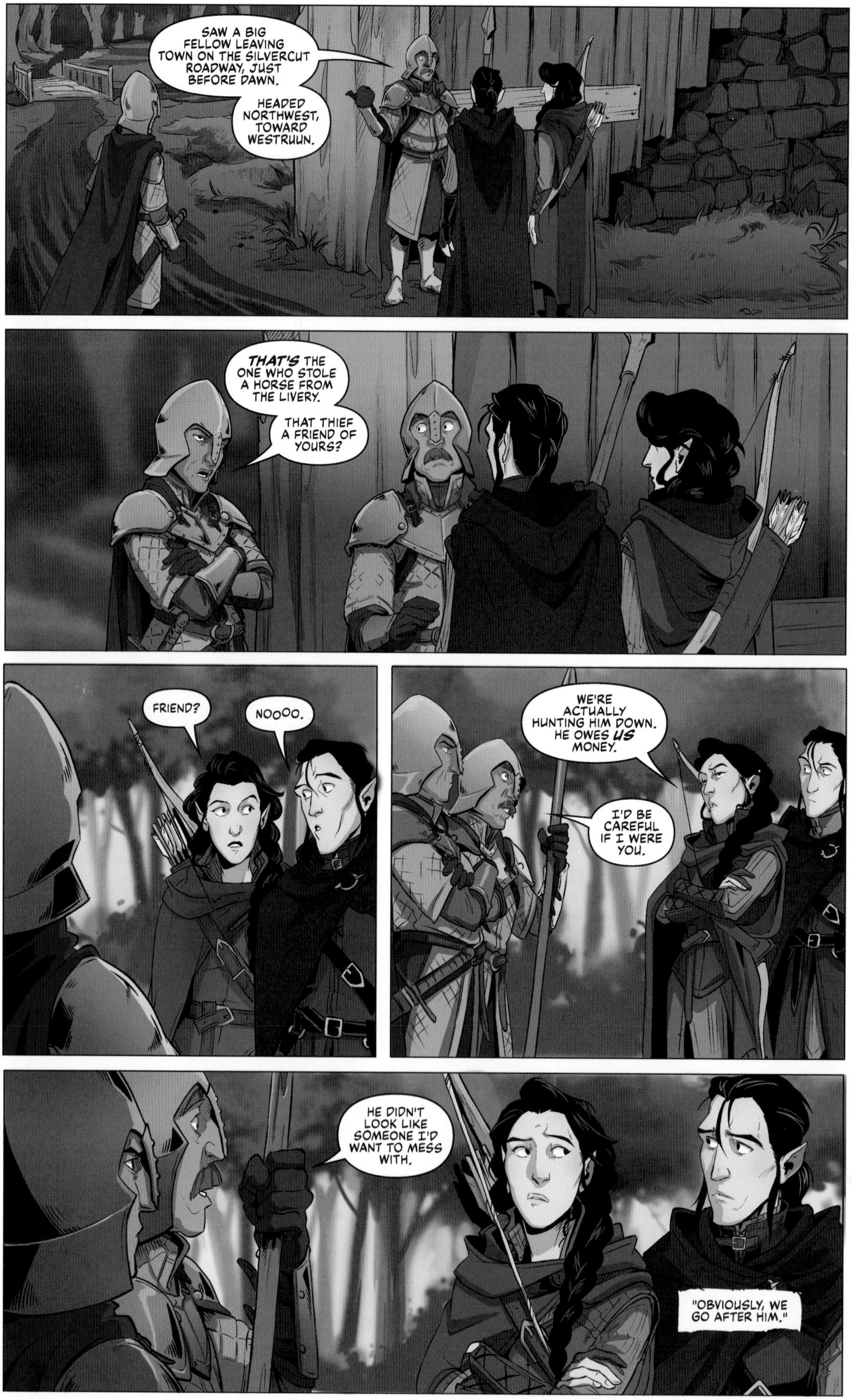
SAW A BIG FELLOW LEAVING TOWN ON THE SILVERCUT ROADWAY, JUST BEFORE DAWN.
HEADED NORTHWEST, TOWARD WESTRUUN.
THAT'S THE ONE WHO STOLE A HORSE FROM THE LIVERY.
THAT THIEF A FRIEND OF YOURS?
FRIEND?
NOOOO.
WE'RE ACTUALLY HUNTING HIM DOWN. HE OWES US MONEY.
I'D BE CAREFUL IF I WERE YOU.
HE DIDN'T LOOK LIKE SOMEONE I'D WANT TO MESS WITH.
"OBVIOUSLY, WE GO AFTER HIM."

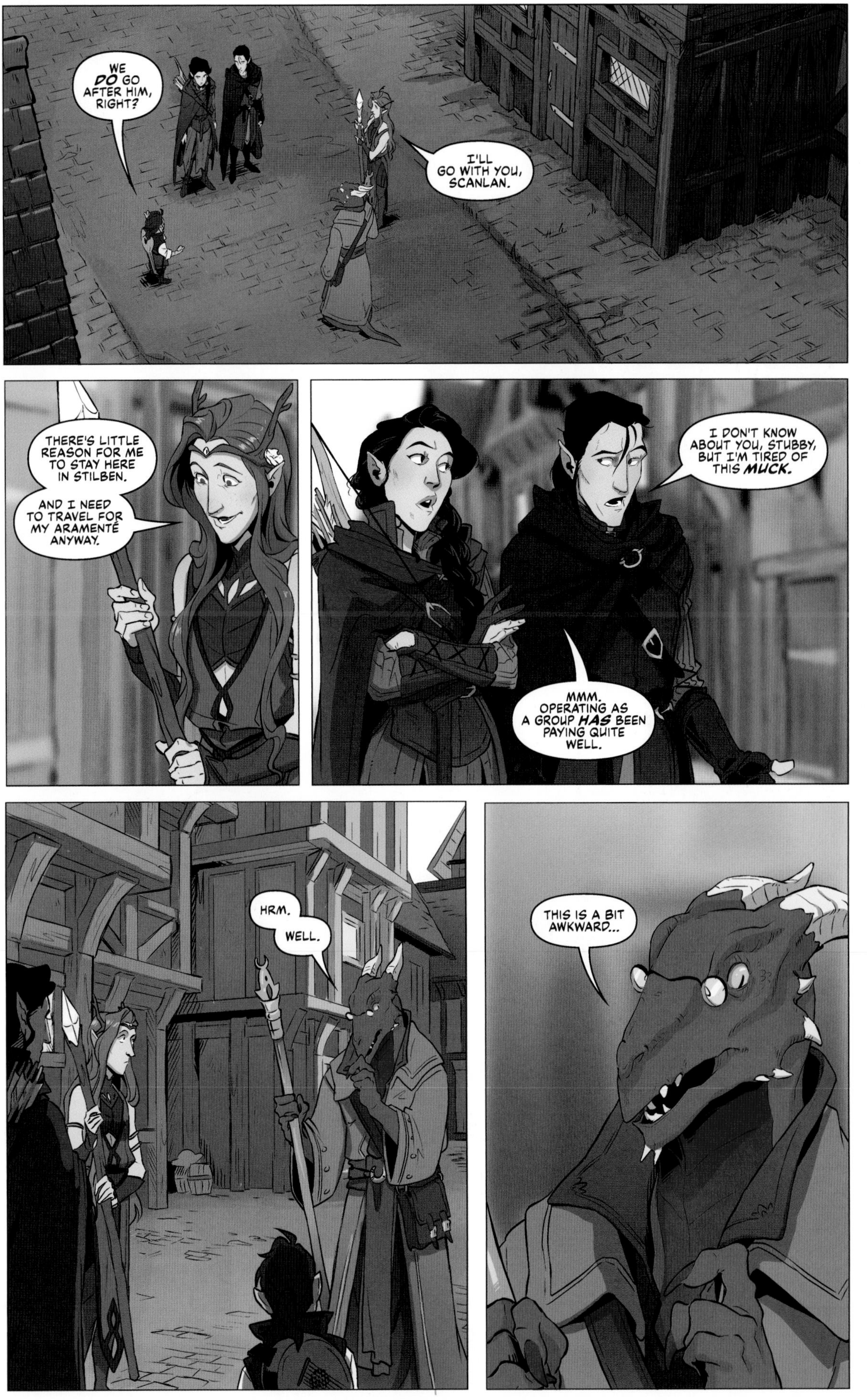
WE DO GO AFTER HIM, RIGHT?
I'LL GO WITH YOU, SCANLAN.
THERE'S LITTLE REASON FOR ME TO STAY HERE IN STILBEN.
AND I NEED TO TRAVEL FOR MY ARAMENTÉ ANYWAY.
I DON'T KNOW ABOUT YOU, STUBBY, BUT I'M TIRED OF THIS MUCK.
MMM. OPERATING AS A GROUP HAS BEEN PAYING QUITE WELL.
HRM.
WELL.
THIS IS A BIT AWKWARD...

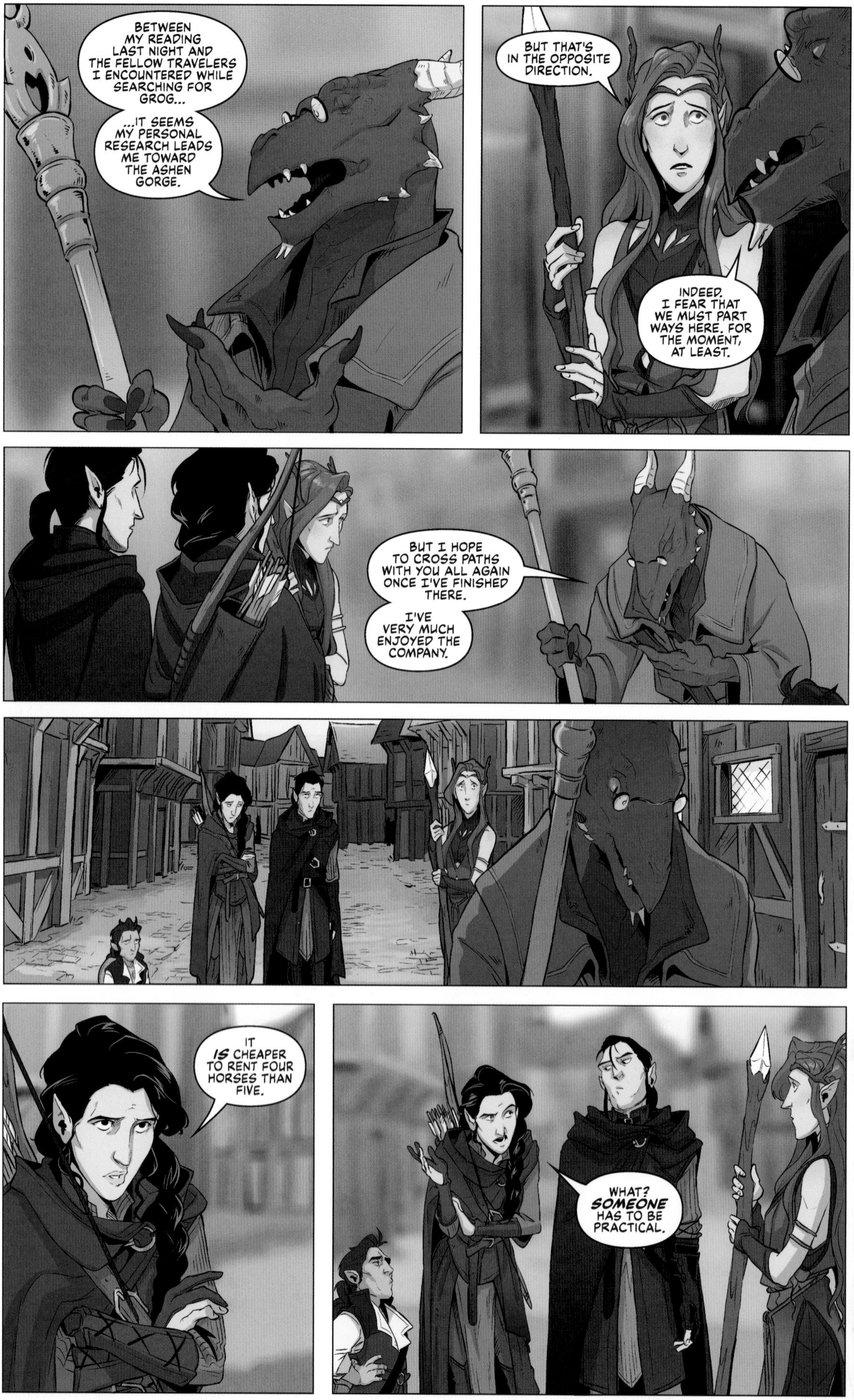
BETWEEN MY READING LAST NIGHT AND THE FELLOW TRAVELERS I ENCOUNTERED WHILE SEARCHING FOR GROG...
...IT SEEMS MY PERSONAL RESEARCH LEADS ME TOWARD THE ASHEN GORGE.
BUT THAT'S IN THE OPPOSITE DIRECTION.
INDEED. I FEAR THAT WE MUST PART WAYS HERE. FOR THE MOMENT, AT LEAST.
BUT I HOPE TO CROSS PATHS WITH YOU ALL AGAIN ONCE I'VE FINISHED THERE.
I'VE VERY MUCH ENJOYED THE COMPANY.
IT *IS* CHEAPER TO RENT FOUR HORSES THAN FIVE.
WHAT? ***SOMEONE*** HAS TO BE PRACTICAL.

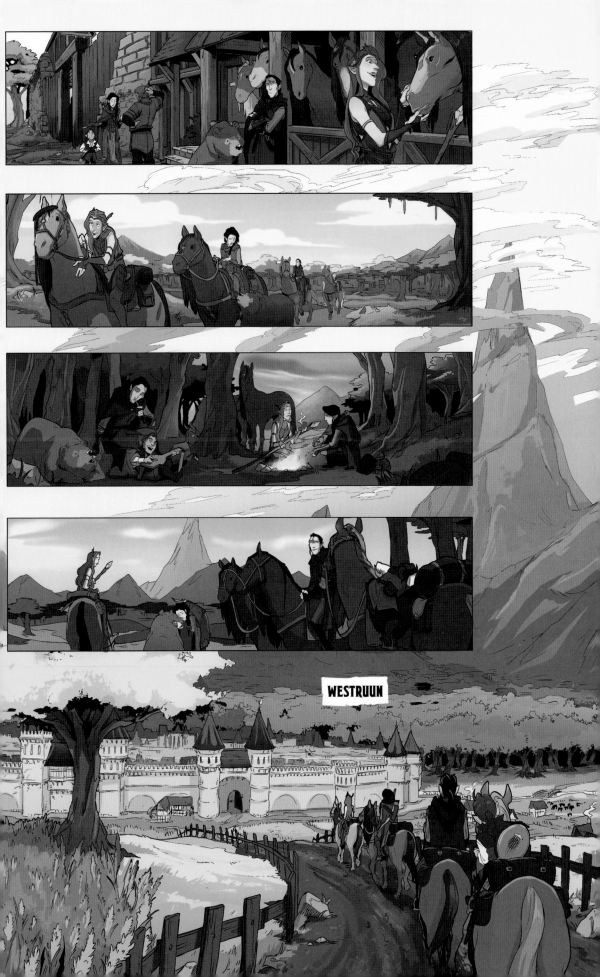

WESTRUUN

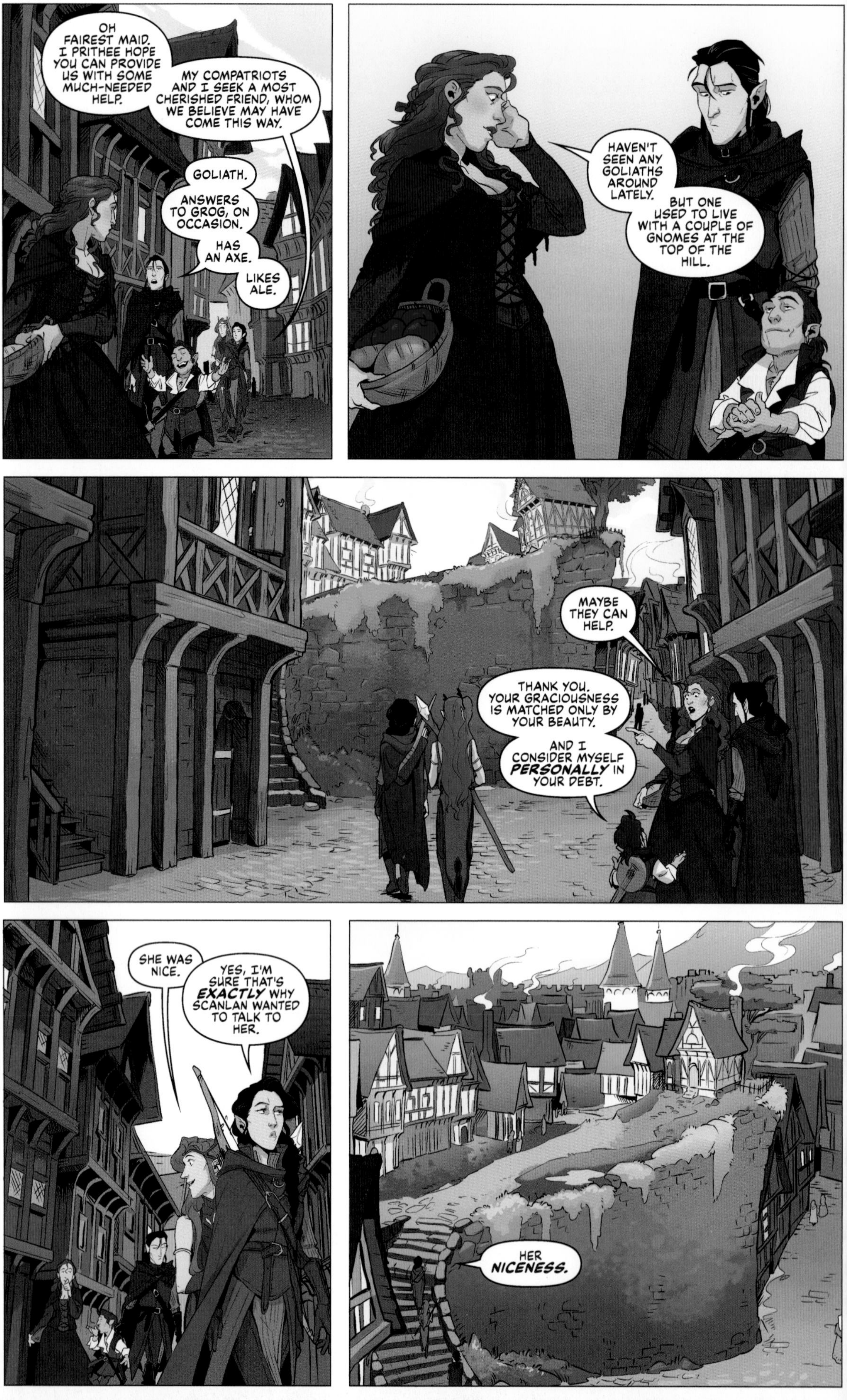
OH FAIREST MAID. I PRITHEE HOPE YOU CAN PROVIDE US WITH SOME MUCH-NEEDED HELP.
MY COMPATRIOTS AND I SEEK A MOST CHERISHED FRIEND, WHOM WE BELIEVE MAY HAVE COME THIS WAY.
GOLIATH.
ANSWERS TO GROG, ON OCCASION.
HAS AN AXE.
LIKES ALE.
HAVEN'T SEEN ANY GOLIATHS AROUND LATELY.
BUT ONE USED TO LIVE WITH A COUPLE OF GNOMES AT THE TOP OF THE HILL.
MAYBE THEY CAN HELP.
THANK YOU. YOUR GRACIOUSNESS IS MATCHED ONLY BY YOUR BEAUTY.
AND I CONSIDER MYSELF ***PERSONALLY*** IN YOUR DEBT.
SHE WAS NICE.
YES, I'M SURE THAT'S ***EXACTLY*** WHY SCANLAN WANTED TO TALK TO HER.
HER ***NICENESS.***

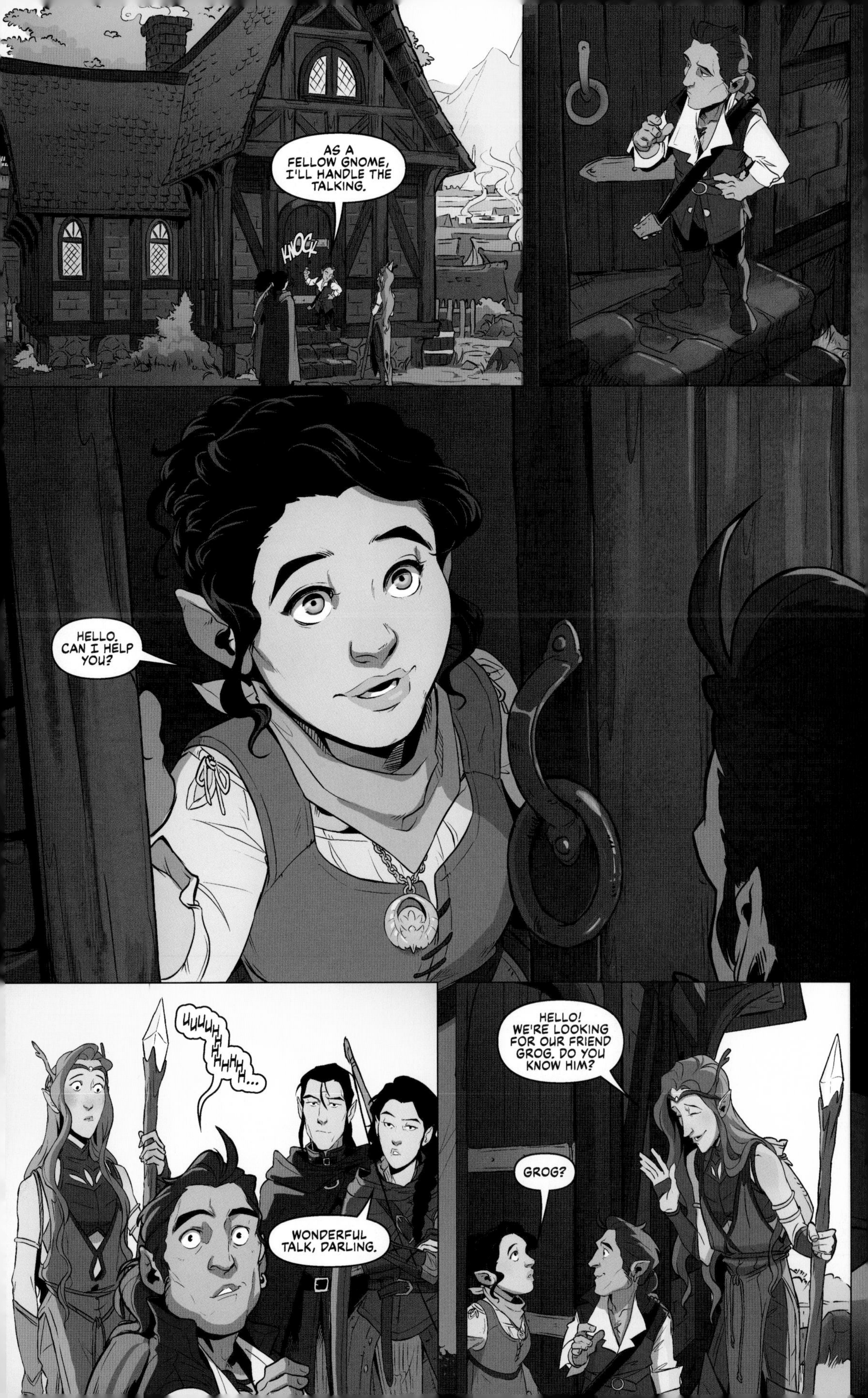
AS A FELLOW GNOME, I'LL HANDLE THE TALKING.
KNOCK
HELLO. CAN I HELP YOU?
UUUUHHHHHHH...
WONDERFUL TALK, DARLING.
HELLO! WE'RE LOOKING FOR OUR FRIEND GROG. DO YOU KNOW HIM?
GROG?

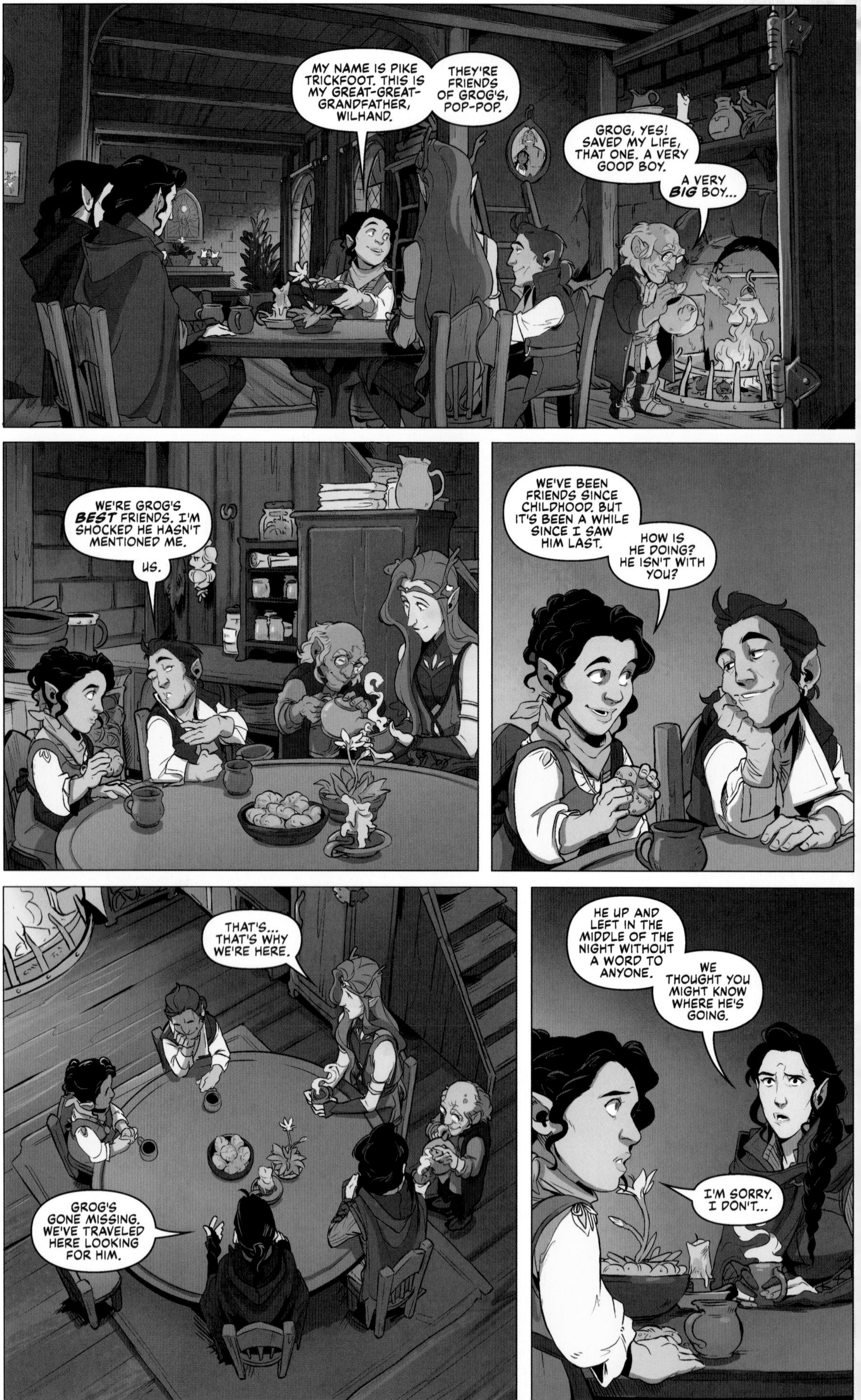

MY NAME IS PIKE TRICKFOOT. THIS IS MY GREAT-GREAT-GRANDFATHER, WILHAND.
THEY'RE FRIENDS OF GROG'S, POP-POP.
GROG, YES! SAVED MY LIFE, THAT ONE. A VERY GOOD BOY.
A VERY BIG BOY...
WE'RE GROG'S BEST FRIENDS. I'M SHOCKED HE HASN'T MENTIONED ME.
US.
WE'VE BEEN FRIENDS SINCE CHILDHOOD. BUT IT'S BEEN A WHILE SINCE I SAW HIM LAST.
HOW IS HE DOING? HE ISN'T WITH YOU?
THAT'S... THAT'S WHY WE'RE HERE.
GROG'S GONE MISSING. WE'VE TRAVELED HERE LOOKING FOR HIM.
HE UP AND LEFT IN THE MIDDLE OF THE NIGHT WITHOUT A WORD TO ANYONE.
WE THOUGHT YOU MIGHT KNOW WHERE HE'S GOING.
I'M SORRY. I DON'T...

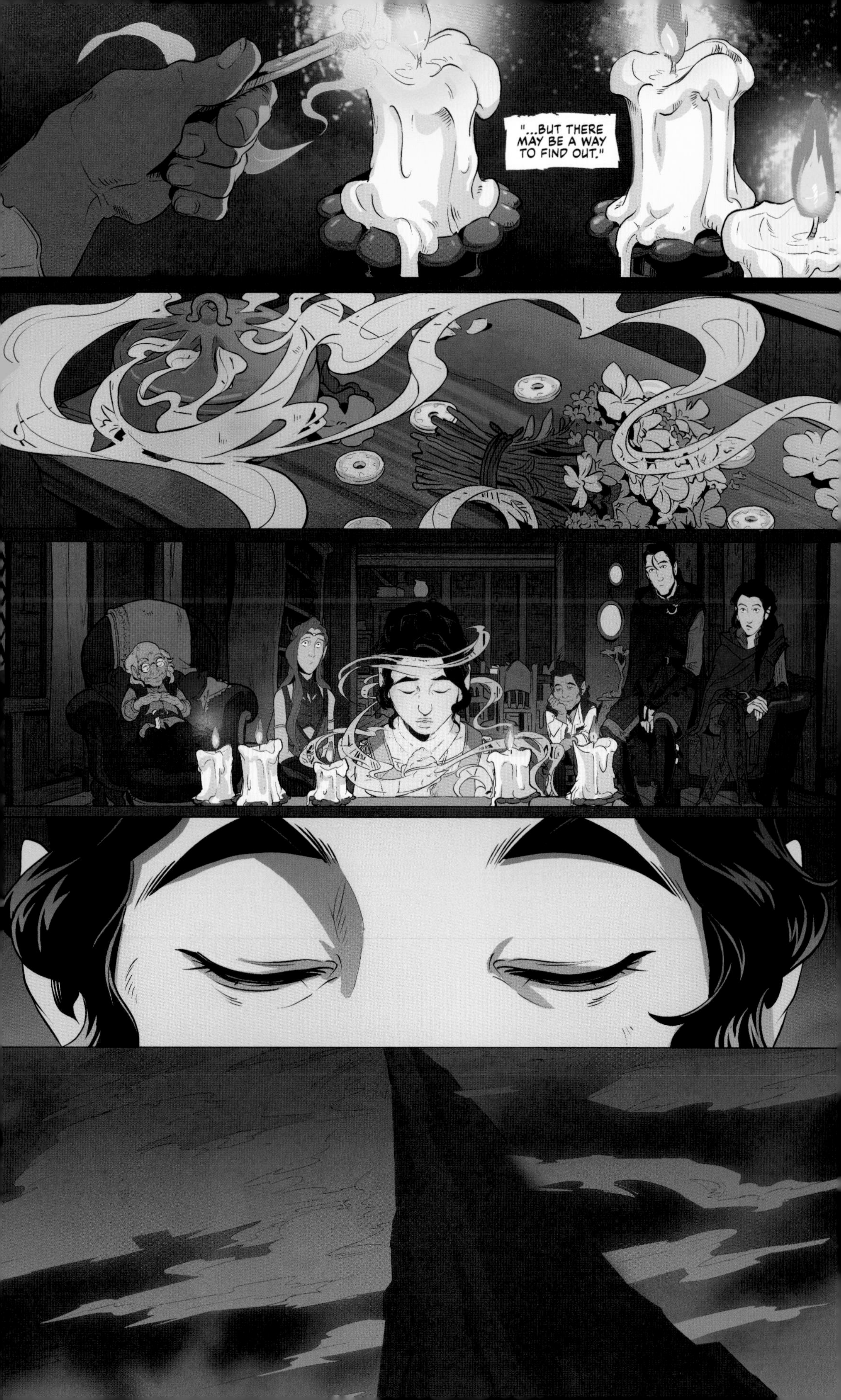
"...BUT THERE MAY BE A WAY TO FIND OUT."

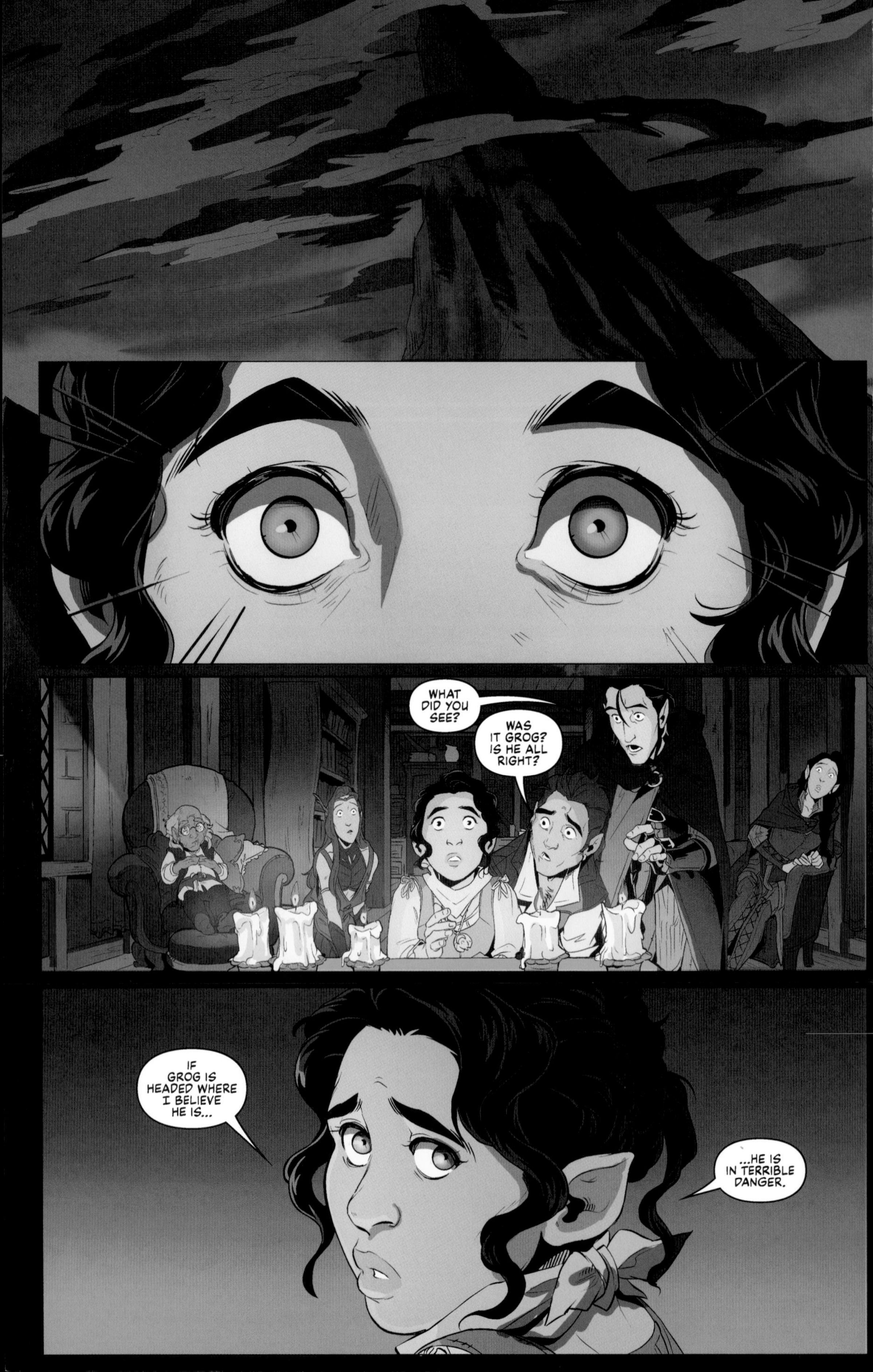
WHAT DID YOU SEE?
WAS IT GROG? IS HE ALL RIGHT?
IF GROG IS HEADED WHERE I BELIEVE HE IS...
...HE IS IN TERRIBLE DANGER.

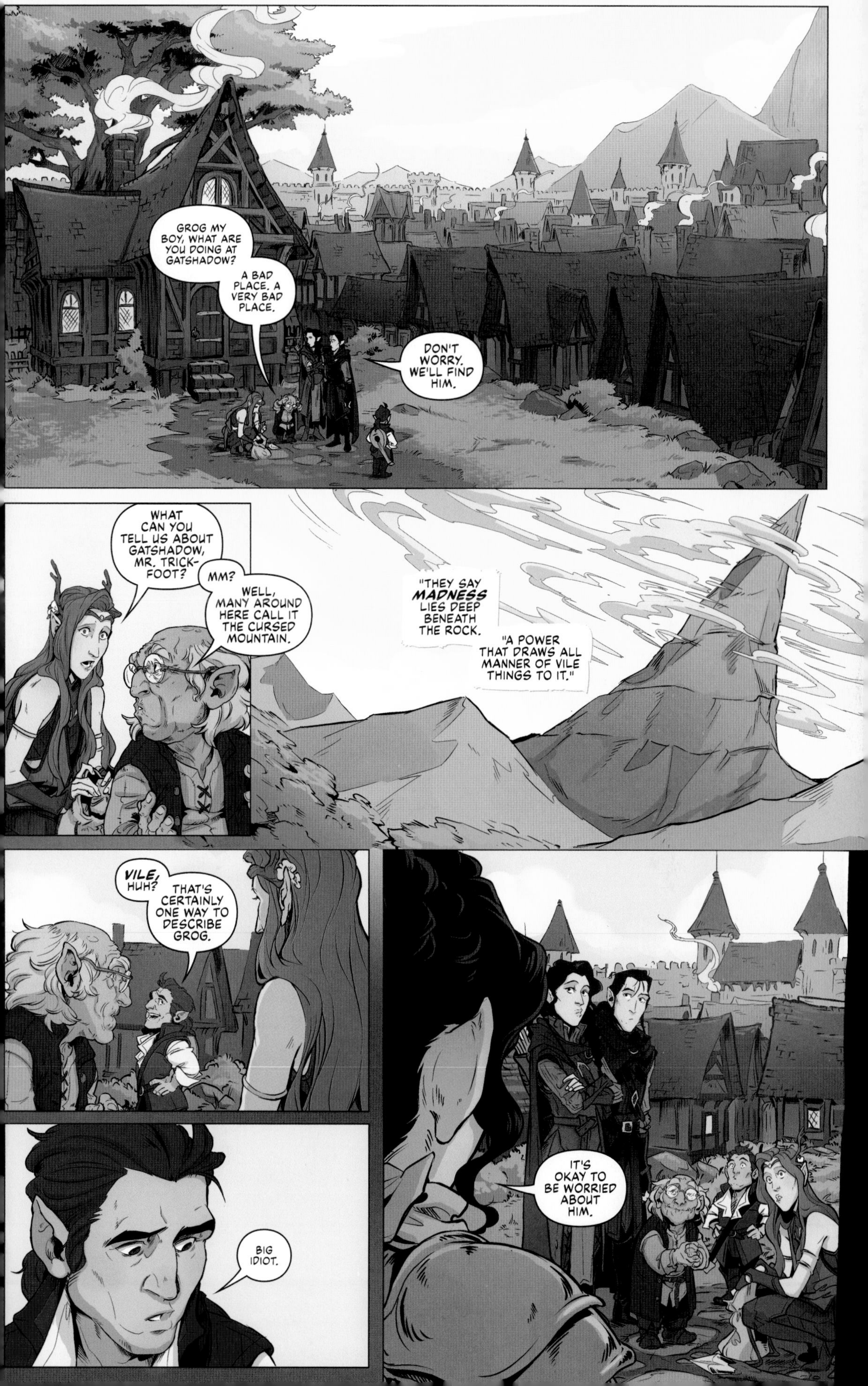
GROG MY BOY, WHAT ARE YOU DOING AT GATSHADOW?
A BAD PLACE. A VERY BAD PLACE.
DON'T WORRY. WE'LL FIND HIM.
WHAT CAN YOU TELL US ABOUT GATSHADOW, MR. TRICK-FOOT?
MM?
WELL, MANY AROUND HERE CALL IT THE CURSED MOUNTAIN.
"THEY SAY MADNESS LIES DEEP BENEATH THE ROCK.
"A POWER THAT DRAWS ALL MANNER OF VILE THINGS TO IT."
VILE, HUH?
THAT'S CERTAINLY ONE WAY TO DESCRIBE GROG.
BIG IDIOT.
IT'S OKAY TO BE WORRIED ABOUT HIM.

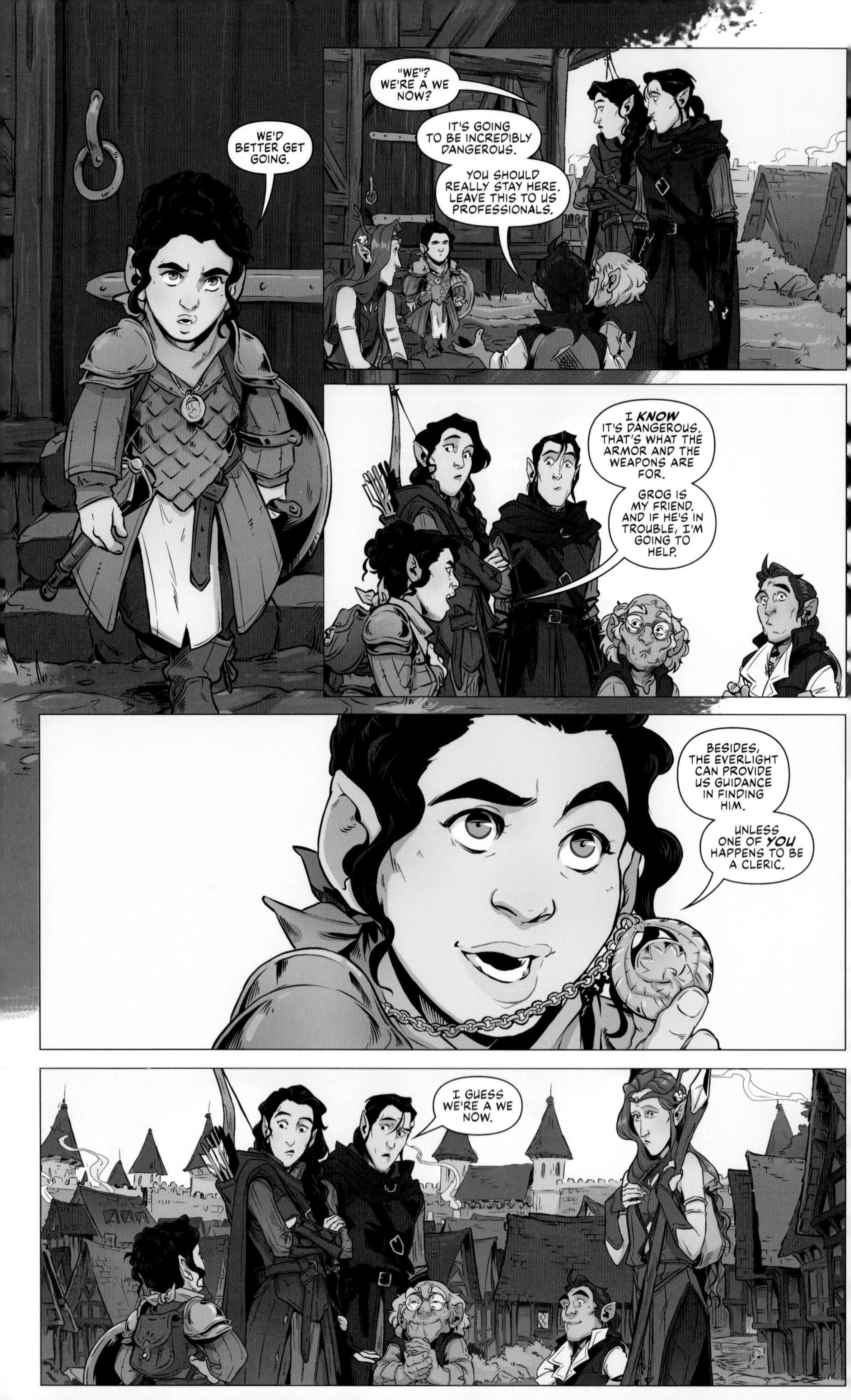
WE'D BETTER GET GOING.
"WE"? WE'RE A WE NOW?
IT'S GOING TO BE INCREDIBLY DANGEROUS.
YOU SHOULD REALLY STAY HERE. LEAVE THIS TO US PROFESSIONALS.
I KNOW IT'S DANGEROUS. THAT'S WHAT THE ARMOR AND THE WEAPONS ARE FOR.
GROG IS MY FRIEND. AND IF HE'S IN TROUBLE, I'M GOING TO HELP.
BESIDES, THE EVERLIGHT CAN PROVIDE US GUIDANCE IN FINDING HIM.
UNLESS ONE OF YOU HAPPENS TO BE A CLERIC.
I GUESS WE'RE A WE NOW.

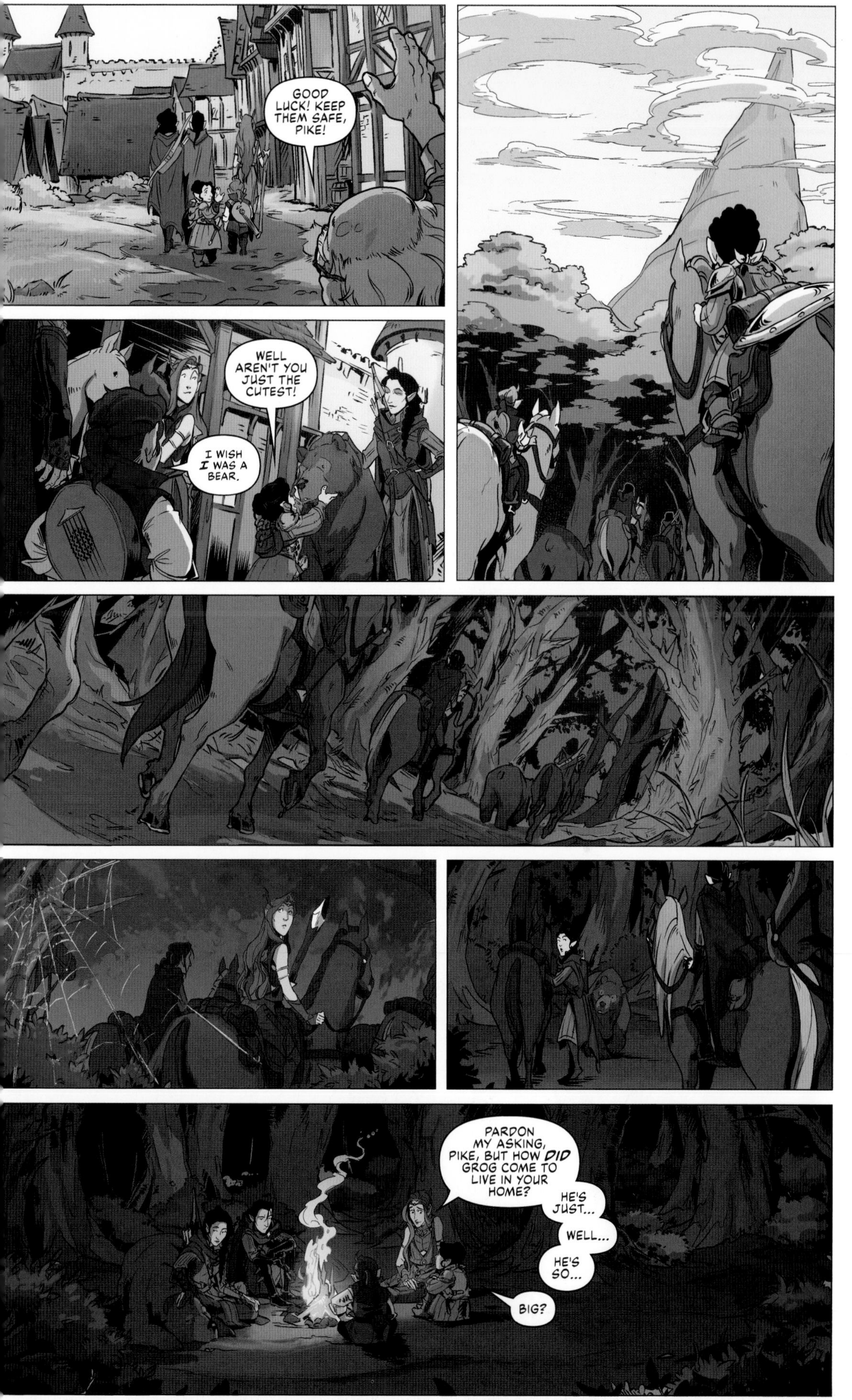
GOOD LUCK! KEEP THEM SAFE, PIKE!
WELL AREN'T YOU JUST THE CUTEST!
I WISH *I* WAS A BEAR.
PARDON MY ASKING, PIKE, BUT HOW *DID* GROG COME TO LIVE IN YOUR HOME?
HE'S JUST...
WELL...
HE'S SO...
BIG?

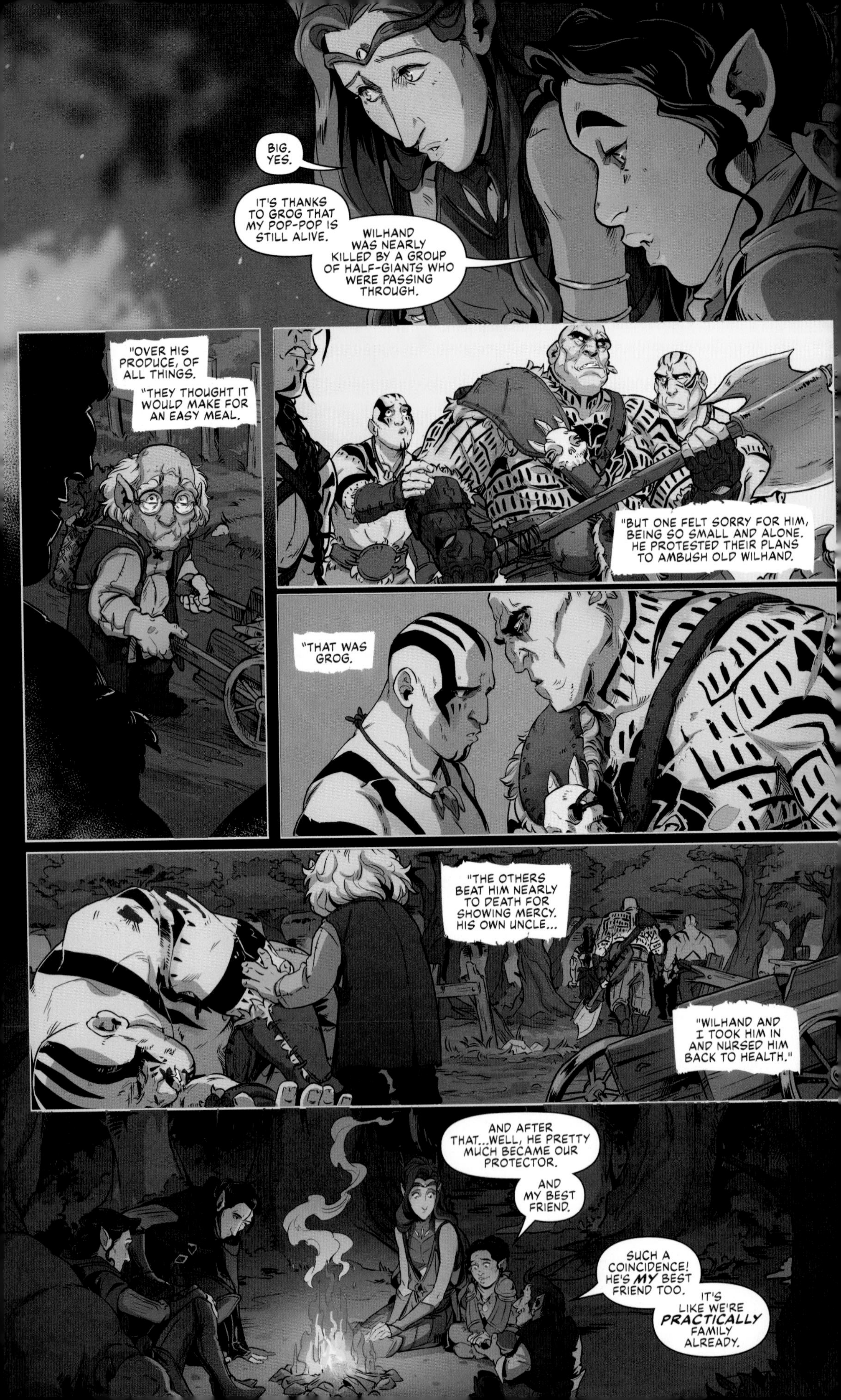
BIG. YES.
IT'S THANKS TO GROG THAT MY POP-POP IS STILL ALIVE.
WILHAND WAS NEARLY KILLED BY A GROUP OF HALF-GIANTS WHO WERE PASSING THROUGH.
"OVER HIS PRODUCE, OF ALL THINGS.
"THEY THOUGHT IT WOULD MAKE FOR AN EASY MEAL.
"BUT ONE FELT SORRY FOR HIM, BEING SO SMALL AND ALONE. HE PROTESTED THEIR PLANS TO AMBUSH OLD WILHAND.
"THAT WAS GROG.
"THE OTHERS BEAT HIM NEARLY TO DEATH FOR SHOWING MERCY. HIS OWN UNCLE...
"WILHAND AND I TOOK HIM IN AND NURSED HIM BACK TO HEALTH."
AND AFTER THAT...WELL, HE PRETTY MUCH BECAME OUR PROTECTOR.
AND MY BEST FRIEND.
SUCH A COINCIDENCE! HE'S *MY* BEST FRIEND TOO.
IT'S LIKE WE'RE ***PRACTICALLY*** FAMILY ALREADY.

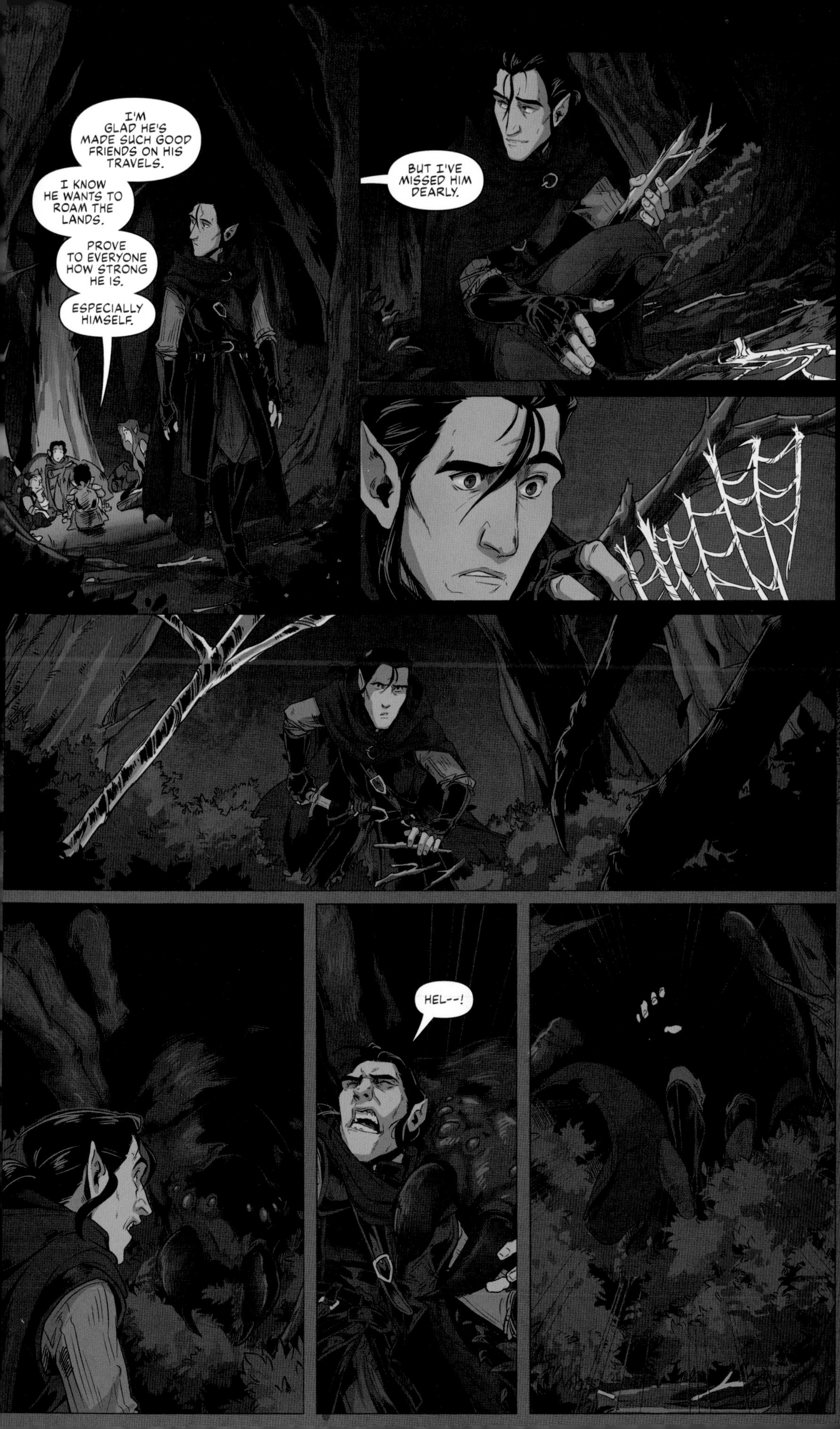
I'M GLAD HE'S MADE SUCH GOOD FRIENDS ON HIS TRAVELS.
I KNOW HE WANTS TO ROAM THE LANDS.
PROVE TO EVERYONE HOW STRONG HE IS.
ESPECIALLY HIMSELF.
BUT I'VE MISSED HIM DEARLY.
HEL--!

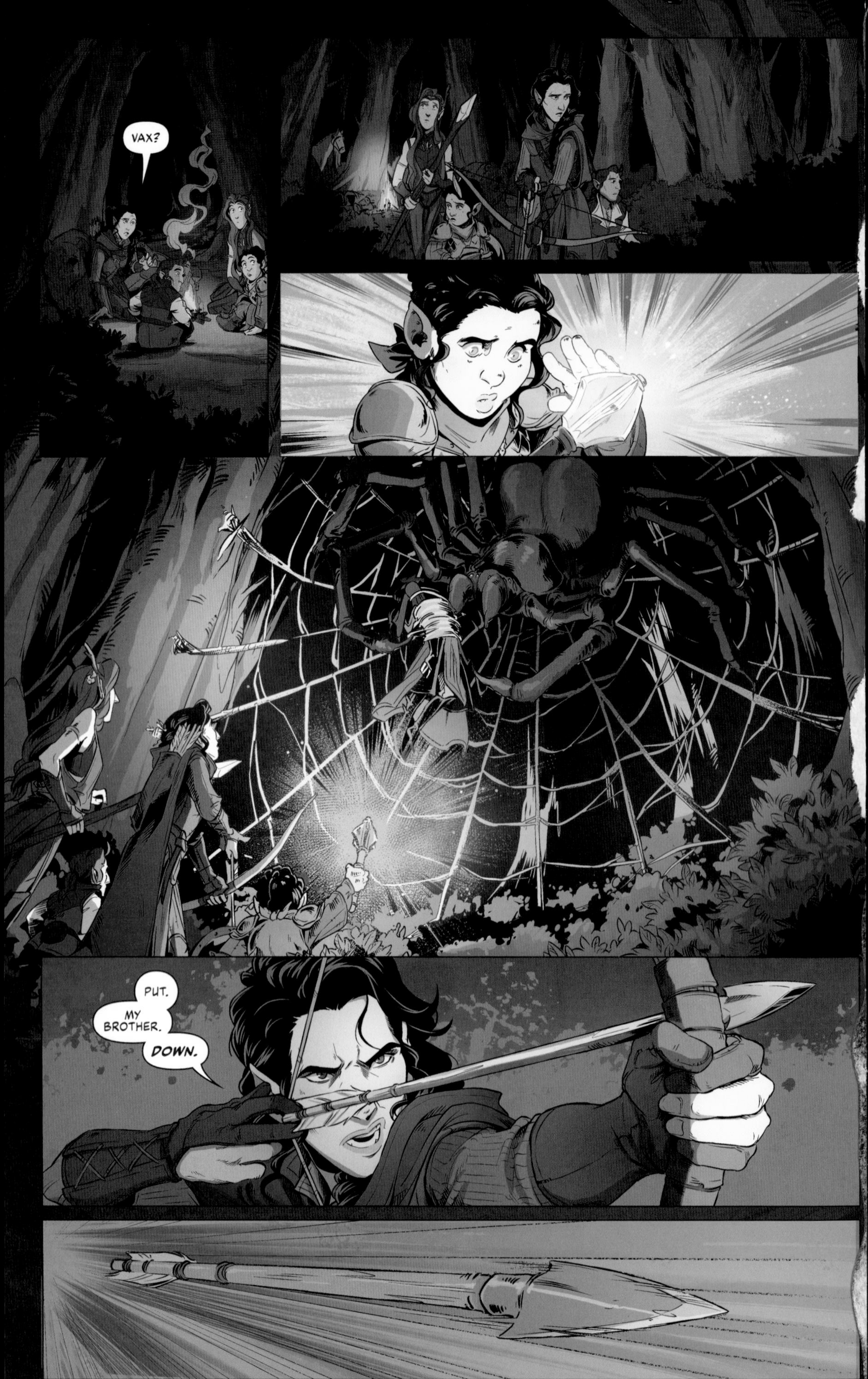
VAX?
PUT.
MY BROTHER.
DOWN.

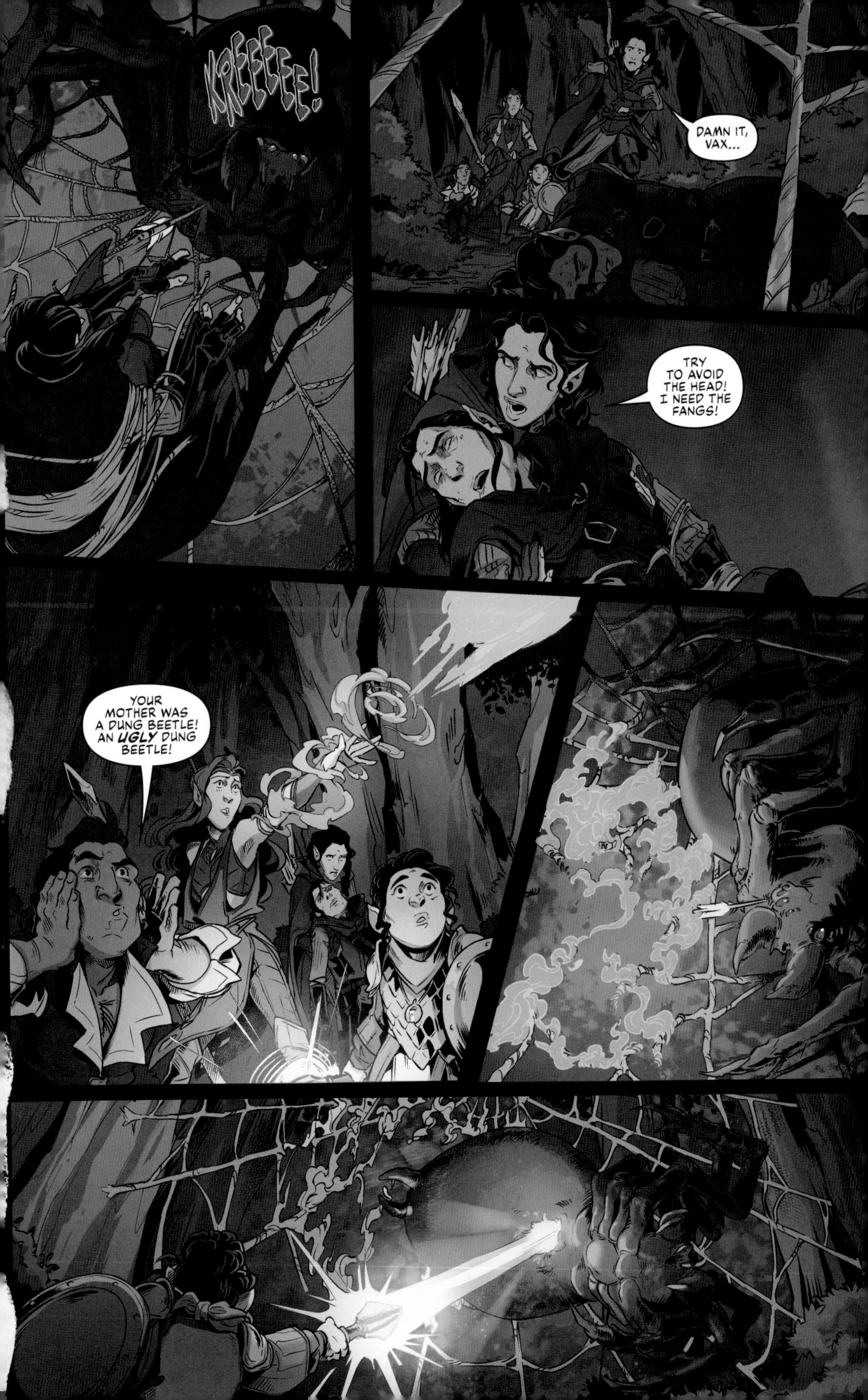
KREEEEEE!
DAMN IT, VAX...
TRY TO AVOID THE HEAD! I NEED THE FANGS!
YOUR MOTHER WAS A DUNG BEETLE! AN UGLY DUNG BEETLE!

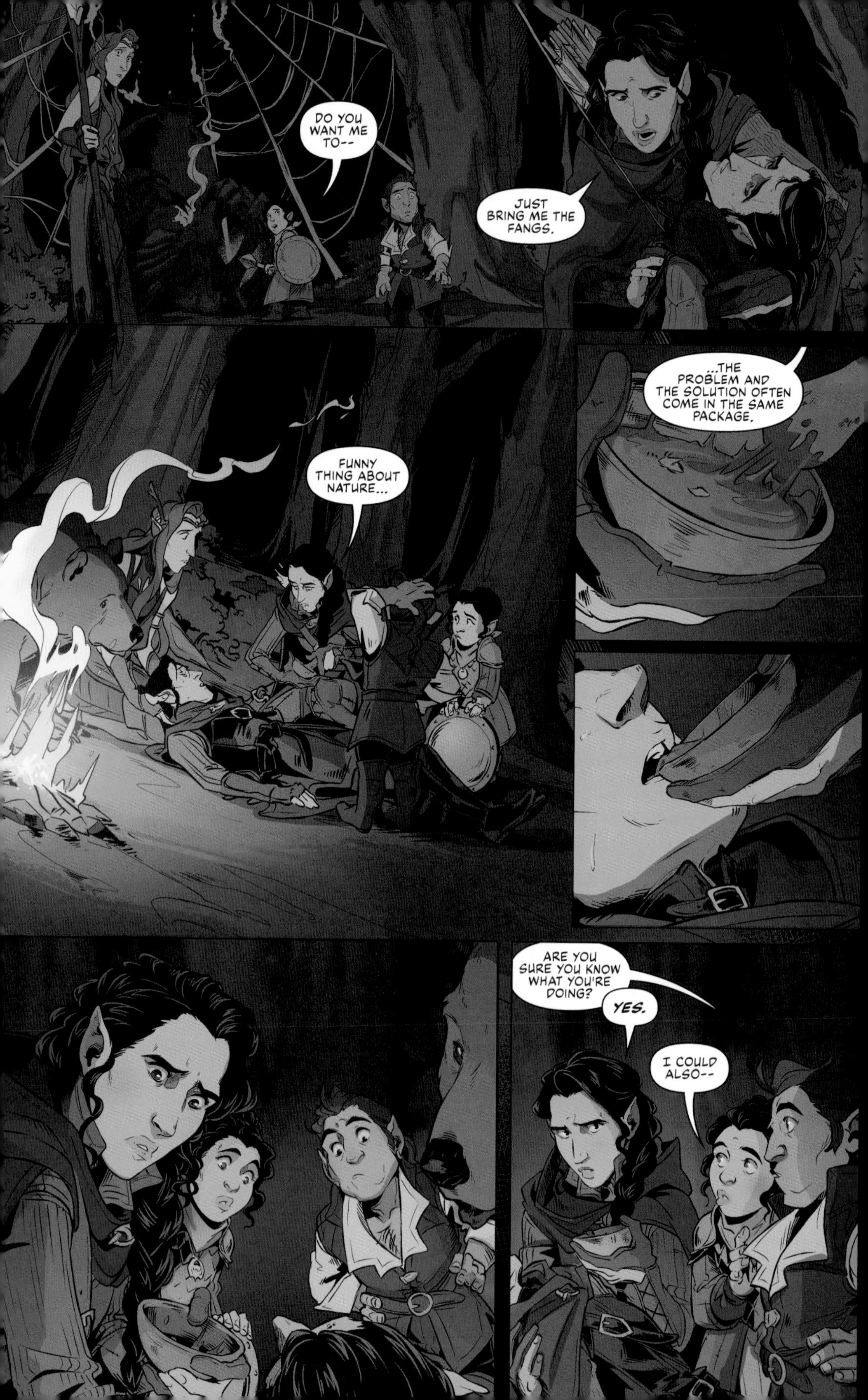
DO YOU WANT ME TO--
JUST BRING ME THE FANGS.
FUNNY THING ABOUT NATURE...
...THE PROBLEM AND THE SOLUTION OFTEN COME IN THE SAME PACKAGE.
ARE YOU SURE YOU KNOW WHAT YOU'RE DOING?
YES.
I COULD ALSO--

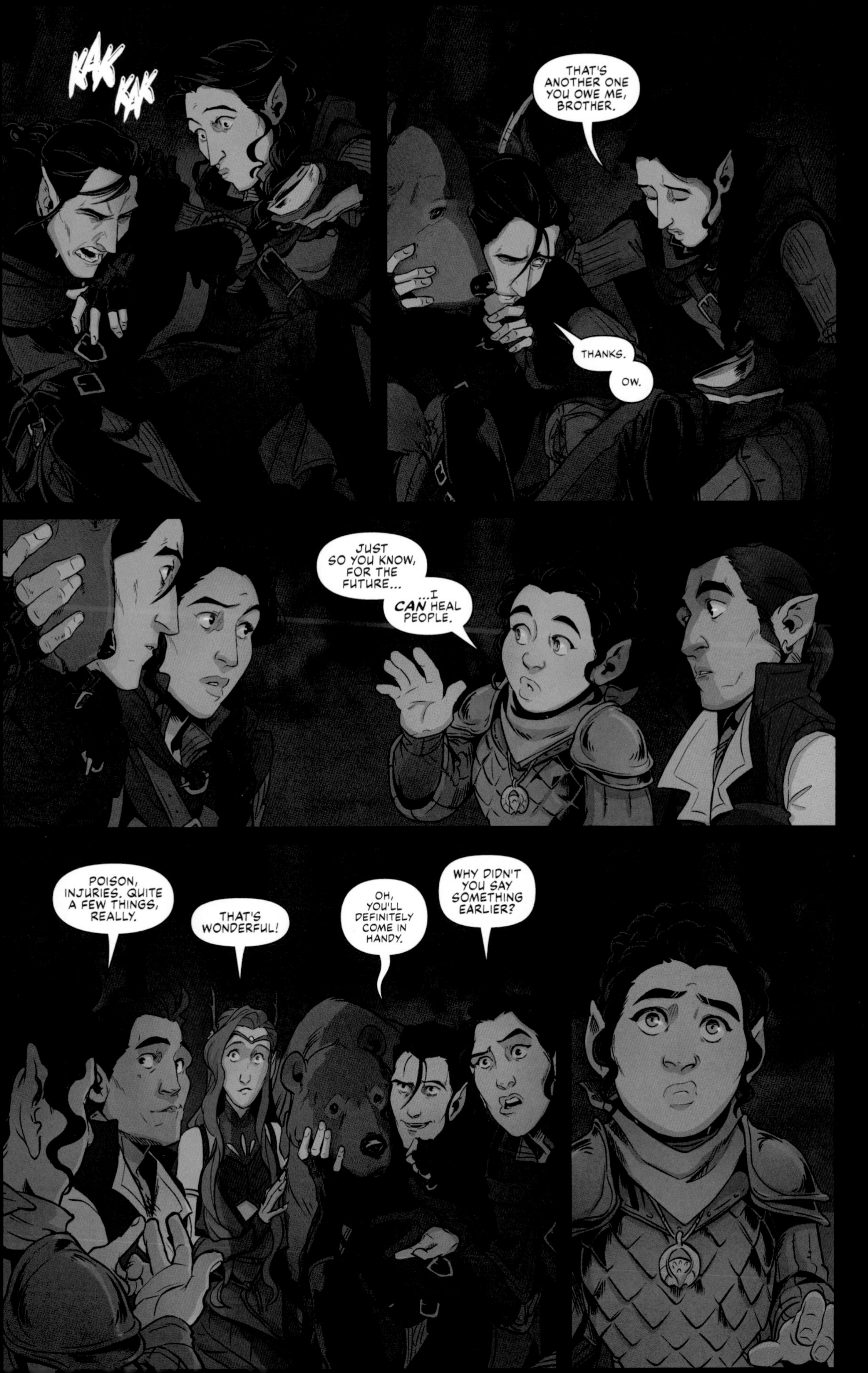
KAK KAK
THAT'S ANOTHER ONE YOU OWE ME, BROTHER.
THANKS.
OW.
JUST SO YOU KNOW, FOR THE FUTURE...
...I CAN HEAL PEOPLE.
POISON, INJURIES. QUITE A FEW THINGS, REALLY.
THAT'S WONDERFUL!
OH, YOU'LL DEFINITELY COME IN HANDY.
WHY DIDN'T YOU SAY SOMETHING EARLIER?

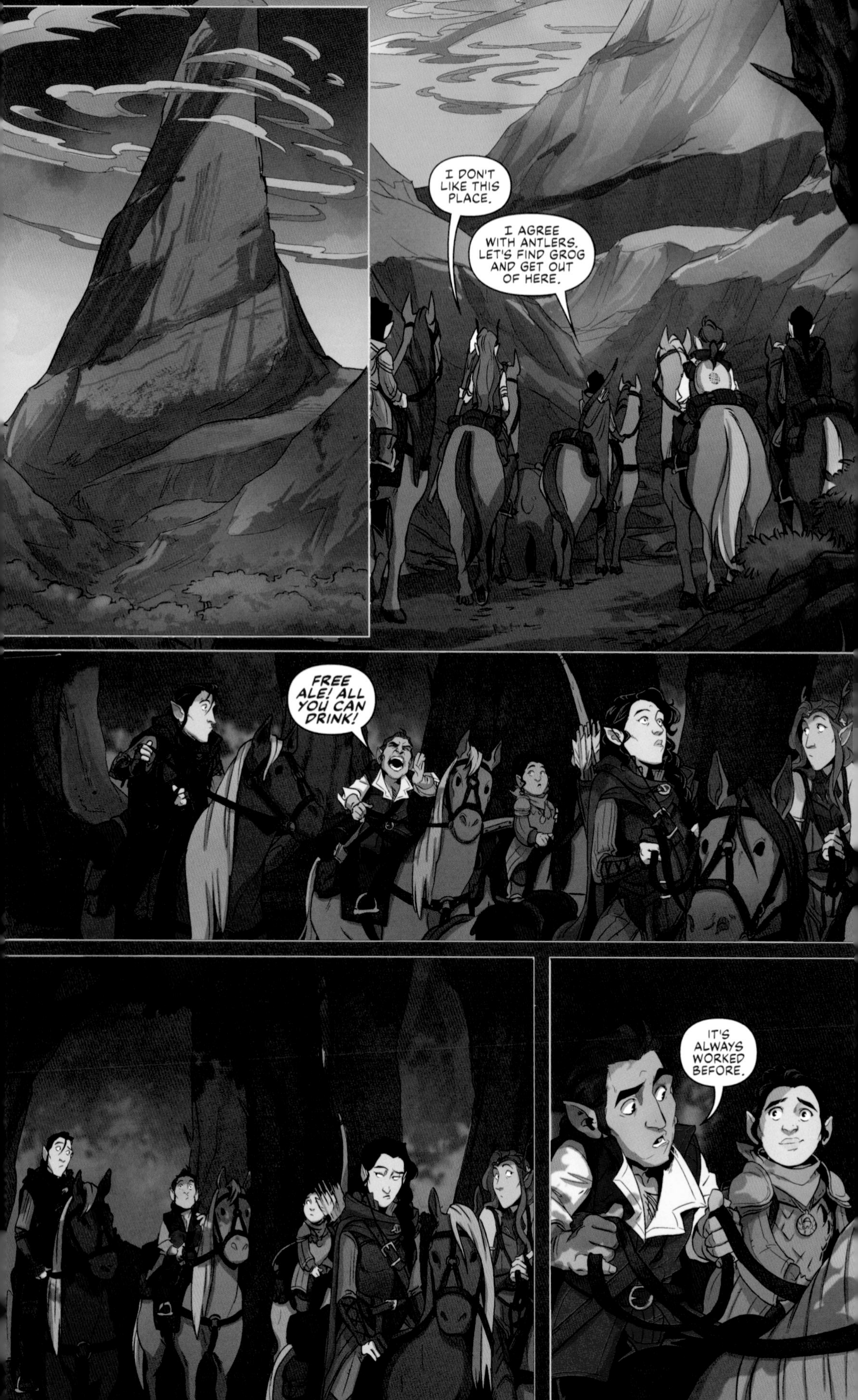
I DON'T LIKE THIS PLACE.
I AGREE WITH ANTLERS. LET'S FIND GROG AND GET OUT OF HERE.
FREE ALE! ALL YOU CAN DRINK!
IT'S ALWAYS WORKED BEFORE.

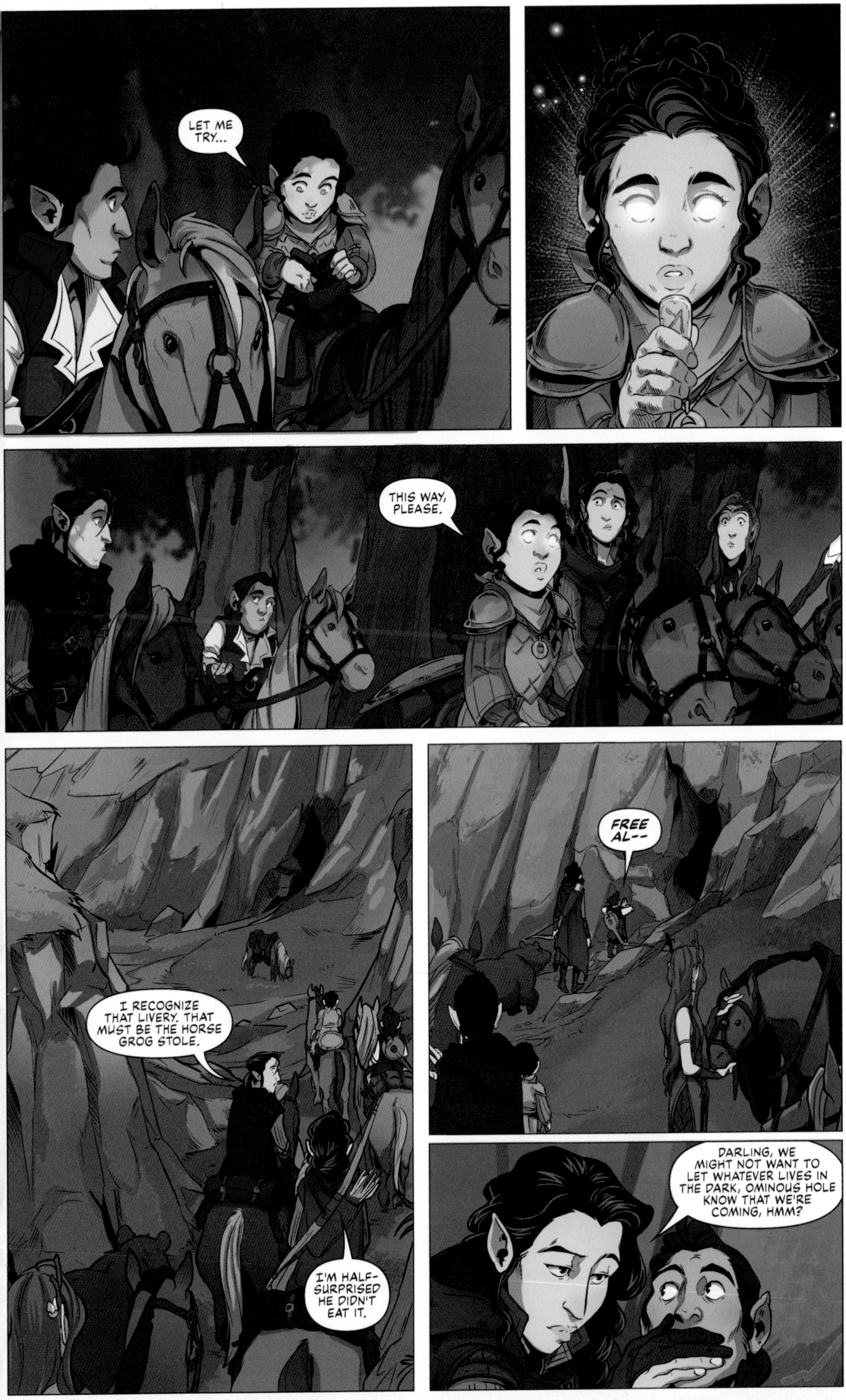
LET ME TRY...
THIS WAY, PLEASE.
I RECOGNIZE THAT LIVERY. THAT MUST BE THE HORSE GROG STOLE.
I'M HALF-SURPRISED HE DIDN'T EAT IT.
FREE AL--
DARLING, WE MIGHT NOT WANT TO LET WHATEVER LIVES IN THE DARK, OMINOUS HOLE KNOW THAT WE'RE COMING, HMM?

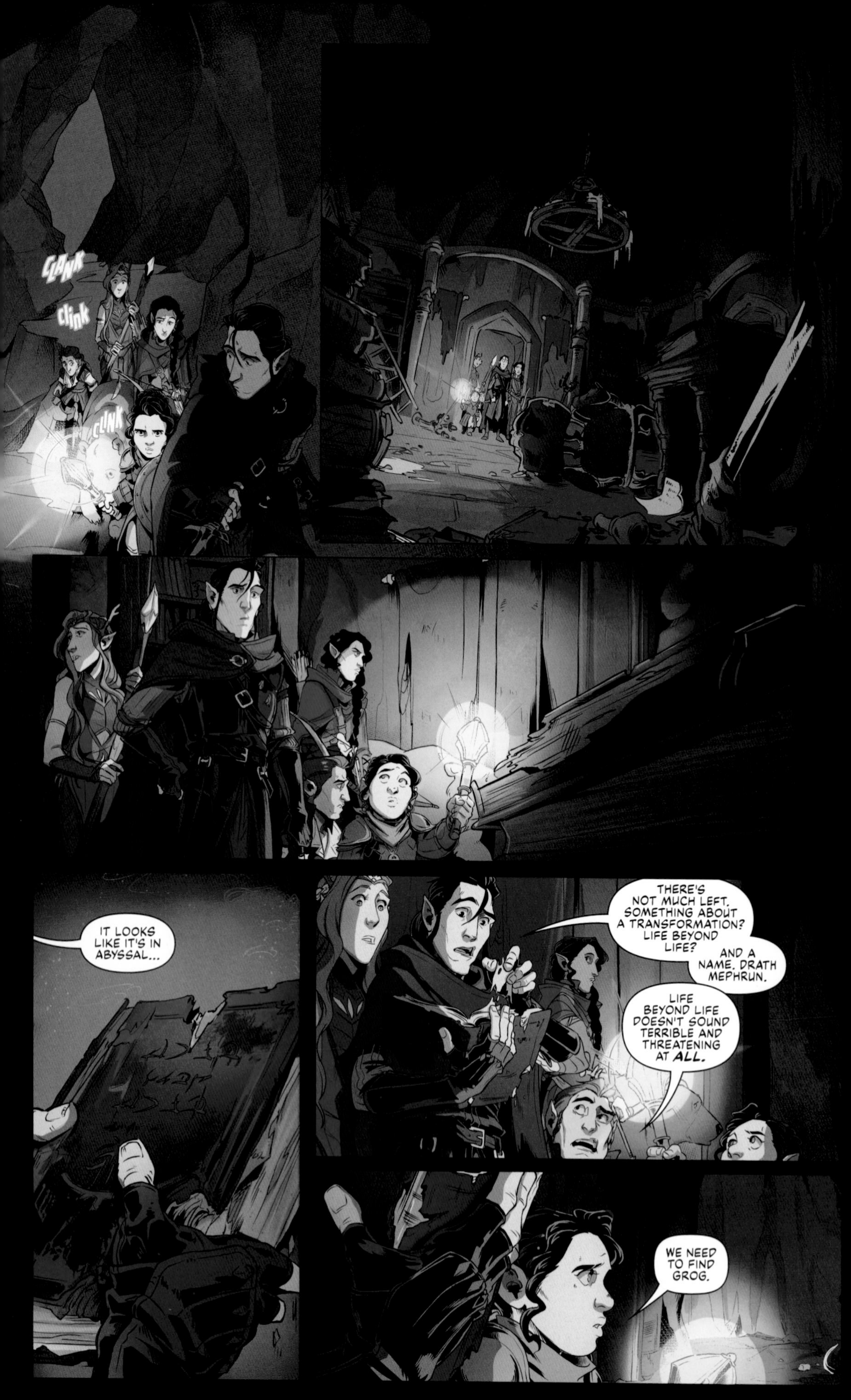
CLANK
clink
CLINK
IT LOOKS LIKE IT'S IN ABYSSAL...
THERE'S NOT MUCH LEFT. SOMETHING ABOUT A TRANSFORMATION? LIFE BEYOND LIFE?
AND A NAME. DRATH MEPHRUN.
LIFE BEYOND LIFE DOESN'T SOUND TERRIBLE AND THREATENING AT ALL.
WE NEED TO FIND GROG.

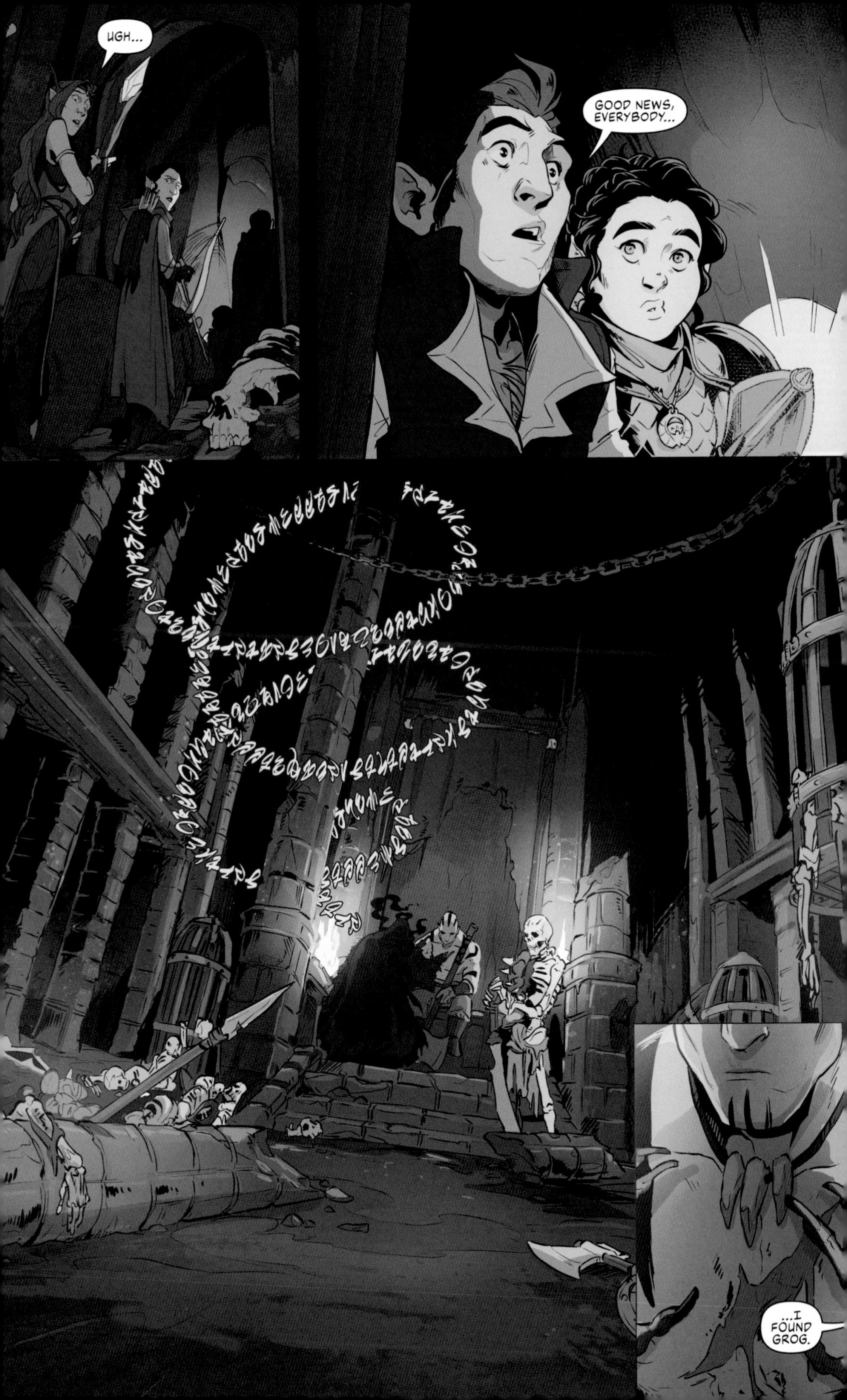
UGH...
GOOD NEWS, EVERYBODY...
...I FOUND GROG.

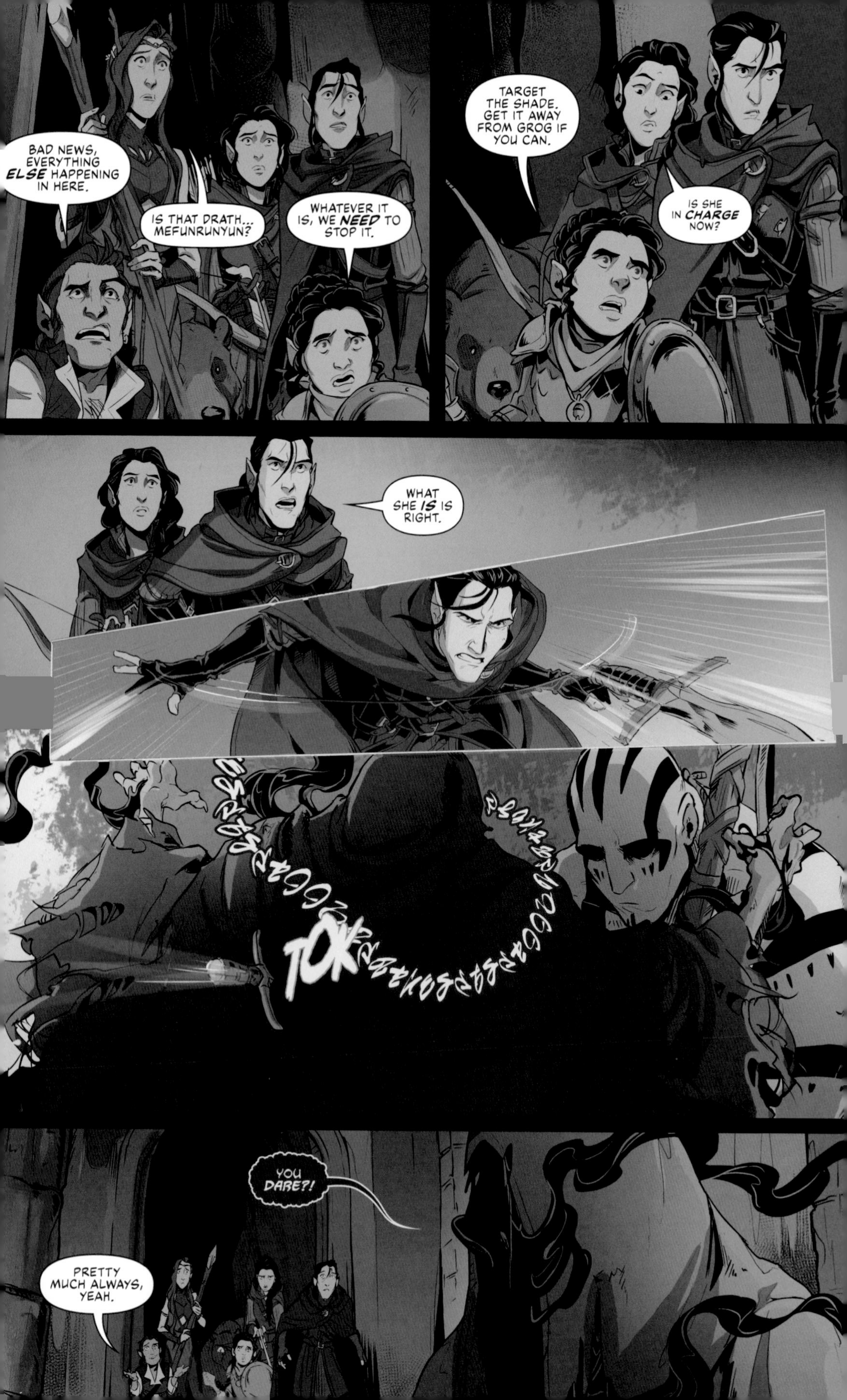
BAD NEWS, EVERYTHING ELSE HAPPENING IN HERE.
IS THAT DRATH... MEFUNRUNYUN?
WHATEVER IT IS, WE NEED TO STOP IT.
TARGET THE SHADE. GET IT AWAY FROM GROG IF YOU CAN.
IS SHE IN CHARGE NOW?
WHAT SHE IS IS RIGHT.
TOK
YOU DARE?!
PRETTY MUCH ALWAYS, YEAH.

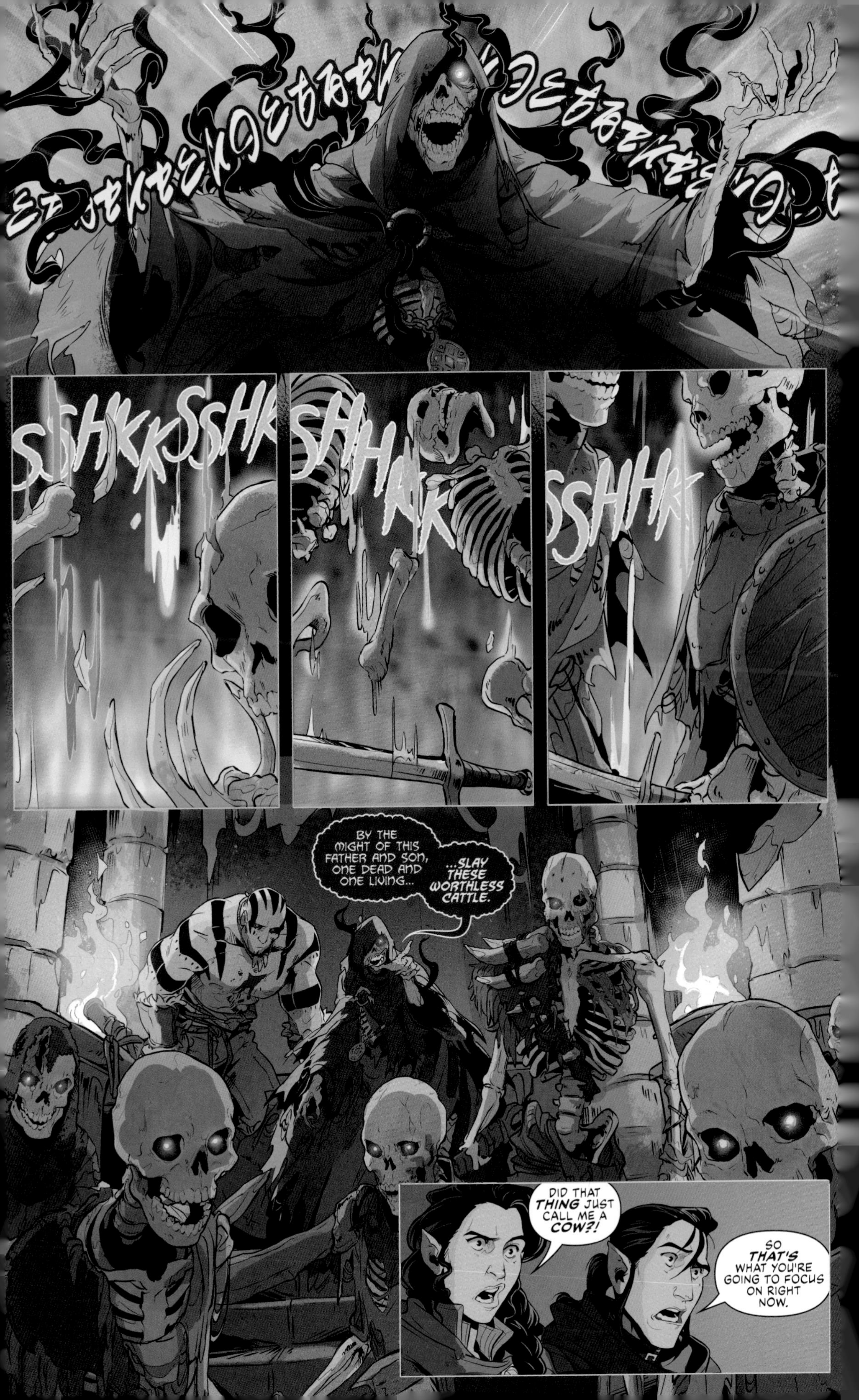
SSHKK
SSHK
SHHK
SSHK
BY THE MIGHT OF THIS FATHER AND SON, ONE DEAD AND ONE LIVING...
...SLAY THESE WORTHLESS CATTLE.
DID THAT THING JUST CALL ME A COW?!
SO THAT'S WHAT YOU'RE GOING TO FOCUS ON RIGHT NOW.

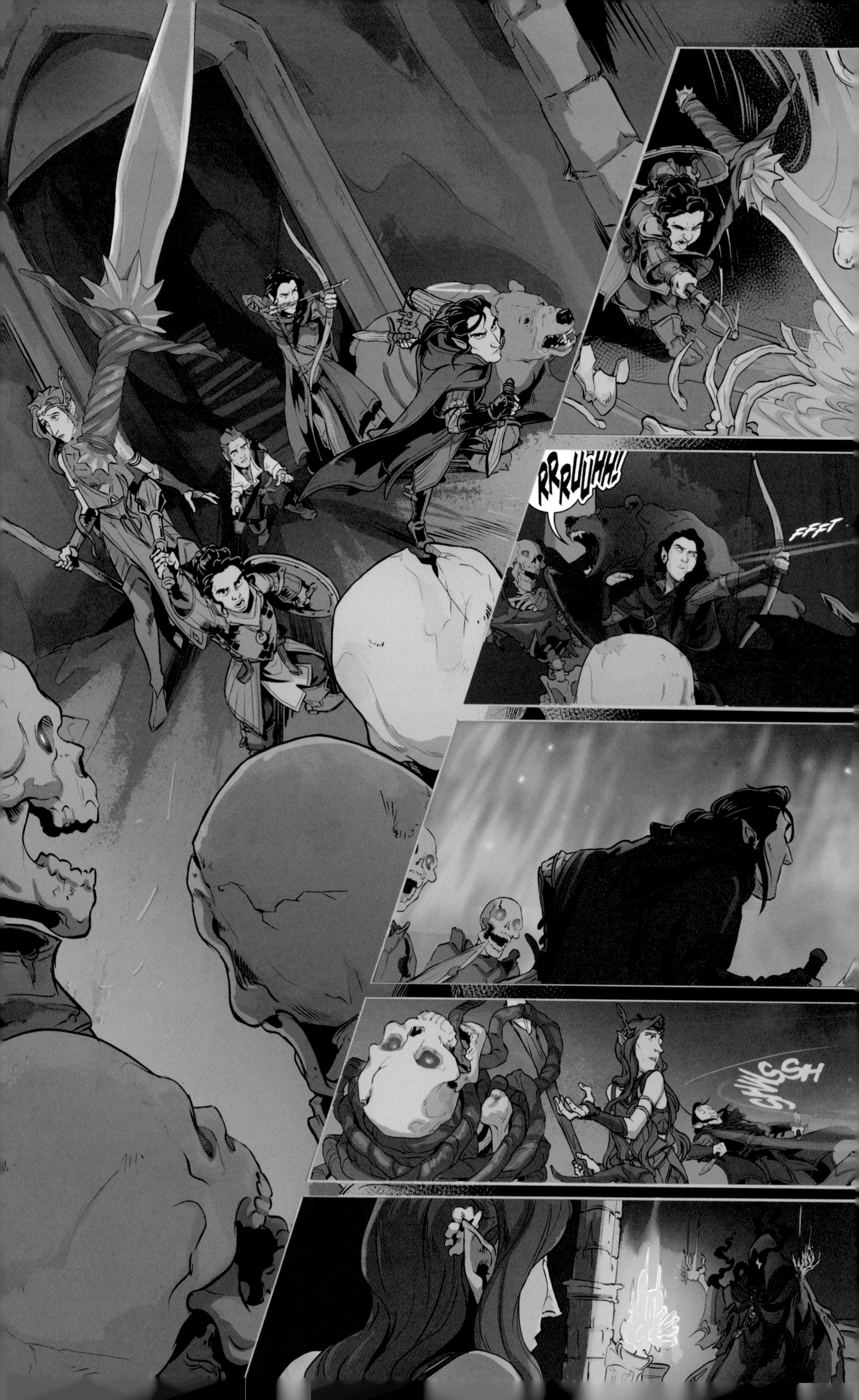
RRRUUHH!
FFFT
SHWSSH

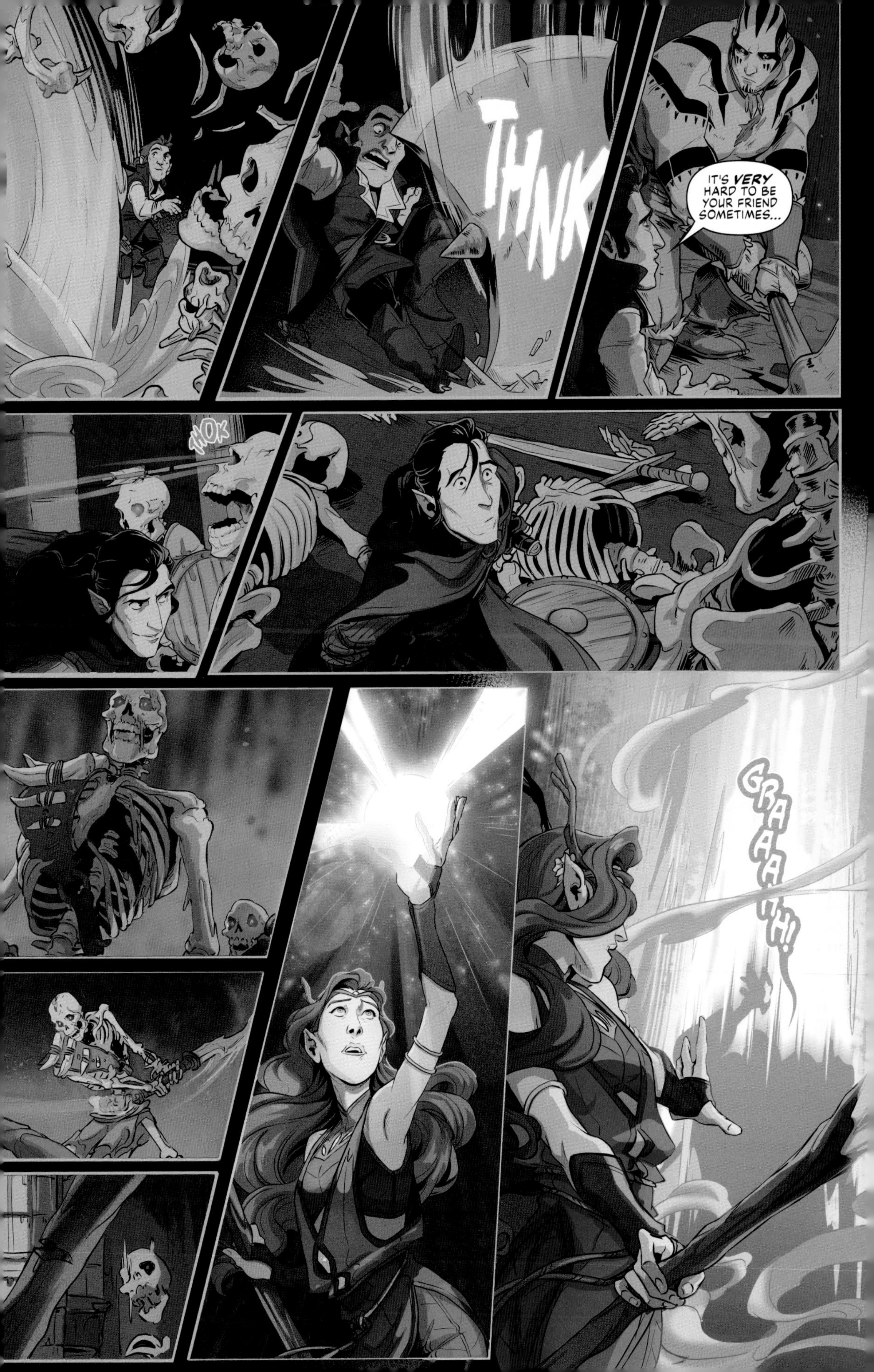
THNK
IT'S **VERY** HARD TO BE YOUR FRIEND SOMETIMES...
THOK
GRAAAAH!

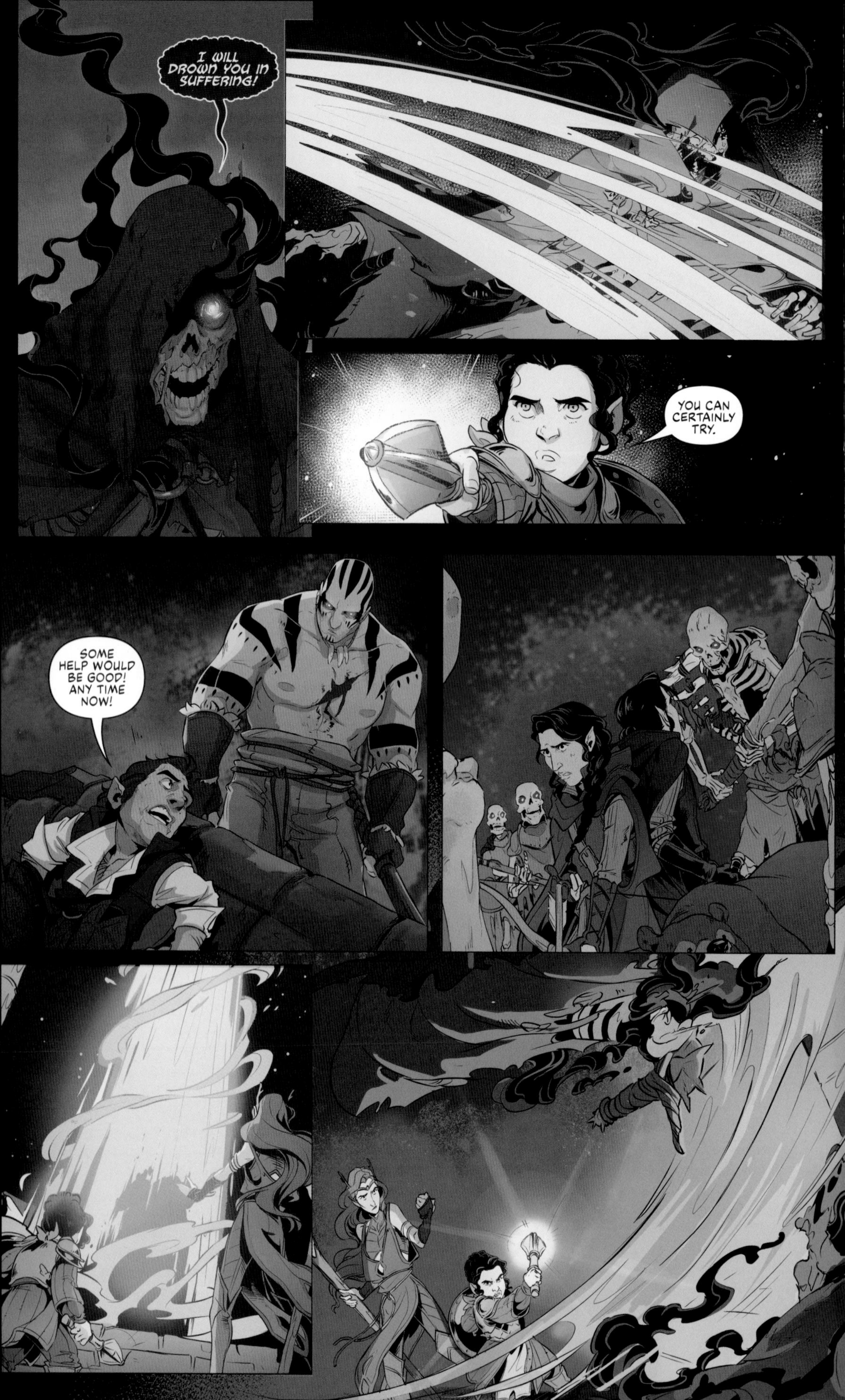
I WILL DROWN YOU IN SUFFERING!
YOU CAN CERTAINLY TRY.
SOME HELP WOULD BE GOOD! ANY TIME NOW!

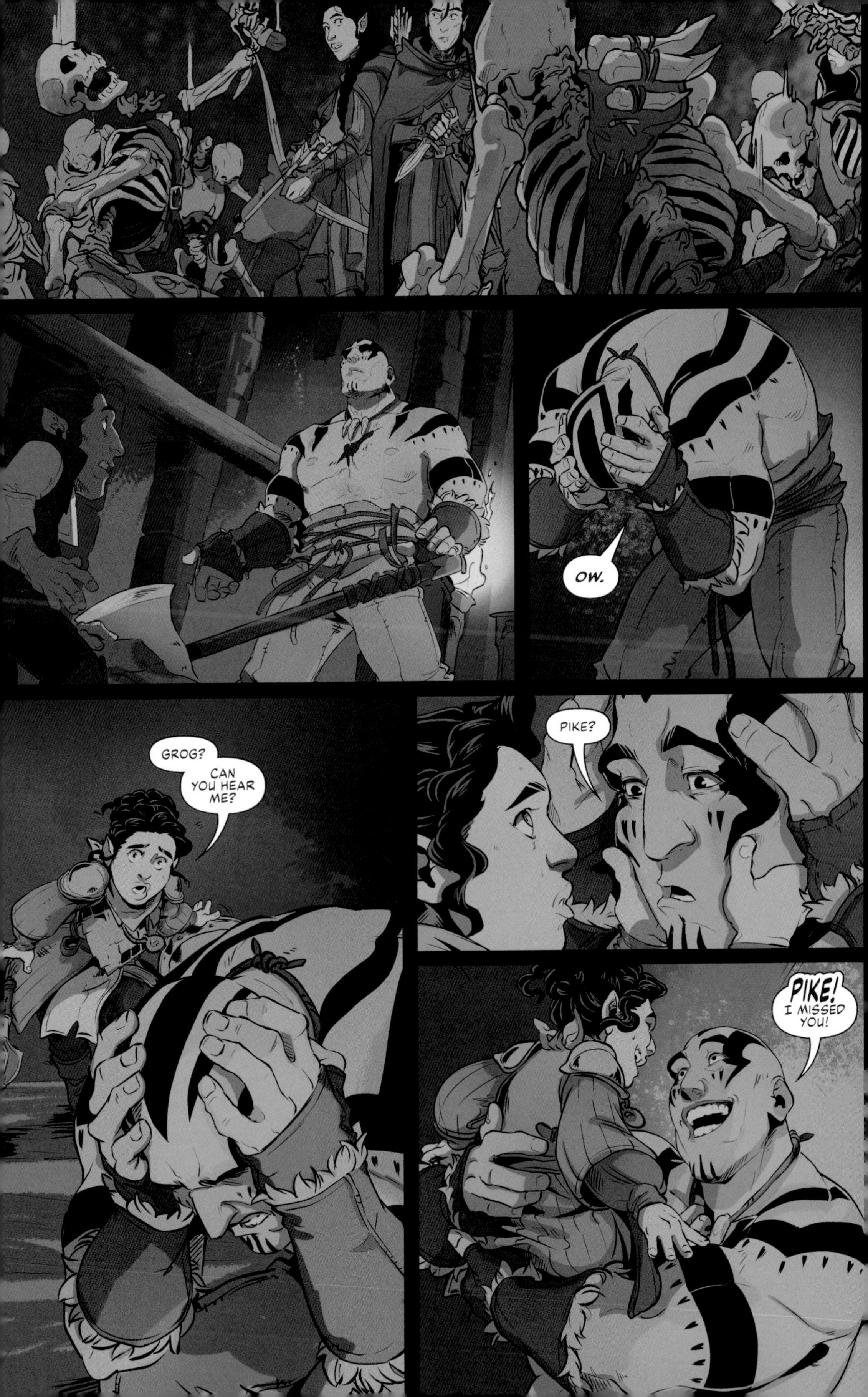
OW.
GROG?
CAN YOU HEAR ME?
PIKE?
PIKE!
I MISSED YOU!

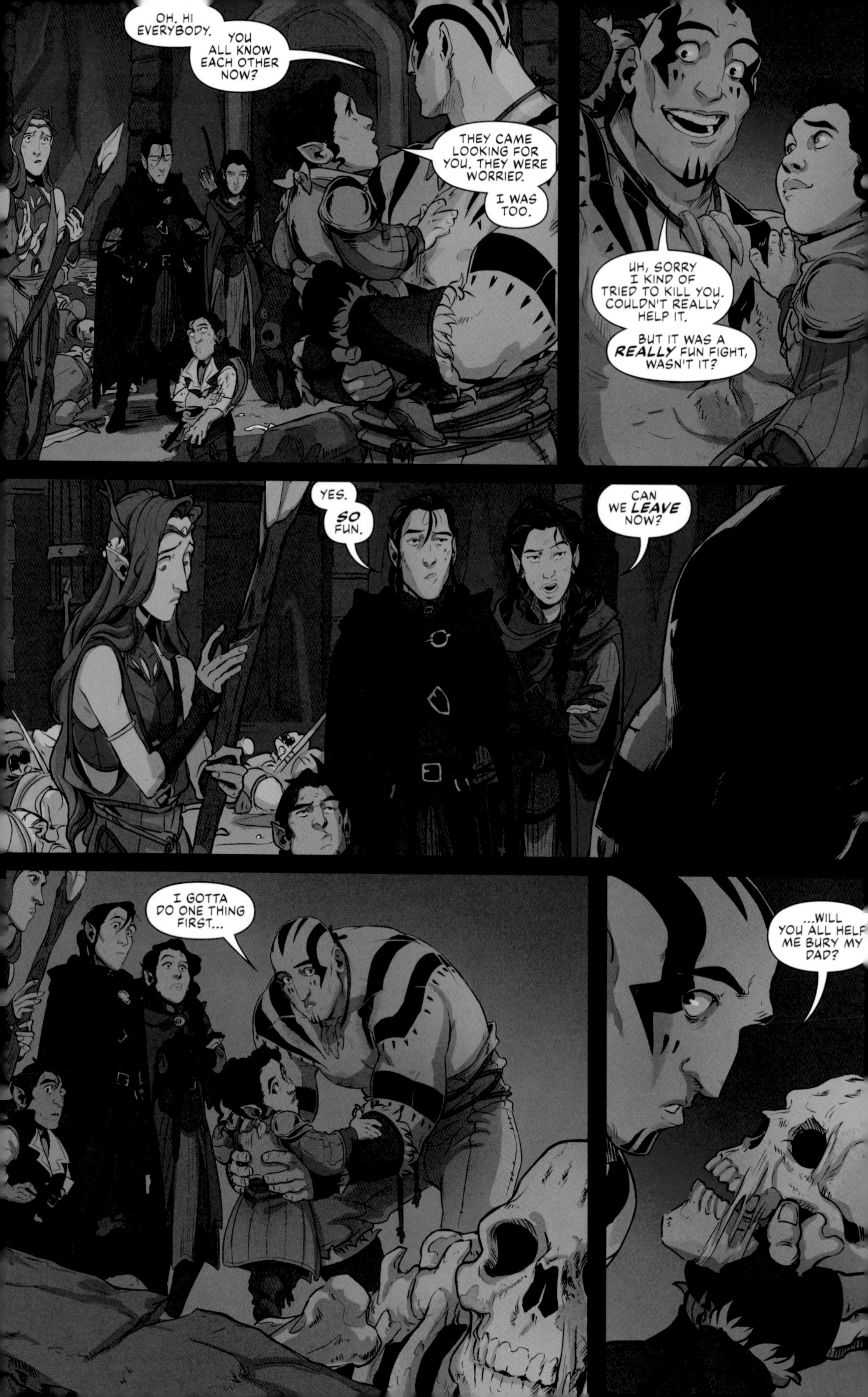
OH. HI EVERYBODY.
YOU ALL KNOW EACH OTHER NOW?
THEY CAME LOOKING FOR YOU. THEY WERE WORRIED.
I WAS TOO.
UH, SORRY I KIND OF TRIED TO KILL YOU. COULDN'T REALLY HELP IT.
BUT IT WAS A REALLY FUN FIGHT, WASN'T IT?
YES. SO FUN.
CAN WE LEAVE NOW?
I GOTTA DO ONE THING FIRST...
...WILL YOU ALL HELP ME BURY MY DAD?

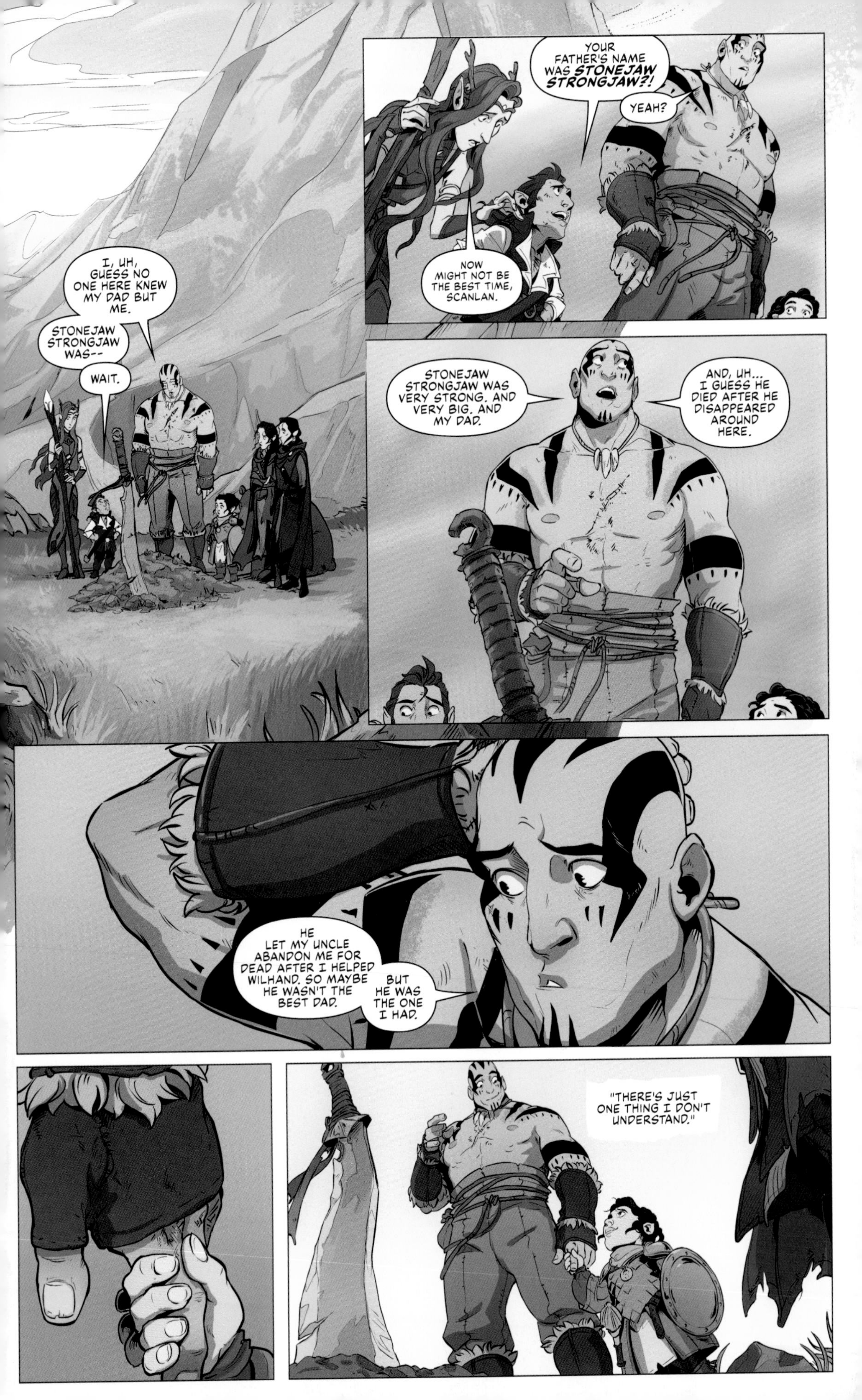
YOUR FATHER'S NAME WAS STONEJAW STRONGJAW?!
YEAH?
NOW MIGHT NOT BE THE BEST TIME, SCANLAN.
I, UH, GUESS NO ONE HERE KNEW MY DAD BUT ME.
STONEJAW STRONGJAW WAS--
WAIT.
STONEJAW STRONGJAW WAS VERY STRONG. AND VERY BIG. AND MY DAD.
AND, UH... I GUESS HE DIED AFTER HE DISAPPEARED AROUND HERE.
HE LET MY UNCLE ABANDON ME FOR DEAD AFTER I HELPED WILHAND. SO MAYBE HE WASN'T THE BEST DAD.
BUT HE WAS THE ONE I HAD.
"THERE'S JUST ONE THING I DON'T UNDERSTAND."

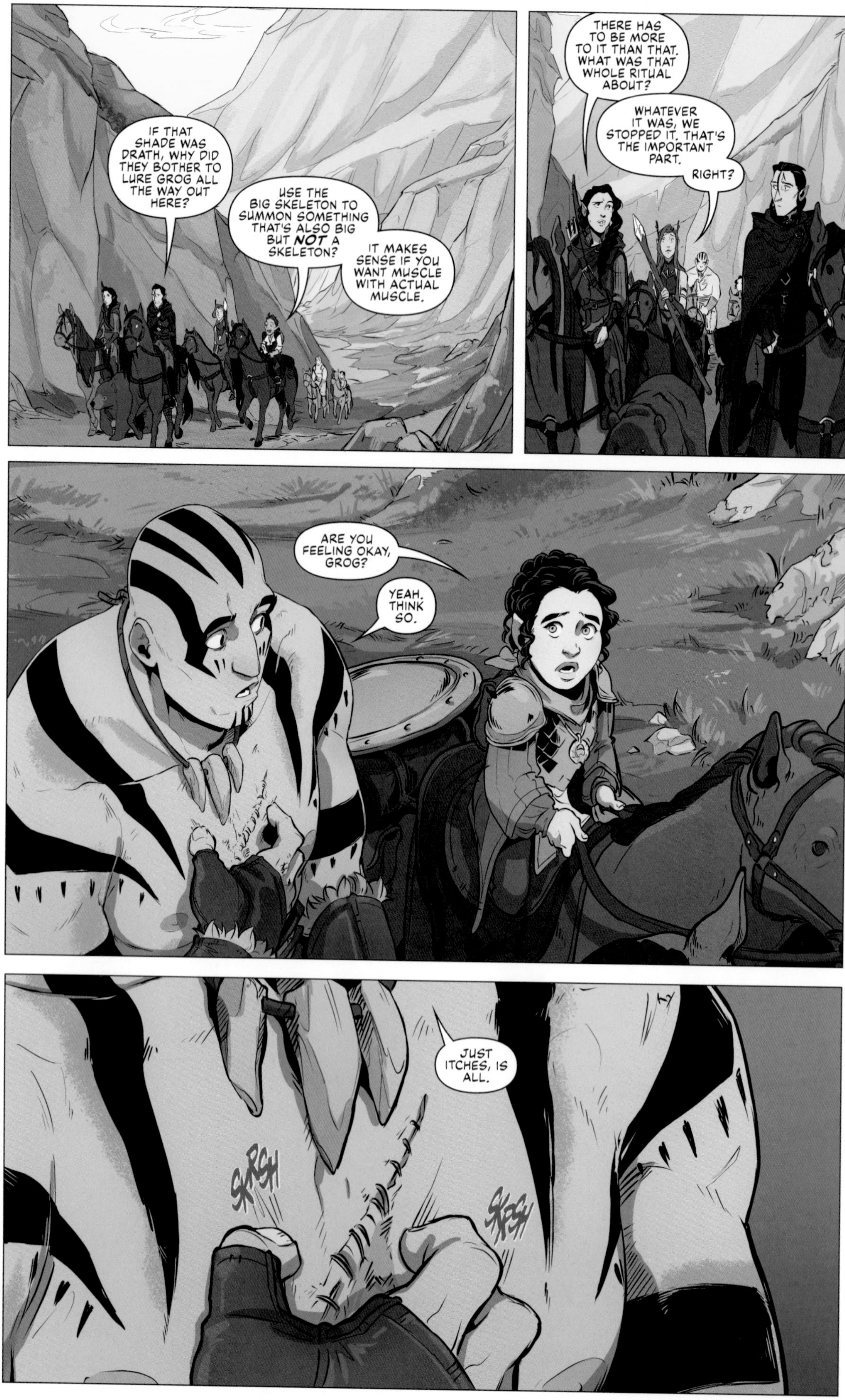
IF THAT SHADE WAS DRATH, WHY DID THEY BOTHER TO LURE GROG ALL THE WAY OUT HERE?
USE THE BIG SKELETON TO SUMMON SOMETHING THAT'S ALSO BIG BUT **NOT** A SKELETON?
IT MAKES SENSE IF YOU WANT MUSCLE WITH ACTUAL MUSCLE.
THERE HAS TO BE MORE TO IT THAN THAT. WHAT WAS THAT WHOLE RITUAL ABOUT?
WHATEVER IT WAS, WE STOPPED IT. THAT'S THE IMPORTANT PART.
RIGHT?
ARE YOU FEELING OKAY, GROG?
YEAH. THINK SO.
JUST ITCHES, IS ALL.
SKRSH
SKRSH

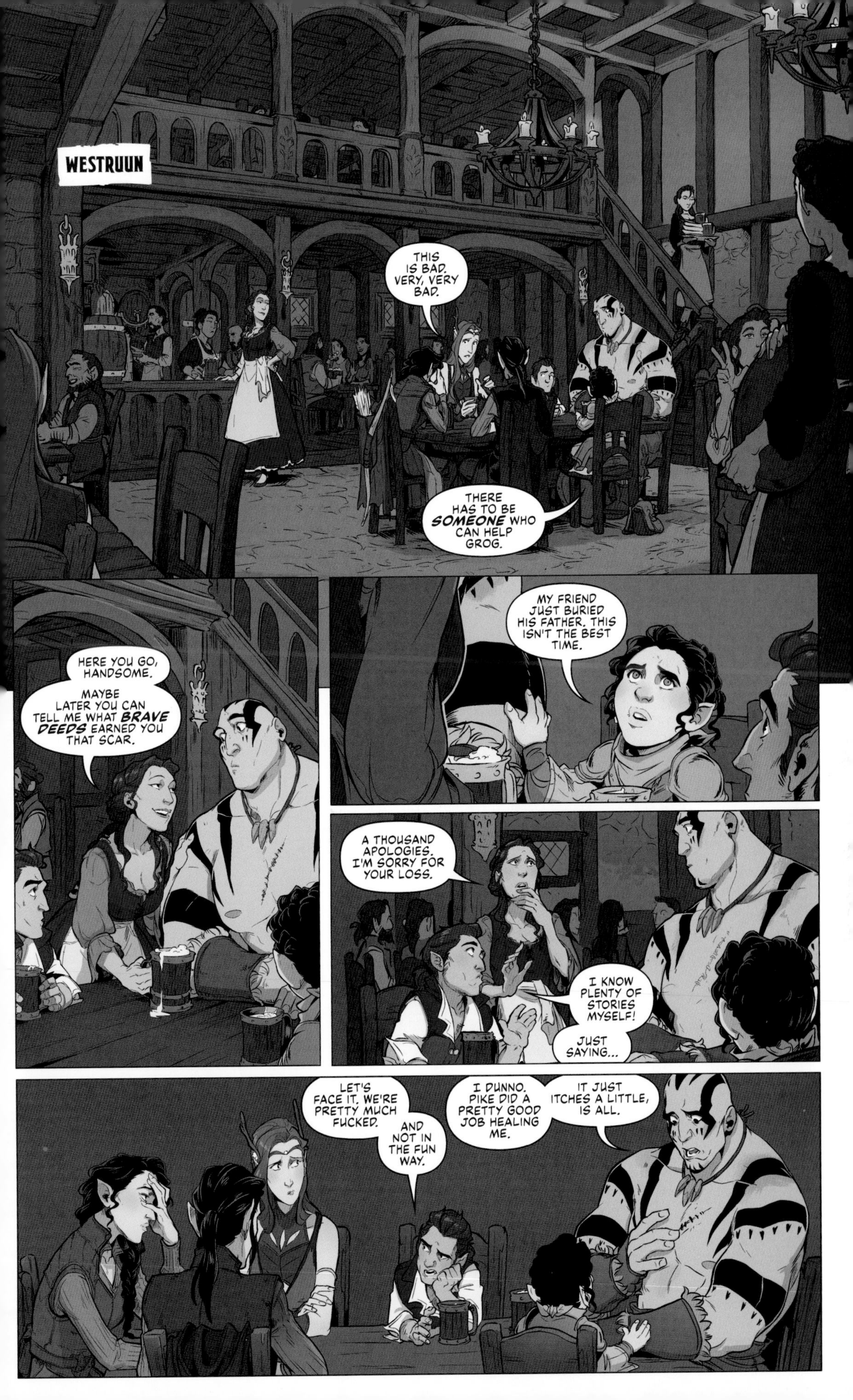
WESTRUUN
THIS IS BAD. VERY, VERY BAD.
THERE HAS TO BE SOMEONE WHO CAN HELP GROG.
HERE YOU GO, HANDSOME.
MAYBE LATER YOU CAN TELL ME WHAT BRAVE DEEDS EARNED YOU THAT SCAR.
MY FRIEND JUST BURIED HIS FATHER. THIS ISN'T THE BEST TIME.
A THOUSAND APOLOGIES. I'M SORRY FOR YOUR LOSS.
I KNOW PLENTY OF STORIES MYSELF!
JUST SAYING...
LET'S FACE IT. WE'RE PRETTY MUCH FUCKED.
AND NOT IN THE FUN WAY.
I DUNNO. PIKE DID A PRETTY GOOD JOB HEALING ME.
IT JUST ITCHES A LITTLE, IS ALL.

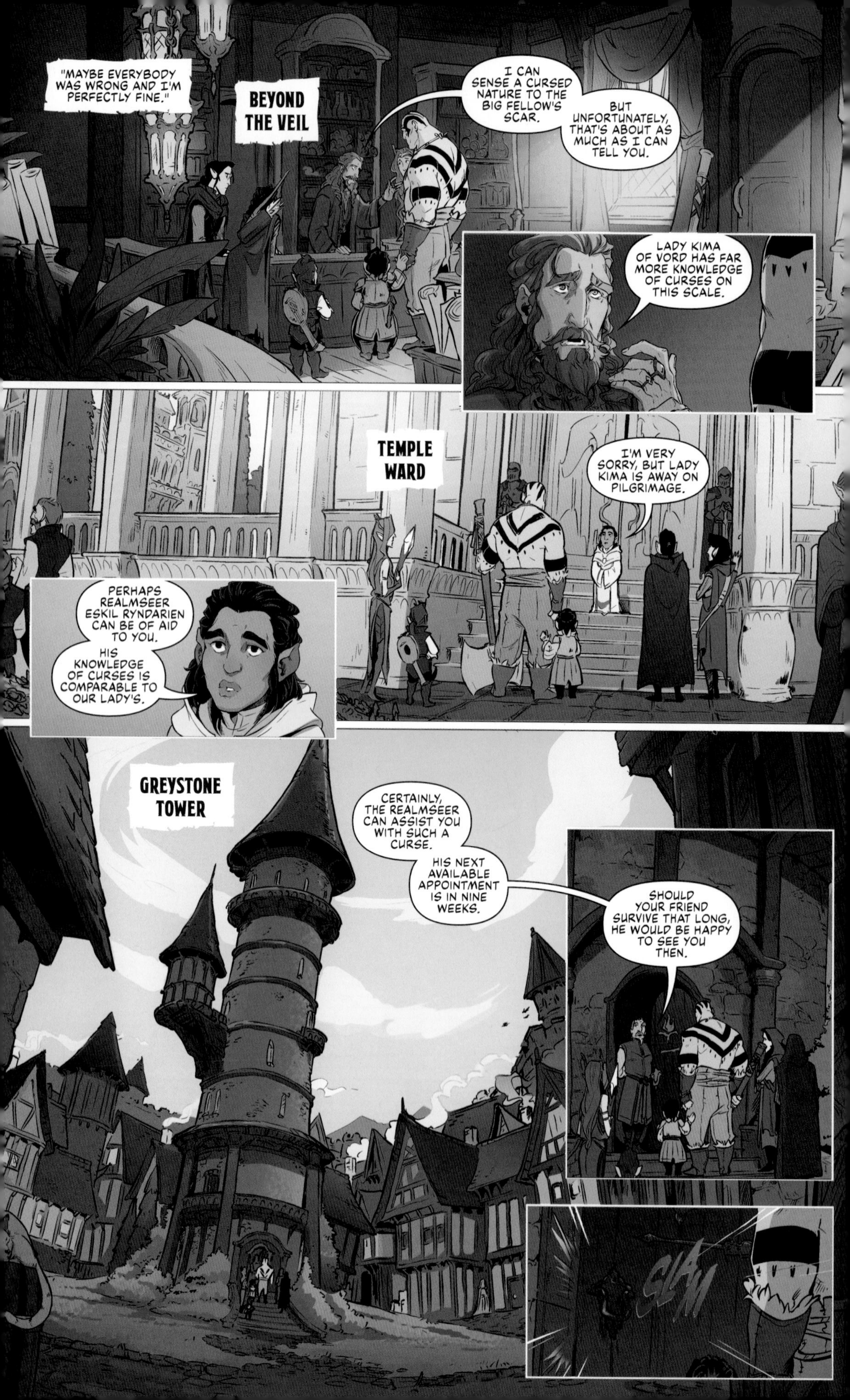
"MAYBE EVERYBODY WAS WRONG AND I'M PERFECTLY FINE."
BEYOND THE VEIL
I CAN SENSE A CURSED NATURE TO THE BIG FELLOW'S SCAR.
BUT UNFORTUNATELY, THAT'S ABOUT AS MUCH AS I CAN TELL YOU.
LADY KIMA OF VORD HAS FAR MORE KNOWLEDGE OF CURSES ON THIS SCALE.
TEMPLE WARD
I'M VERY SORRY, BUT LADY KIMA IS AWAY ON PILGRIMAGE.
PERHAPS REALMSEER ESKIL RYNDARIEN CAN BE OF AID TO YOU.
HIS KNOWLEDGE OF CURSES IS COMPARABLE TO OUR LADY'S.
GREYSTONE TOWER
CERTAINLY, THE REALMSEER CAN ASSIST YOU WITH SUCH A CURSE.
HIS NEXT AVAILABLE APPOINTMENT IS IN NINE WEEKS.
SHOULD YOUR FRIEND SURVIVE THAT LONG, HE WOULD BE HAPPY TO SEE YOU THEN.
SLAM

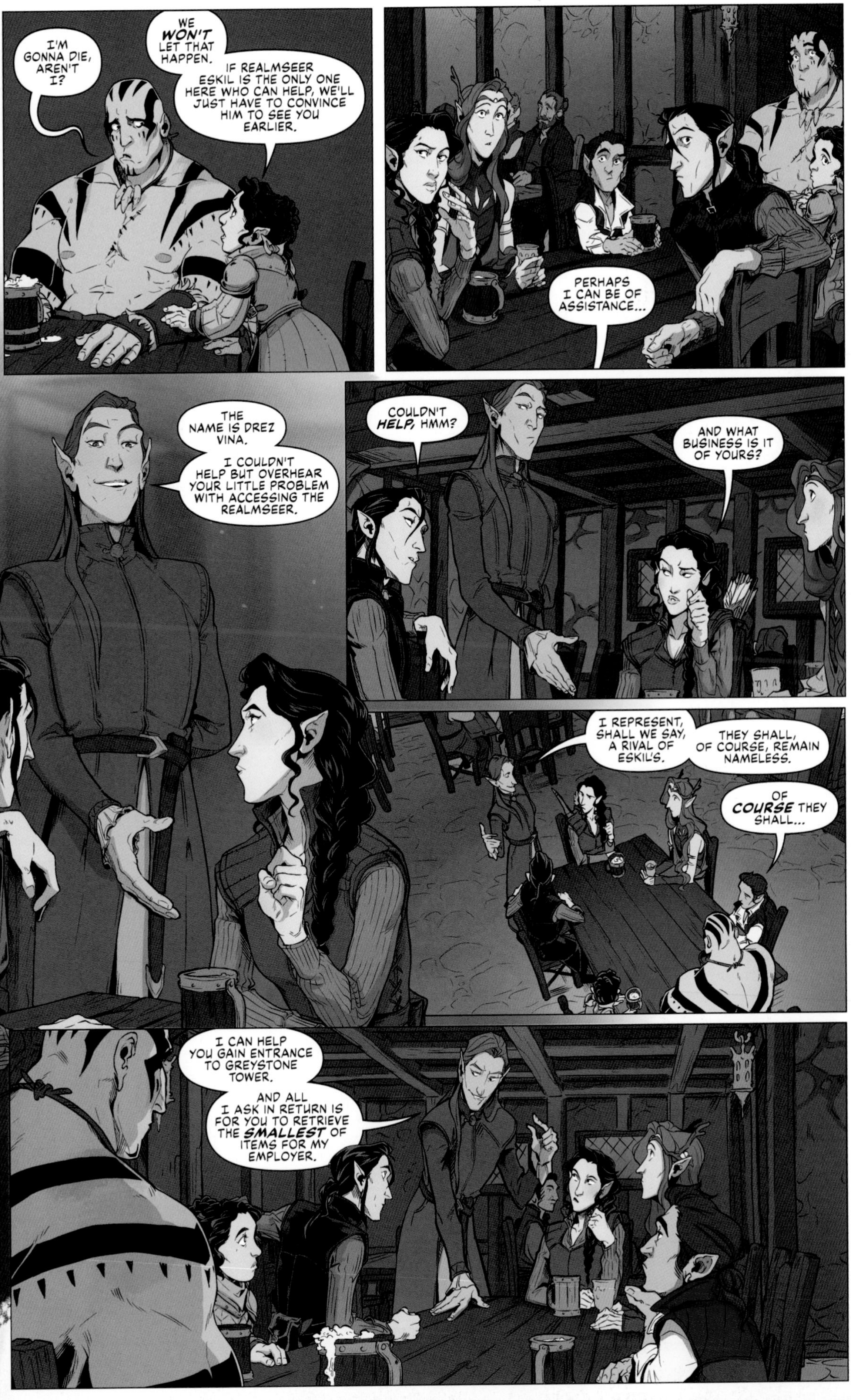
I'M GONNA DIE, AREN'T I?
WE WON'T LET THAT HAPPEN.
IF REALMSEER ESKIL IS THE ONLY ONE HERE WHO CAN HELP, WE'LL JUST HAVE TO CONVINCE HIM TO SEE YOU EARLIER.
PERHAPS I CAN BE OF ASSISTANCE...
THE NAME IS DREZ VINA.
I COULDN'T HELP BUT OVERHEAR YOUR LITTLE PROBLEM WITH ACCESSING THE REALMSEER.
COULDN'T HELP, HMM?
AND WHAT BUSINESS IS IT OF YOURS?
I REPRESENT, SHALL WE SAY, A RIVAL OF ESKIL'S.
THEY SHALL, OF COURSE, REMAIN NAMELESS.
OF COURSE THEY SHALL...
I CAN HELP YOU GAIN ENTRANCE TO GREYSTONE TOWER.
AND ALL I ASK IN RETURN IS FOR YOU TO RETRIEVE THE SMALLEST OF ITEMS FOR MY EMPLOYER.

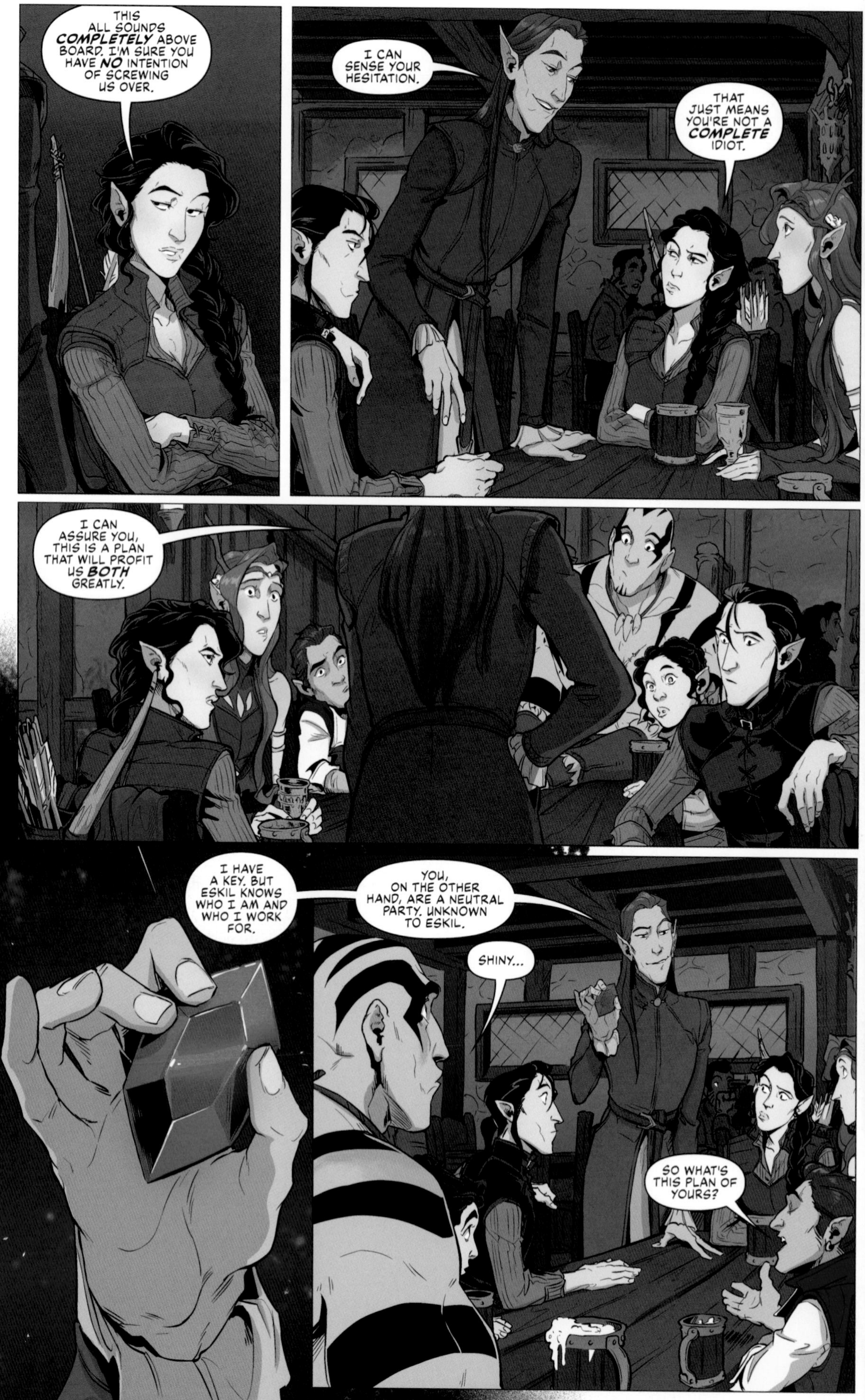
THIS ALL SOUNDS COMPLETELY ABOVE BOARD. I'M SURE YOU HAVE NO INTENTION OF SCREWING US OVER.
I CAN SENSE YOUR HESITATION.
THAT JUST MEANS YOU'RE NOT A COMPLETE IDIOT.
I CAN ASSURE YOU, THIS IS A PLAN THAT WILL PROFIT US BOTH GREATLY.
I HAVE A KEY. BUT ESKIL KNOWS WHO I AM AND WHO I WORK FOR.
YOU, ON THE OTHER HAND, ARE A NEUTRAL PARTY. UNKNOWN TO ESKIL.
SHINY...
SO WHAT'S THIS PLAN OF YOURS?

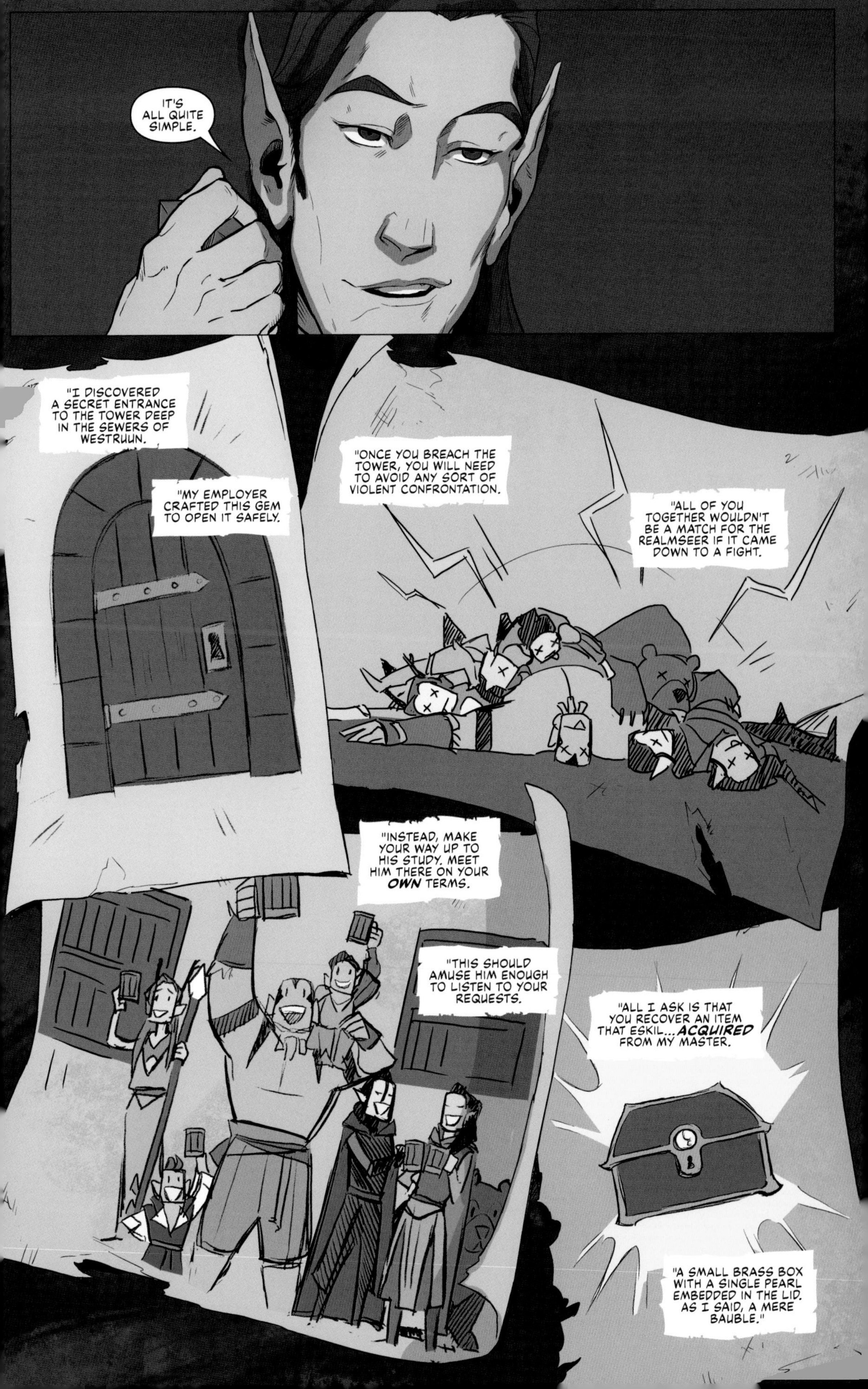
IT'S ALL QUITE SIMPLE.
"I DISCOVERED A SECRET ENTRANCE TO THE TOWER DEEP IN THE SEWERS OF WESTRUUN.
"MY EMPLOYER CRAFTED THIS GEM TO OPEN IT SAFELY.
"ONCE YOU BREACH THE TOWER, YOU WILL NEED TO AVOID ANY SORT OF VIOLENT CONFRONTATION.
"ALL OF YOU TOGETHER WOULDN'T BE A MATCH FOR THE REALMSEER IF IT CAME DOWN TO A FIGHT.
"INSTEAD, MAKE YOUR WAY UP TO HIS STUDY. MEET HIM THERE ON YOUR *OWN* TERMS.
"THIS SHOULD AMUSE HIM ENOUGH TO LISTEN TO YOUR REQUESTS.
"ALL I ASK IS THAT YOU RECOVER AN ITEM THAT ESKIL... *ACQUIRED* FROM MY MASTER.
"A SMALL BRASS BOX WITH A SINGLE PEARL EMBEDDED IN THE LID. AS I SAID, A MERE BAUBLE."

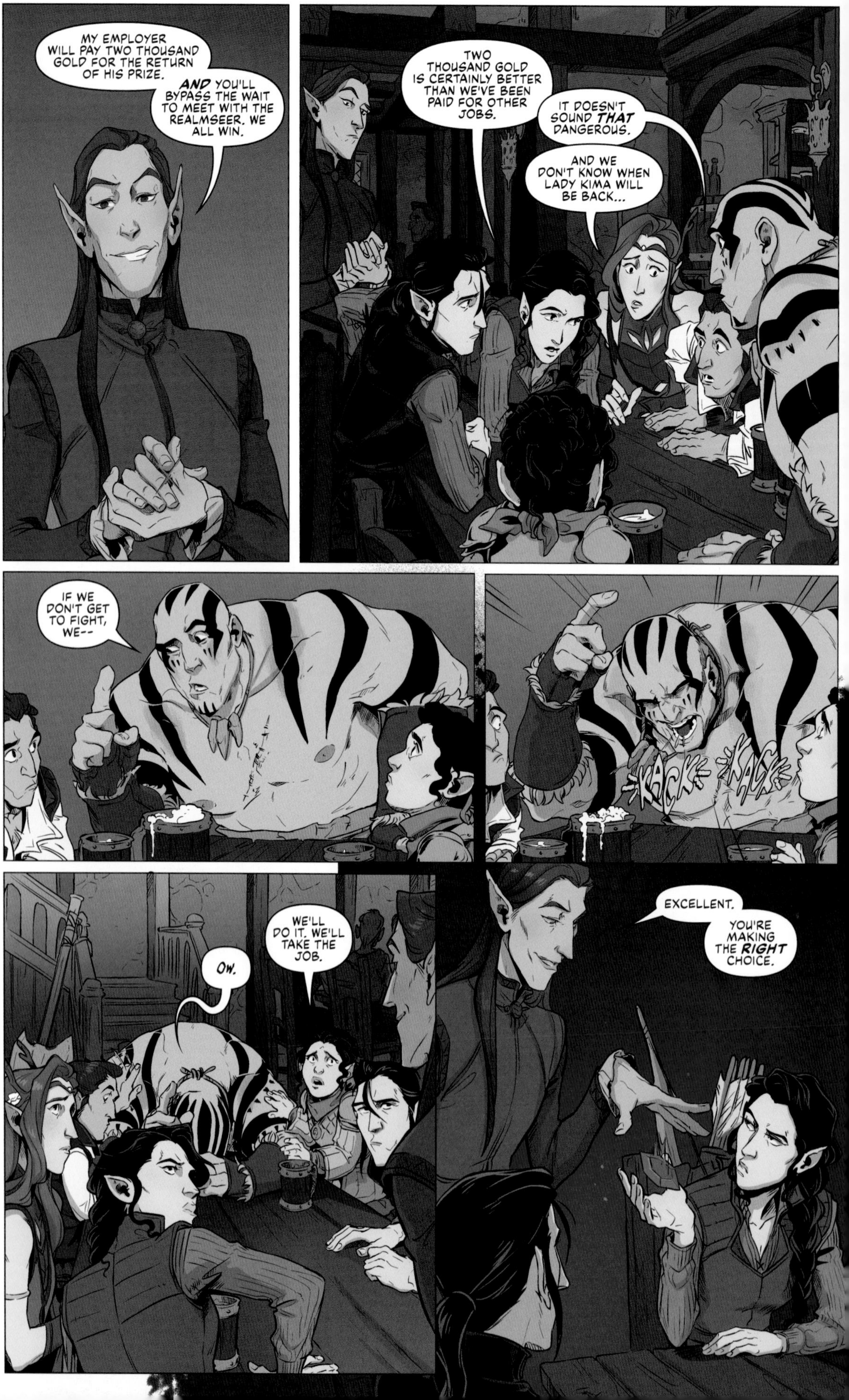
MY EMPLOYER WILL PAY TWO THOUSAND GOLD FOR THE RETURN OF HIS PRIZE.
AND YOU'LL BYPASS THE WAIT TO MEET WITH THE REALMSEER. WE ALL WIN.
TWO THOUSAND GOLD IS CERTAINLY BETTER THAN WE'VE BEEN PAID FOR OTHER JOBS.
IT DOESN'T SOUND THAT DANGEROUS.
AND WE DON'T KNOW WHEN LADY KIMA WILL BE BACK...
IF WE DON'T GET TO FIGHT, WE--
KACK- KACK
OW.
WE'LL DO IT. WE'LL TAKE THE JOB.
EXCELLENT.
YOU'RE MAKING THE RIGHT CHOICE.

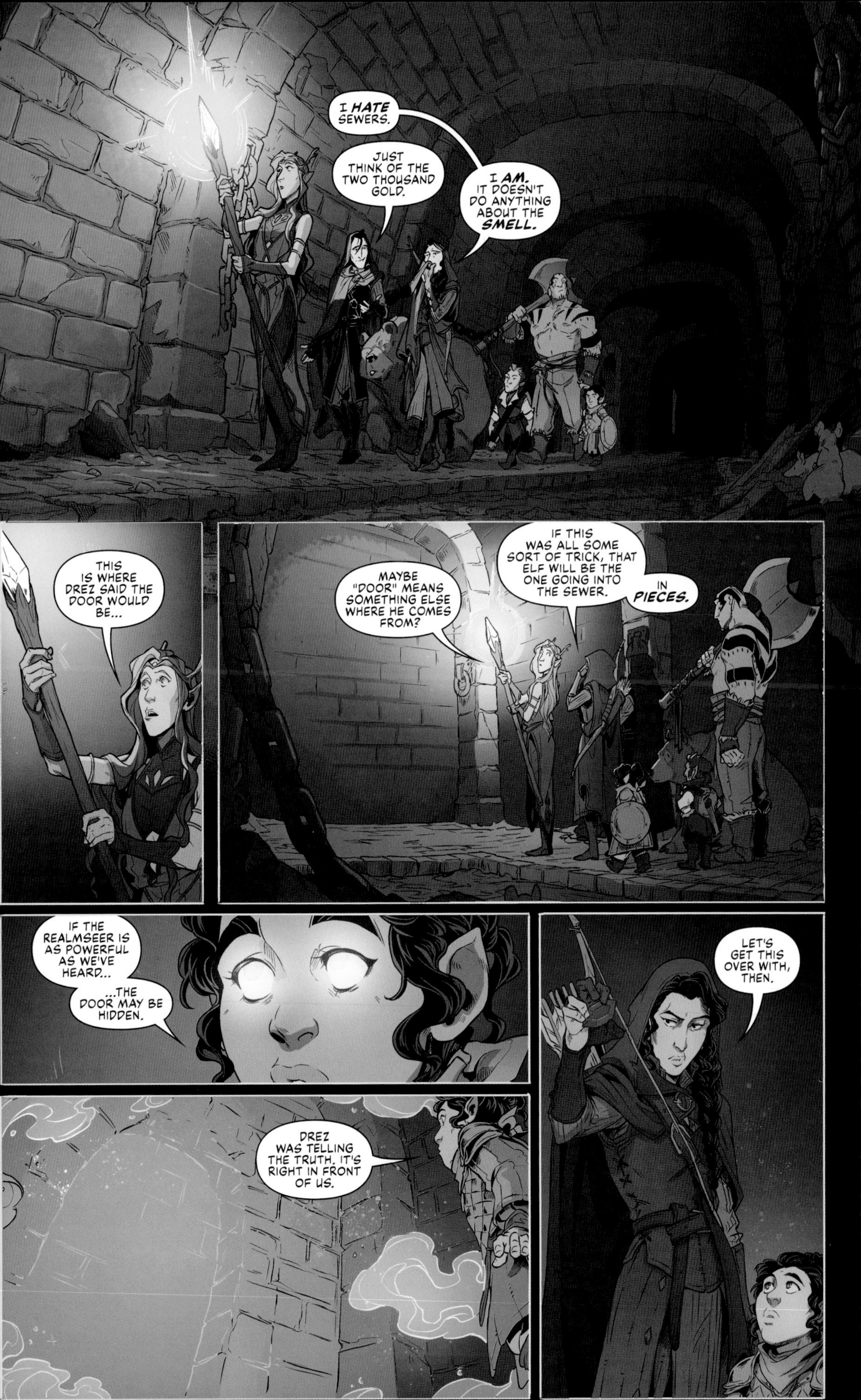
I HATE SEWERS.
JUST THINK OF THE TWO THOUSAND GOLD.
I AM. IT DOESN'T DO ANYTHING ABOUT THE SMELL.
THIS IS WHERE DREZ SAID THE DOOR WOULD BE...
MAYBE "DOOR" MEANS SOMETHING ELSE WHERE HE COMES FROM?
IF THIS WAS ALL SOME SORT OF TRICK, THAT ELF WILL BE THE ONE GOING INTO THE SEWER.
IN PIECES.
IF THE REALMSEER IS AS POWERFUL AS WE'VE HEARD...
...THE DOOR MAY BE HIDDEN.
LET'S GET THIS OVER WITH, THEN.
DREZ WAS TELLING THE TRUTH. IT'S RIGHT IN FRONT OF US.

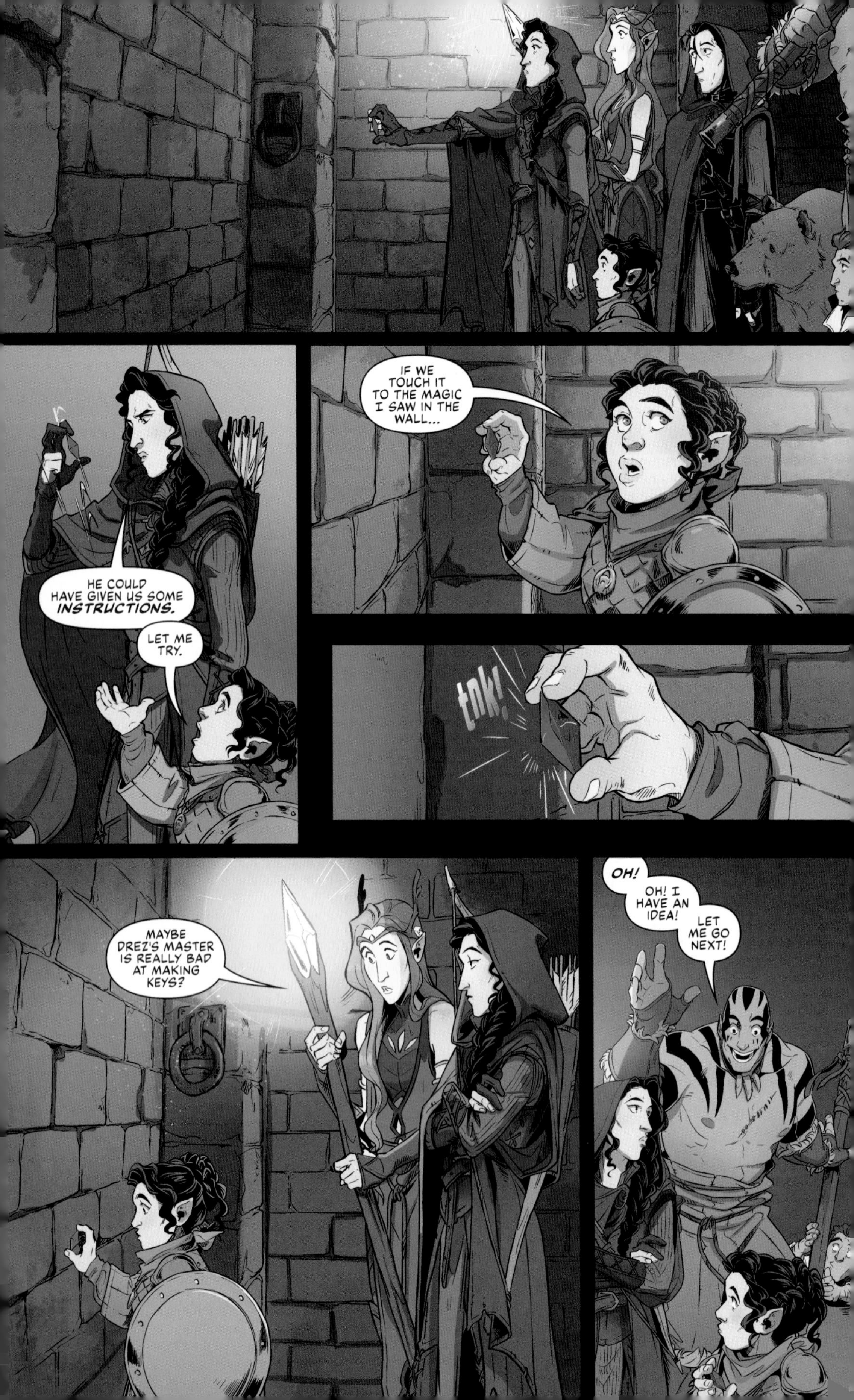

HE COULD HAVE GIVEN US SOME INSTRUCTIONS.
LET ME TRY.
IF WE TOUCH IT TO THE MAGIC I SAW IN THE WALL...
tok!
MAYBE DREZ'S MASTER IS REALLY BAD AT MAKING KEYS?
OH!
OH! I HAVE AN IDEA!
LET ME GO NEXT!

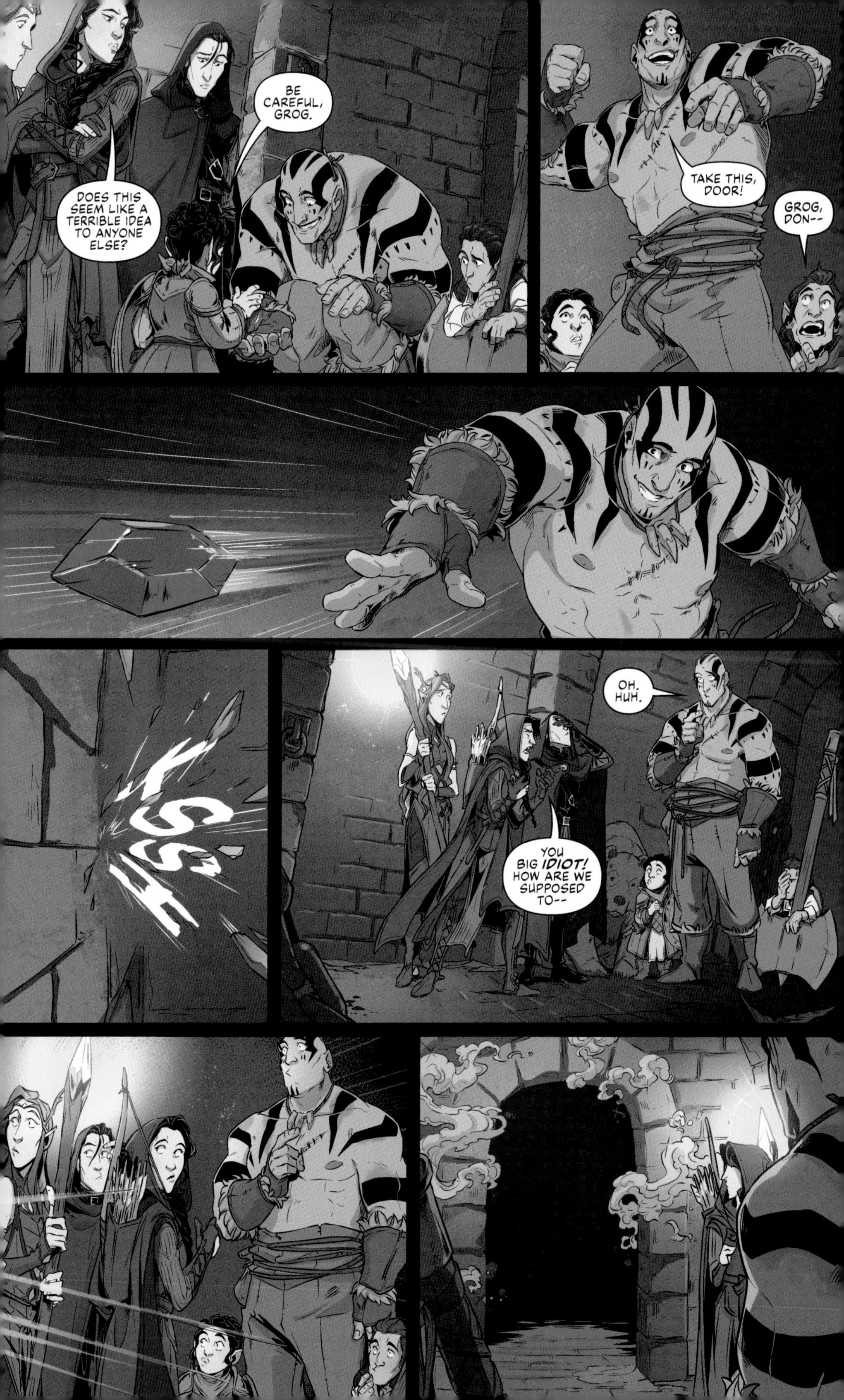
DOES THIS SEEM LIKE A TERRIBLE IDEA TO ANYONE ELSE?
BE CAREFUL, GROG.
TAKE THIS, DOOR!
GROG, DON--
OH. HUH.
YOU BIG *IDIOT!* HOW ARE WE SUPPOSED TO--

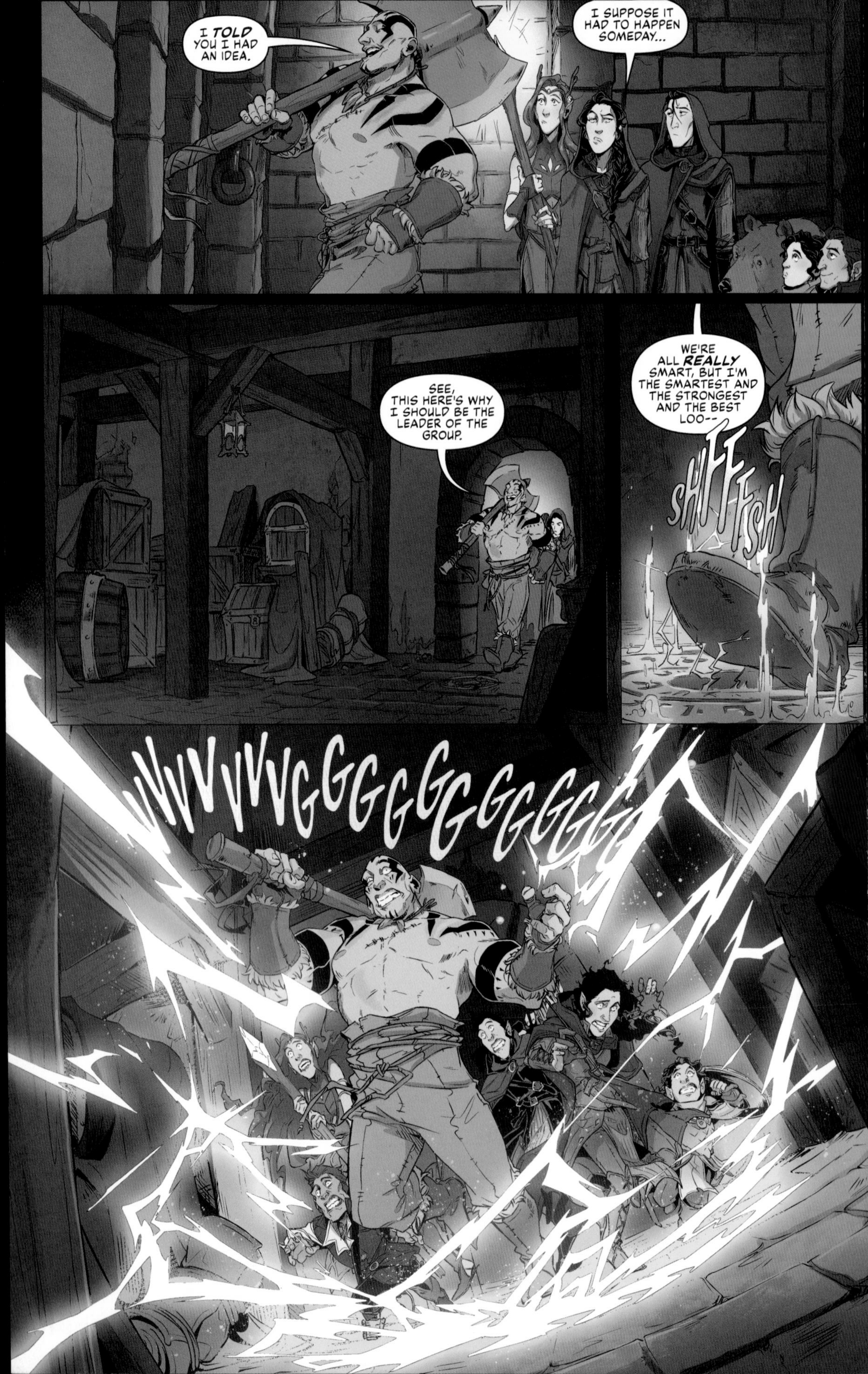
I *TOLD* YOU I HAD AN IDEA.
I SUPPOSE IT HAD TO HAPPEN SOMEDAY...
SEE, THIS HERE'S WHY I SHOULD BE THE LEADER OF THE GROUP.
WE'RE ALL *REALLY* SMART, BUT I'M THE SMARTEST AND THE STRONGEST AND THE BEST LOO--
SHFFFSH
VVVVVVVVGGGGGGGGGG

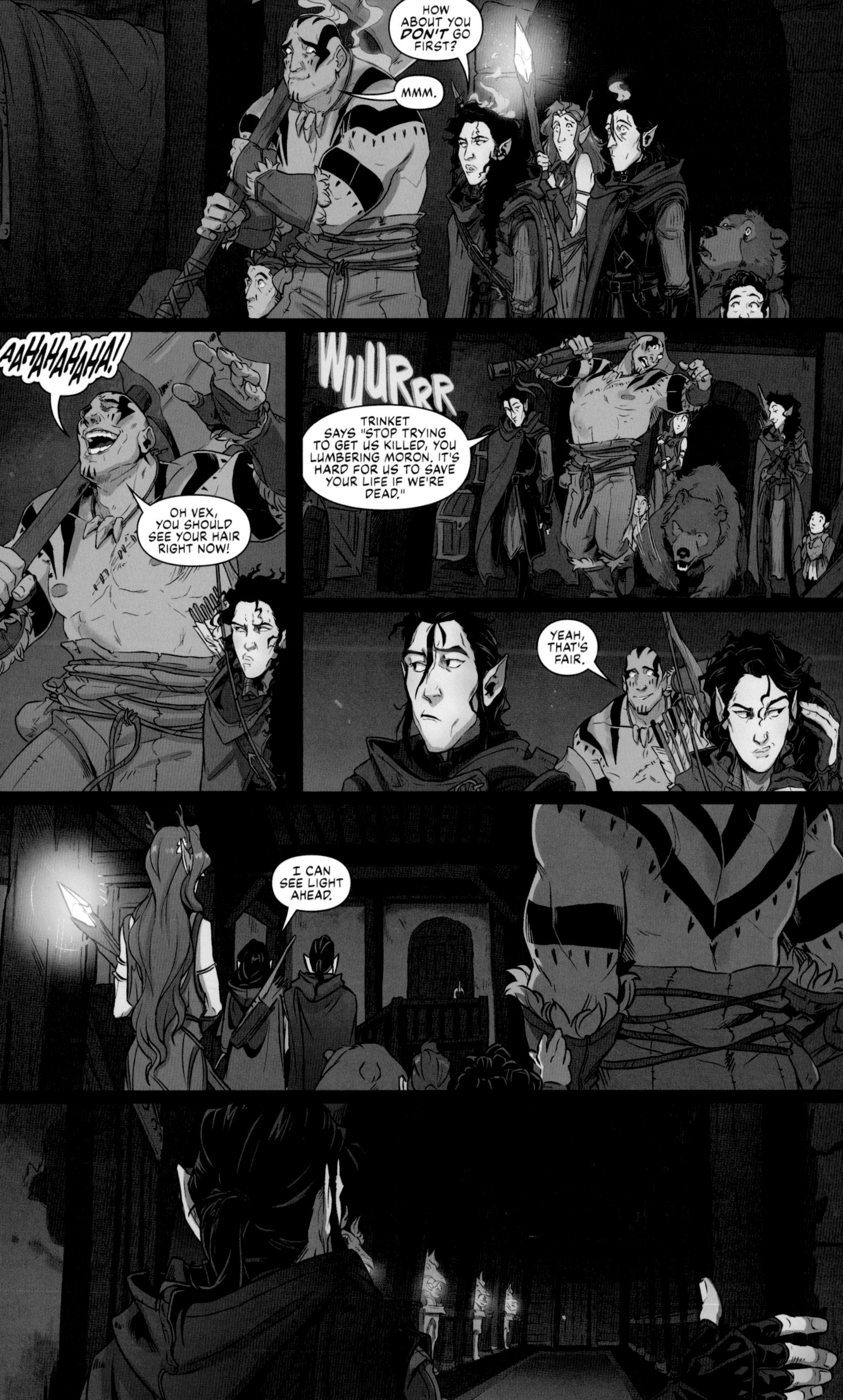
HOW ABOUT YOU *DON'T* GO FIRST?
MMM.
AAHAHAHAHA!
OH VEX, YOU SHOULD SEE YOUR HAIR RIGHT NOW!
WUURRR
TRINKET SAYS "STOP TRYING TO GET US KILLED, YOU LUMBERING MORON. IT'S HARD FOR US TO SAVE YOUR LIFE IF WE'RE DEAD."
YEAH, THAT'S FAIR.
I CAN SEE LIGHT AHEAD.

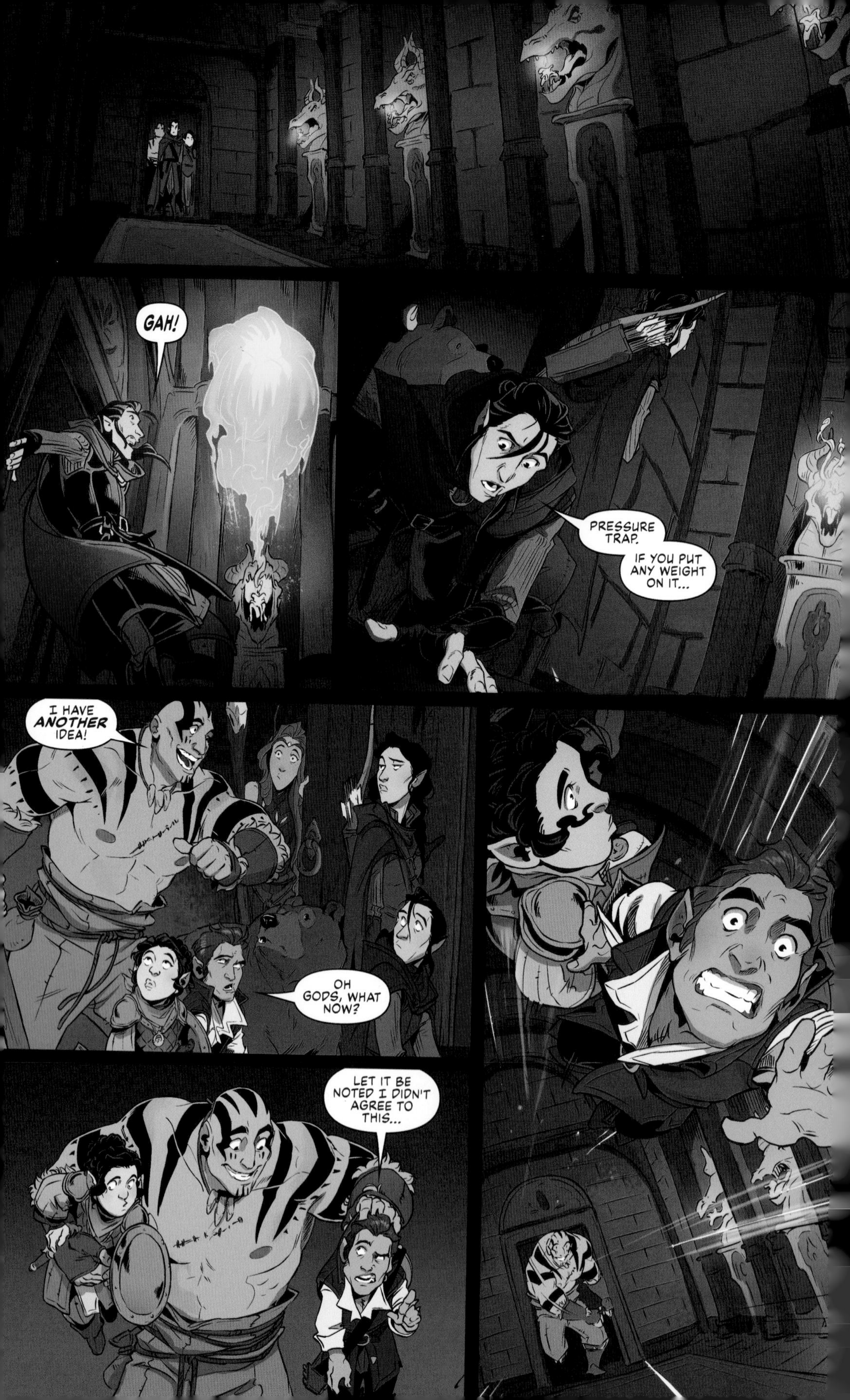
GAH!
PRESSURE TRAP.
IF YOU PUT ANY WEIGHT ON IT...
I HAVE **ANOTHER** IDEA!
OH GODS, WHAT NOW?
LET IT BE NOTED I DIDN'T AGREE TO THIS...

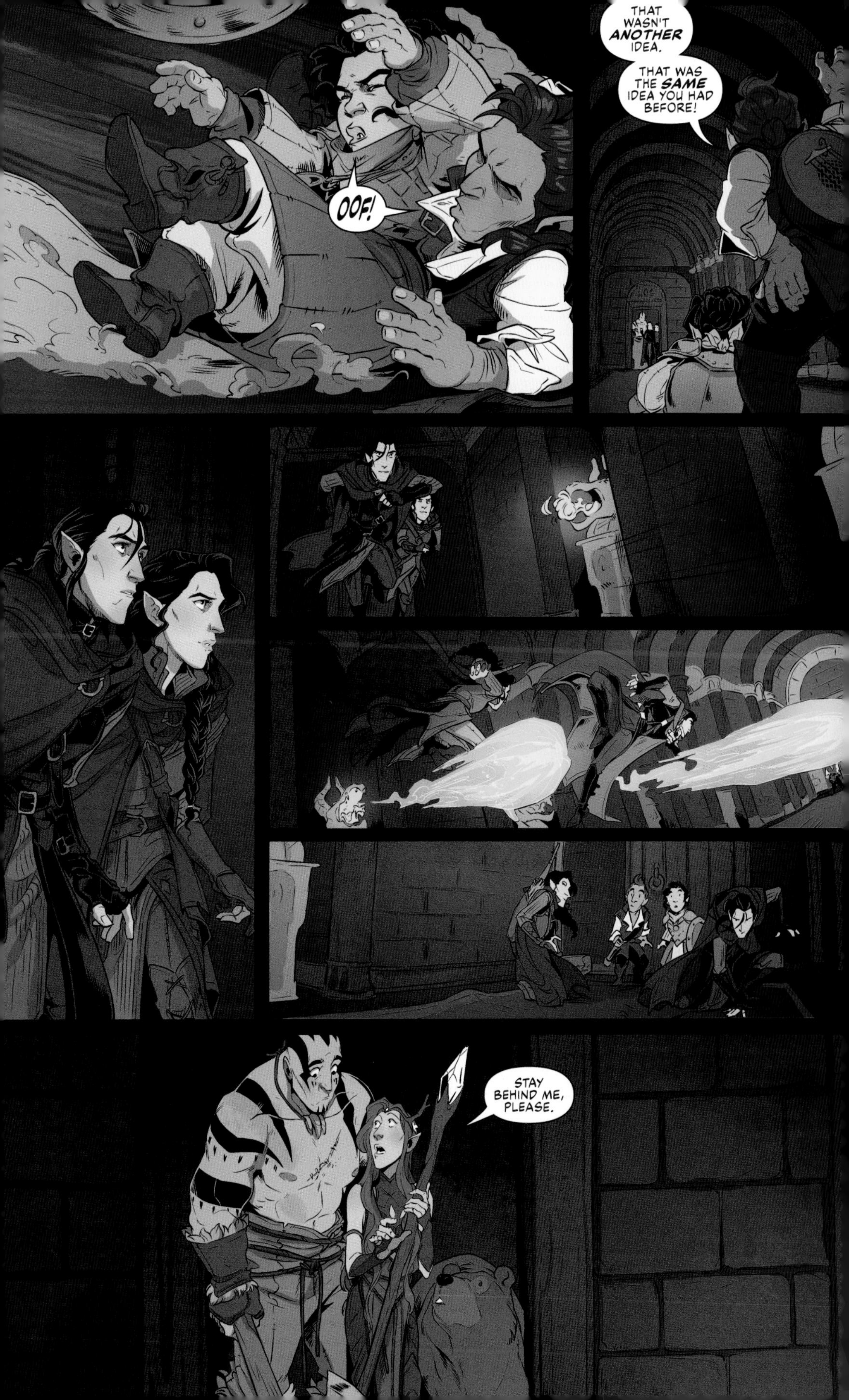
OOF!
THAT WASN'T ANOTHER IDEA.
THAT WAS THE SAME IDEA YOU HAD BEFORE!
STAY BEHIND ME, PLEASE.

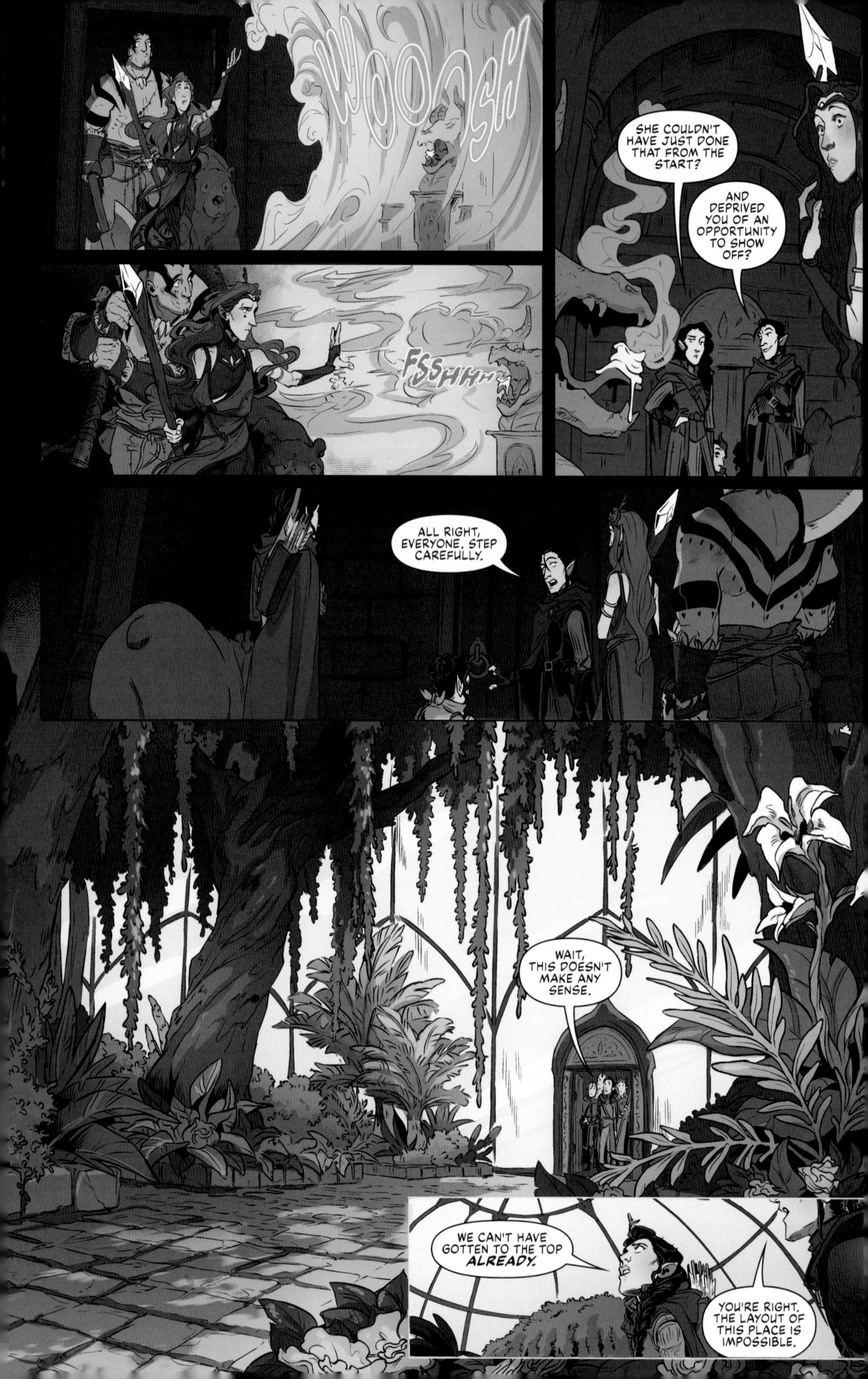
WOOOSH
FSSHHH
SHE COULDN'T HAVE JUST DONE THAT FROM THE START?
AND DEPRIVED YOU OF AN OPPORTUNITY TO SHOW OFF?
ALL RIGHT, EVERYONE. STEP CAREFULLY.
WAIT, THIS DOESN'T MAKE ANY SENSE.
WE CAN'T HAVE GOTTEN TO THE TOP *ALREADY.*
YOU'RE RIGHT. THE LAYOUT OF THIS PLACE IS IMPOSSIBLE.

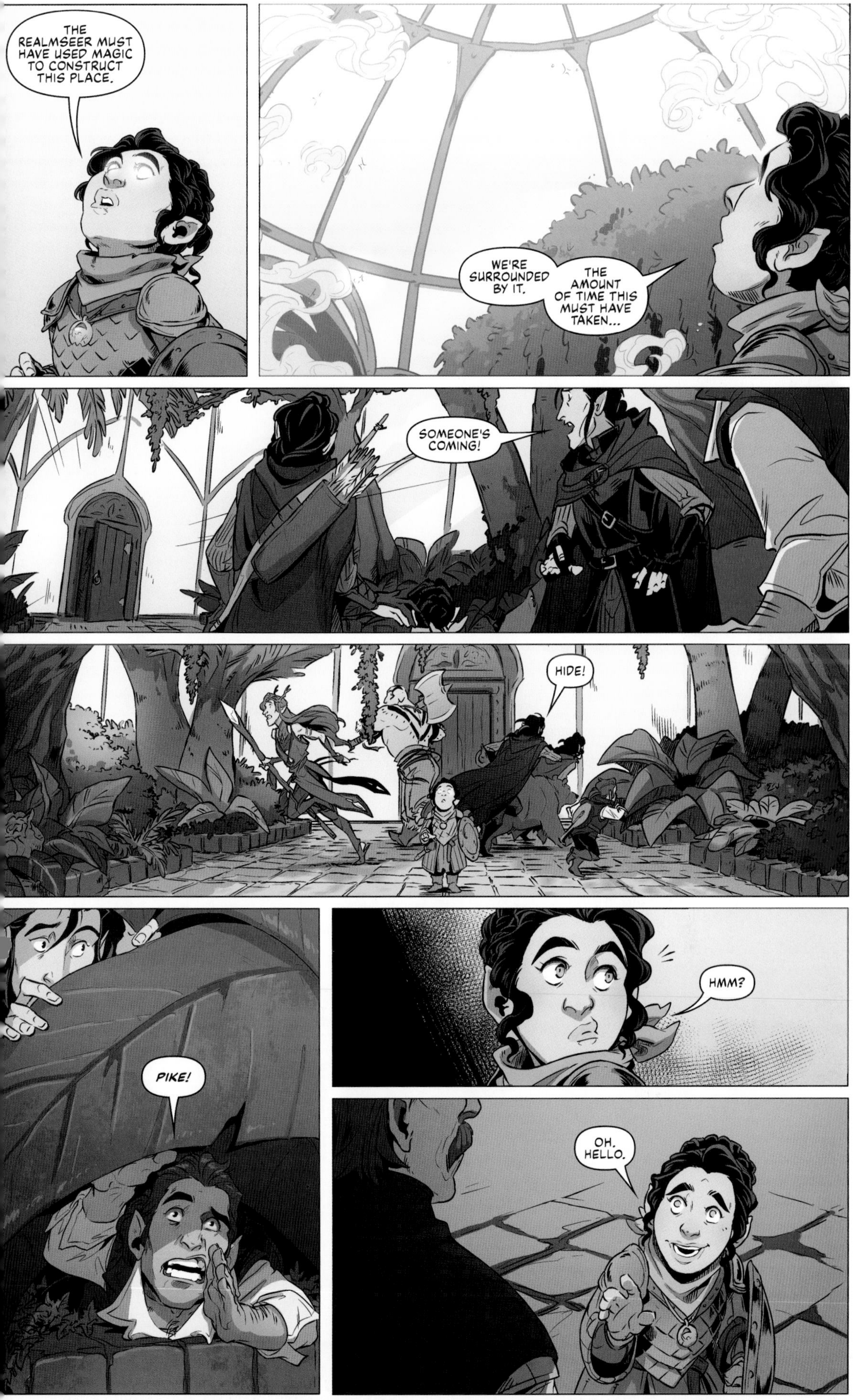
THE REALMSEER MUST HAVE USED MAGIC TO CONSTRUCT THIS PLACE.
WE'RE SURROUNDED BY IT.
THE AMOUNT OF TIME THIS MUST HAVE TAKEN...
SOMEONE'S COMING!
HIDE!
PIKE!
HMM?
OH. HELLO.

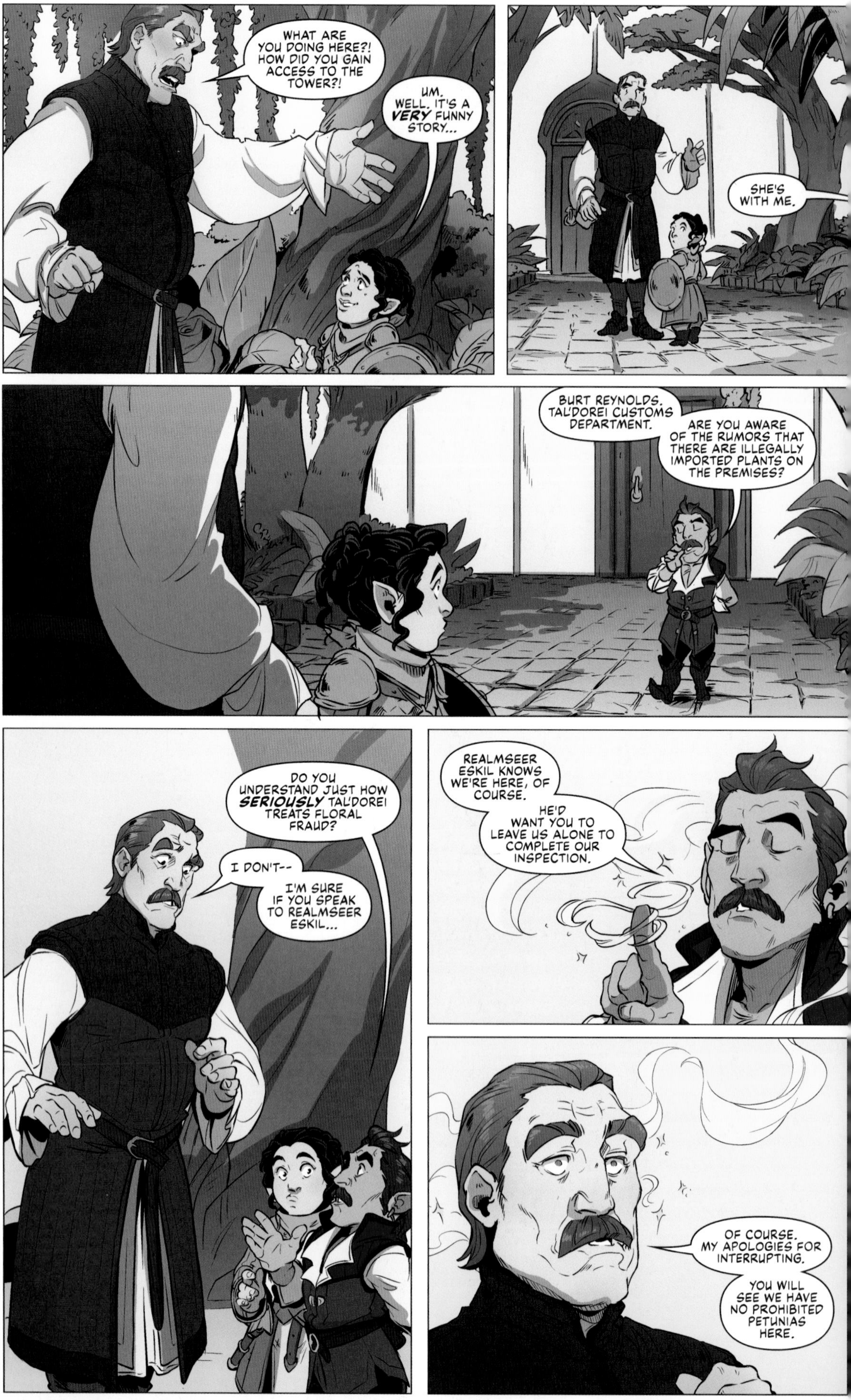
WHAT ARE YOU DOING HERE?! HOW DID YOU GAIN ACCESS TO THE TOWER?!
UM. WELL, IT'S A VERY FUNNY STORY...
SHE'S WITH ME.
BURT REYNOLDS. TAL'DOREI CUSTOMS DEPARTMENT.
ARE YOU AWARE OF THE RUMORS THAT THERE ARE ILLEGALLY IMPORTED PLANTS ON THE PREMISES?
DO YOU UNDERSTAND JUST HOW SERIOUSLY TAL'DOREI TREATS FLORAL FRAUD?
I DON'T--
I'M SURE IF YOU SPEAK TO REALMSEER ESKIL...
REALMSEER ESKIL KNOWS WE'RE HERE, OF COURSE.
HE'D WANT YOU TO LEAVE US ALONE TO COMPLETE OUR INSPECTION.
OF COURSE. MY APOLOGIES FOR INTERRUPTING.
YOU WILL SEE WE HAVE NO PROHIBITED PETUNIAS HERE.

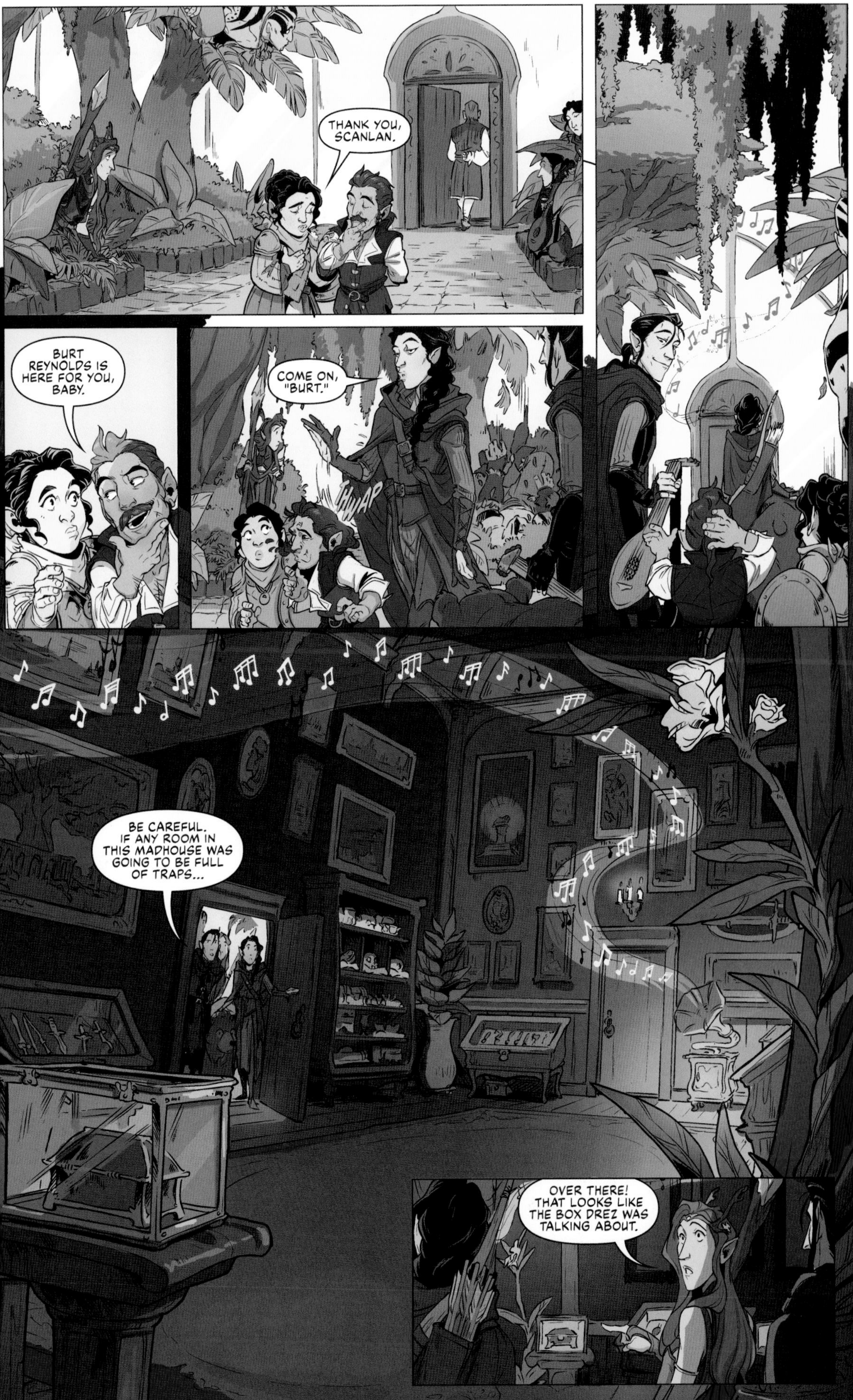
THANK YOU, SCANLAN.
BURT REYNOLDS IS HERE FOR YOU, BABY.
COME ON, "BURT."
THWAP
BE CAREFUL. IF ANY ROOM IN THIS MADHOUSE WAS GOING TO BE FULL OF TRAPS...
OVER THERE! THAT LOOKS LIKE THE BOX DREZ WAS TALKING ABOUT.

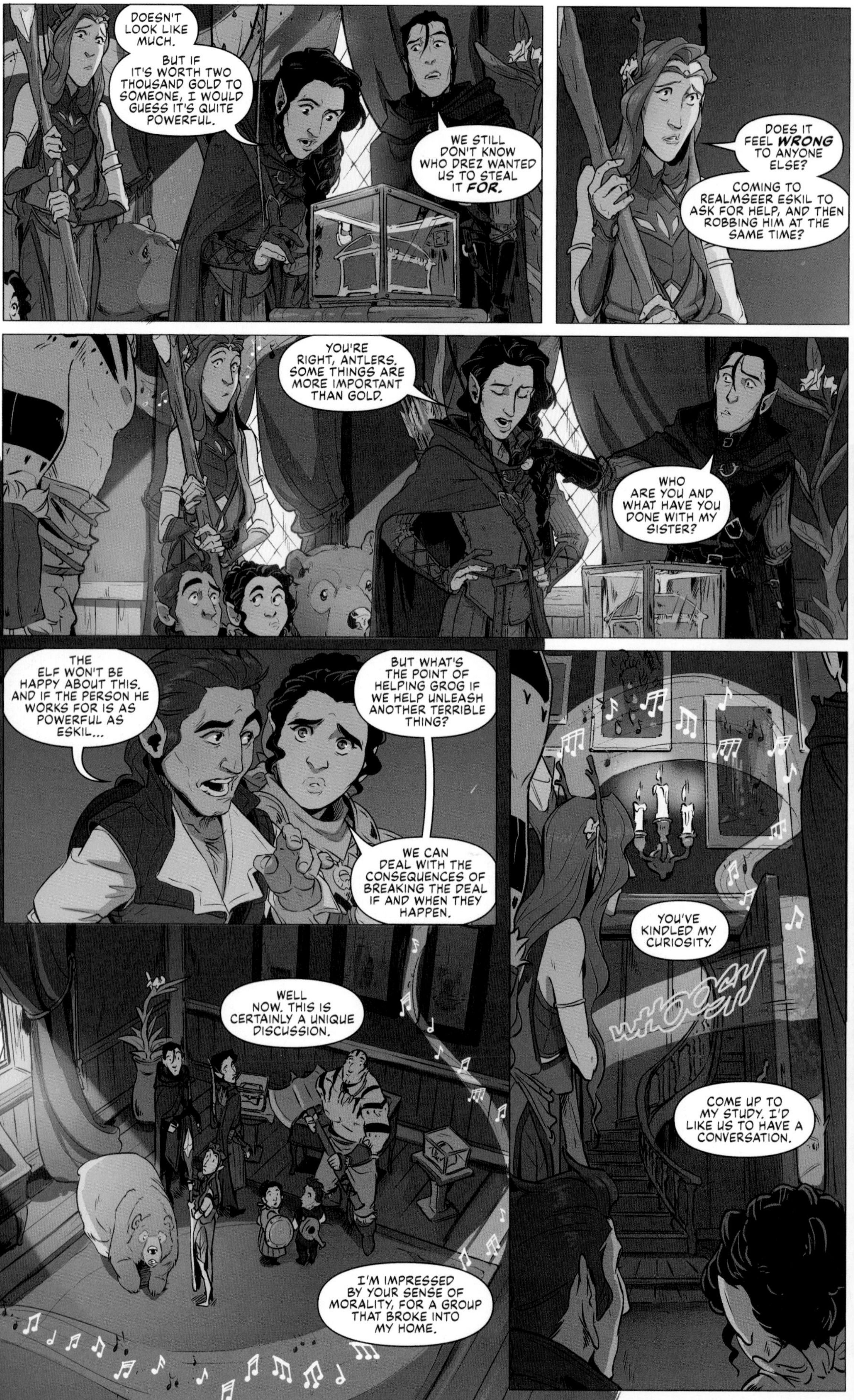
DOESN'T LOOK LIKE MUCH.
BUT IF IT'S WORTH TWO THOUSAND GOLD TO SOMEONE, I WOULD GUESS IT'S QUITE POWERFUL.
WE STILL DON'T KNOW WHO DREZ WANTED US TO STEAL IT *FOR.*
DOES IT FEEL *WRONG* TO ANYONE ELSE?
COMING TO REALMSEER ESKIL TO ASK FOR HELP, AND THEN ROBBING HIM AT THE SAME TIME?
YOU'RE RIGHT, ANTLERS. SOME THINGS ARE MORE IMPORTANT THAN GOLD.
WHO ARE YOU AND WHAT HAVE YOU DONE WITH MY SISTER?
THE ELF WON'T BE HAPPY ABOUT THIS. AND IF THE PERSON HE WORKS FOR IS AS POWERFUL AS ESKIL...
BUT WHAT'S THE POINT OF HELPING GROG IF WE HELP UNLEASH ANOTHER TERRIBLE THING?
WE CAN DEAL WITH THE CONSEQUENCES OF BREAKING THE DEAL IF AND WHEN THEY HAPPEN.
WELL NOW. THIS IS CERTAINLY A UNIQUE DISCUSSION.
I'M IMPRESSED BY YOUR SENSE OF MORALITY, FOR A GROUP THAT BROKE INTO MY HOME.
YOU'VE KINDLED MY CURIOSITY.
WHOOSH
COME UP TO MY STUDY. I'D LIKE US TO HAVE A CONVERSATION.

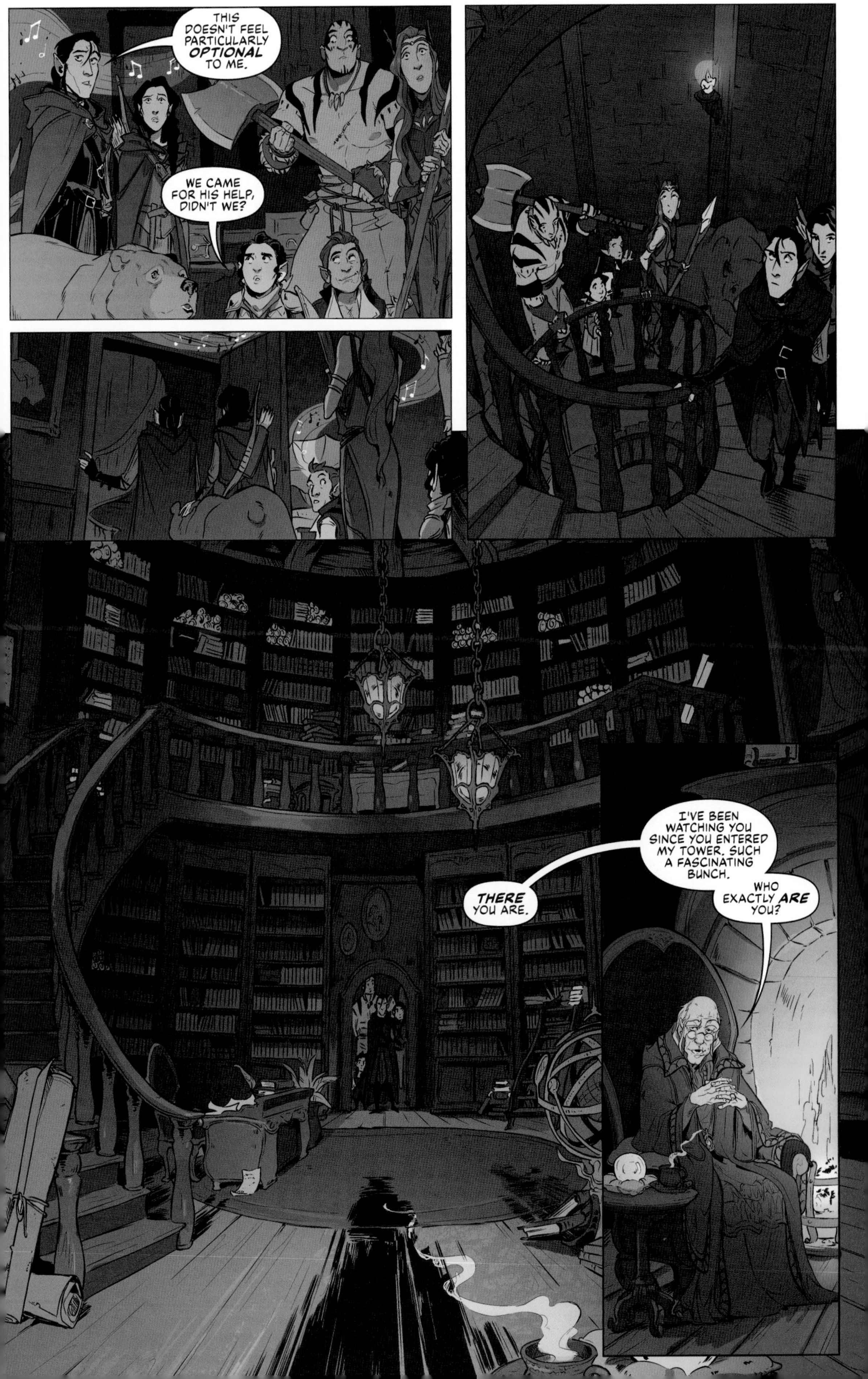
THIS DOESN'T FEEL PARTICULARLY OPTIONAL TO ME.
WE CAME FOR HIS HELP, DIDN'T WE?
THERE YOU ARE.
I'VE BEEN WATCHING YOU SINCE YOU ENTERED MY TOWER. SUCH A FASCINATING BUNCH.
WHO EXACTLY ARE YOU?

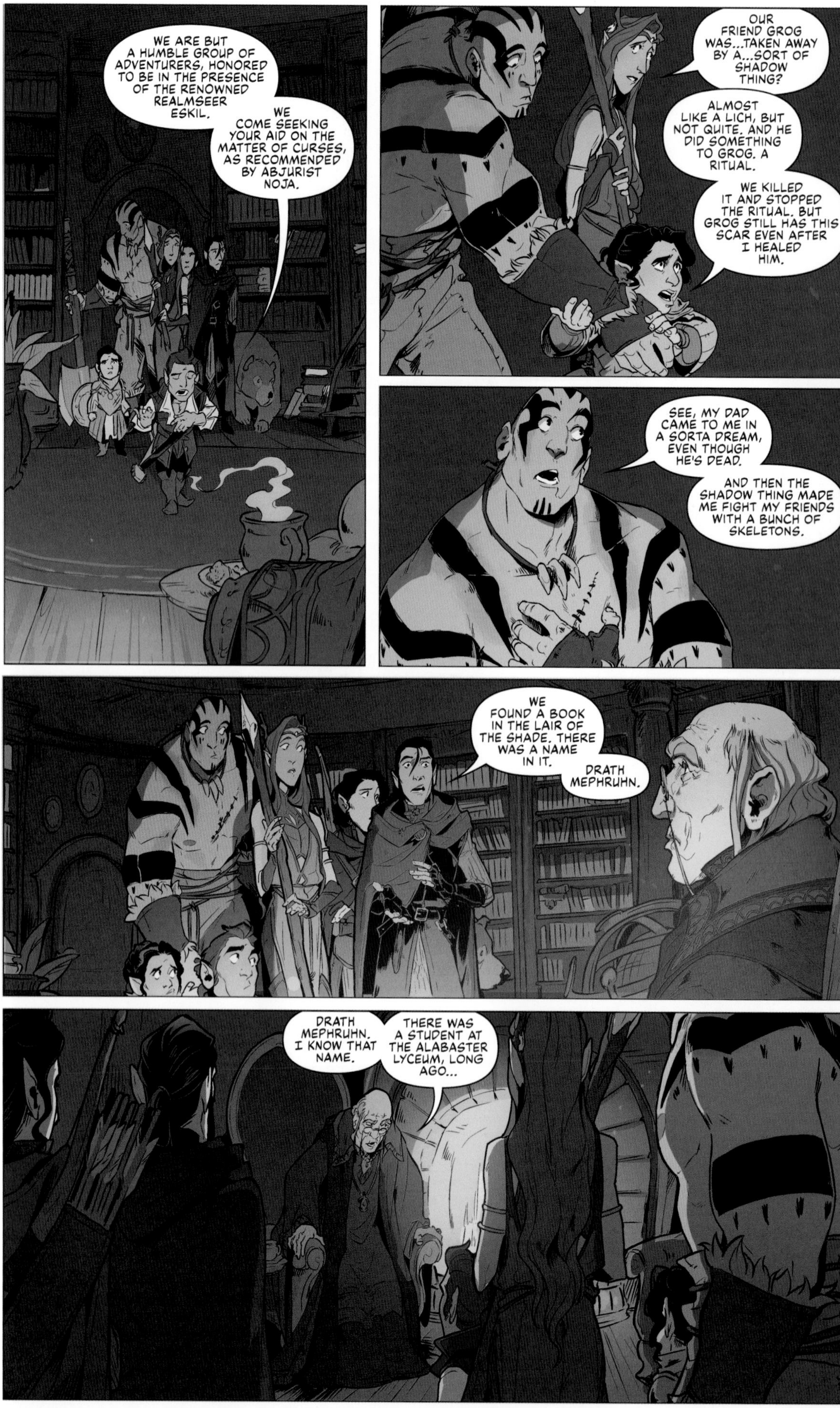
WE ARE BUT A HUMBLE GROUP OF ADVENTURERS, HONORED TO BE IN THE PRESENCE OF THE RENOWNED REALMSEER ESKIL.
WE COME SEEKING YOUR AID ON THE MATTER OF CURSES, AS RECOMMENDED BY ABJURIST NOJA.
OUR FRIEND GROG WAS...TAKEN AWAY BY A...SORT OF SHADOW THING?
ALMOST LIKE A LICH, BUT NOT QUITE. AND HE DID SOMETHING TO GROG. A RITUAL.
WE KILLED IT AND STOPPED THE RITUAL. BUT GROG STILL HAS THIS SCAR EVEN AFTER I HEALED HIM.
SEE, MY DAD CAME TO ME IN A SORTA DREAM, EVEN THOUGH HE'S DEAD.
AND THEN THE SHADOW THING MADE ME FIGHT MY FRIENDS WITH A BUNCH OF SKELETONS.
WE FOUND A BOOK IN THE LAIR OF THE SHADE. THERE WAS A NAME IN IT.
DRATH MEPHRUHN.
DRATH MEPHRUHN. I KNOW THAT NAME.
THERE WAS A STUDENT AT THE ALABASTER LYCEUM, LONG AGO...

HE WAS OUSTED FROM THE COLLEGE AT A YOUNG AGE, DABBLING IN DARK, FORBIDDEN THINGS.

LET ME TAKE A LOOK AT THIS SCAR OF YOURS.

COULD YOU COUGH FOR ME, MY LARGE FRIEND?

UH HURM!

KACK

KACK

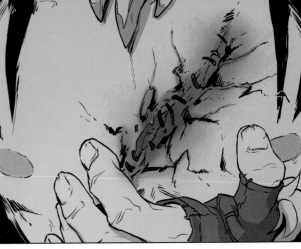

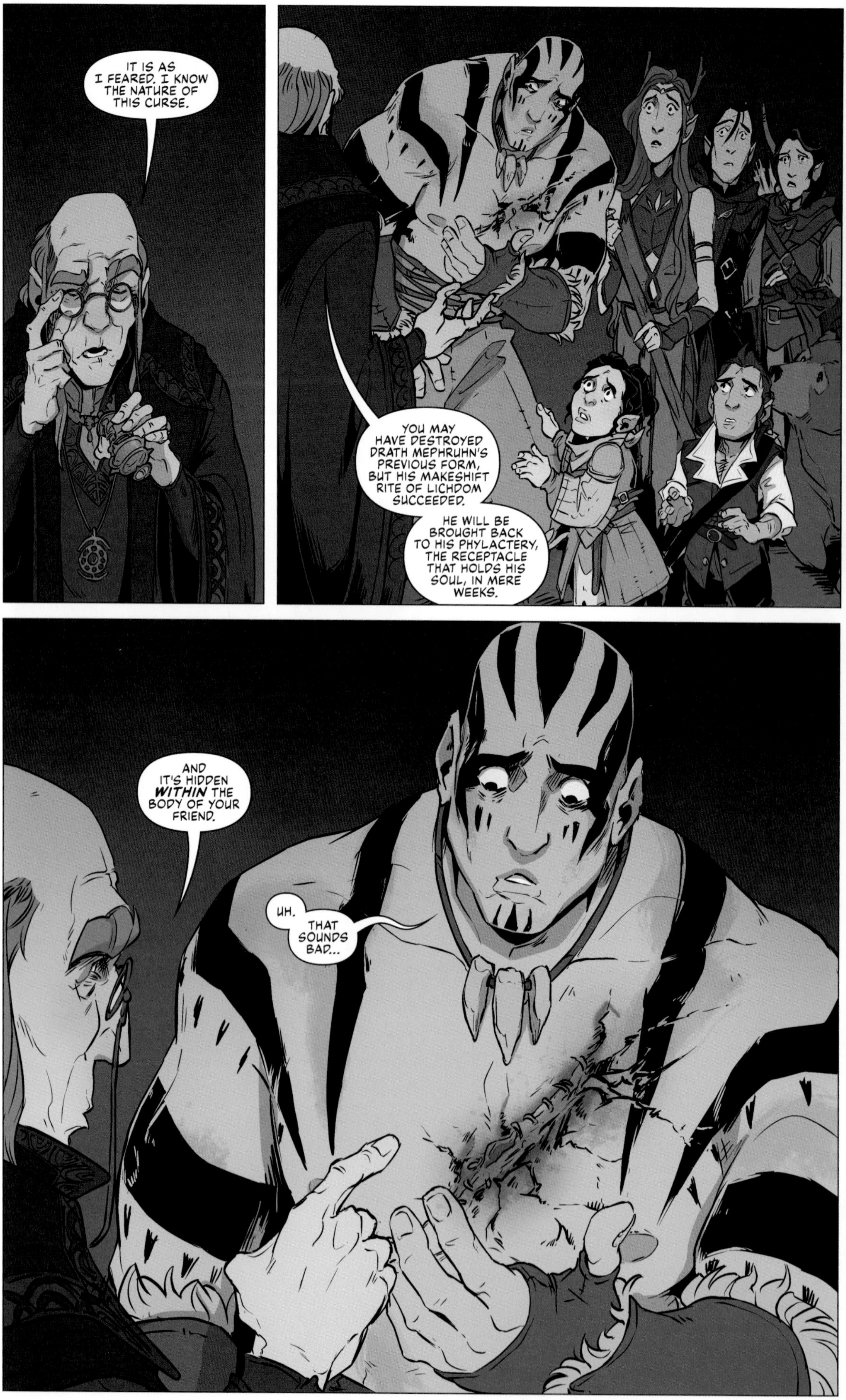
IT IS AS I FEARED. I KNOW THE NATURE OF THIS CURSE.
YOU MAY HAVE DESTROYED DRATH MEPHRUHN'S PREVIOUS FORM, BUT HIS MAKESHIFT RITE OF LICHDOM SUCCEEDED.
HE WILL BE BROUGHT BACK TO HIS PHYLACTERY, THE RECEPTACLE THAT HOLDS HIS SOUL, IN MERE WEEKS.
AND IT'S HIDDEN **WITHIN** THE BODY OF YOUR FRIEND.
UH. THAT SOUNDS BAD...

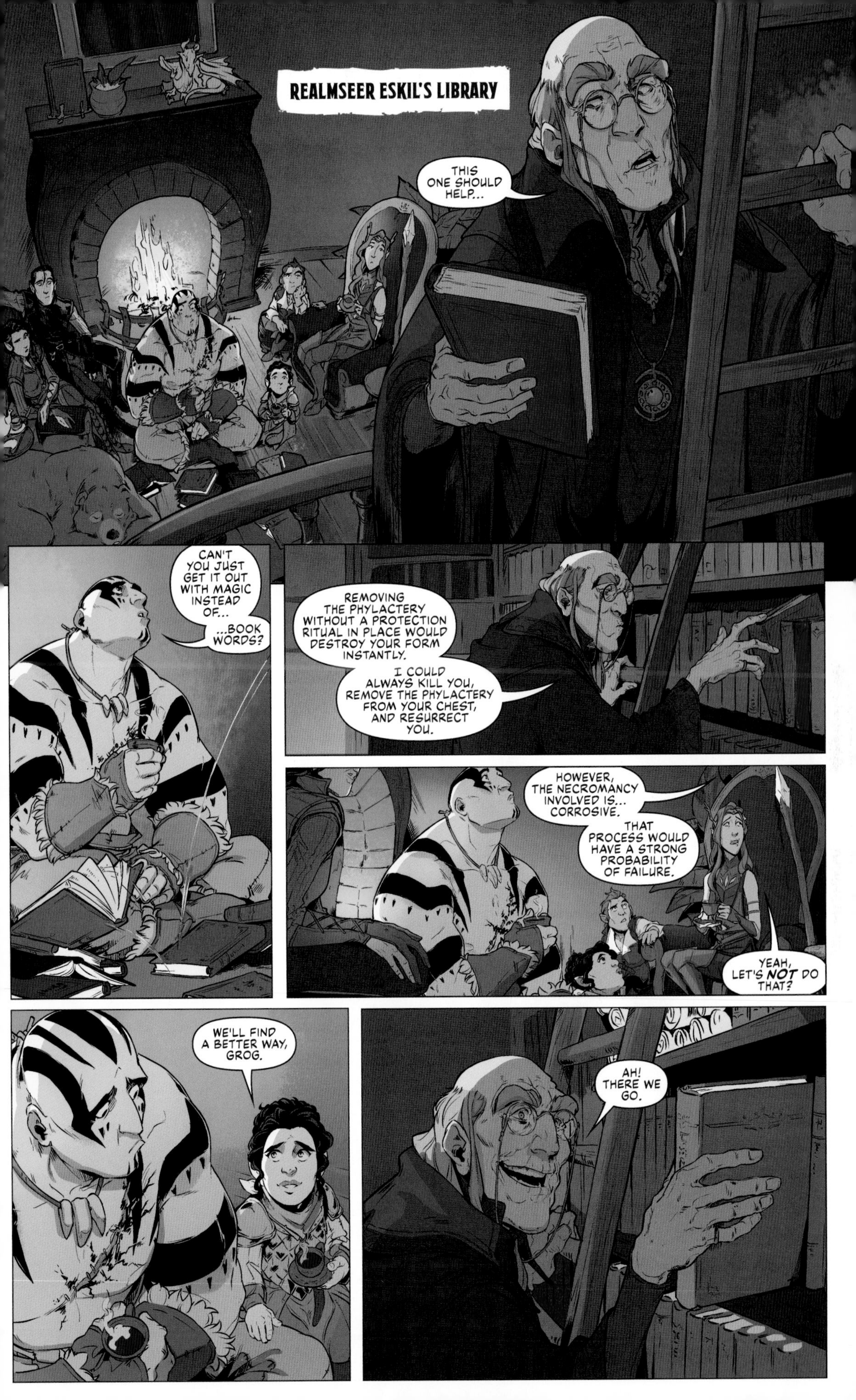
REALMSEER ESKIL'S LIBRARY
THIS ONE SHOULD HELP...
CAN'T YOU JUST GET IT OUT WITH MAGIC INSTEAD OF...
...BOOK WORDS?
REMOVING THE PHYLACTERY WITHOUT A PROTECTION RITUAL IN PLACE WOULD DESTROY YOUR FORM INSTANTLY.
I COULD ALWAYS KILL YOU, REMOVE THE PHYLACTERY FROM YOUR CHEST, AND RESURRECT YOU.
HOWEVER, THE NECROMANCY INVOLVED IS... CORROSIVE.
THAT PROCESS WOULD HAVE A STRONG PROBABILITY OF FAILURE.
YEAH, LET'S ***NOT*** DO THAT?
WE'LL FIND A BETTER WAY, GROG.
AH! THERE WE GO.

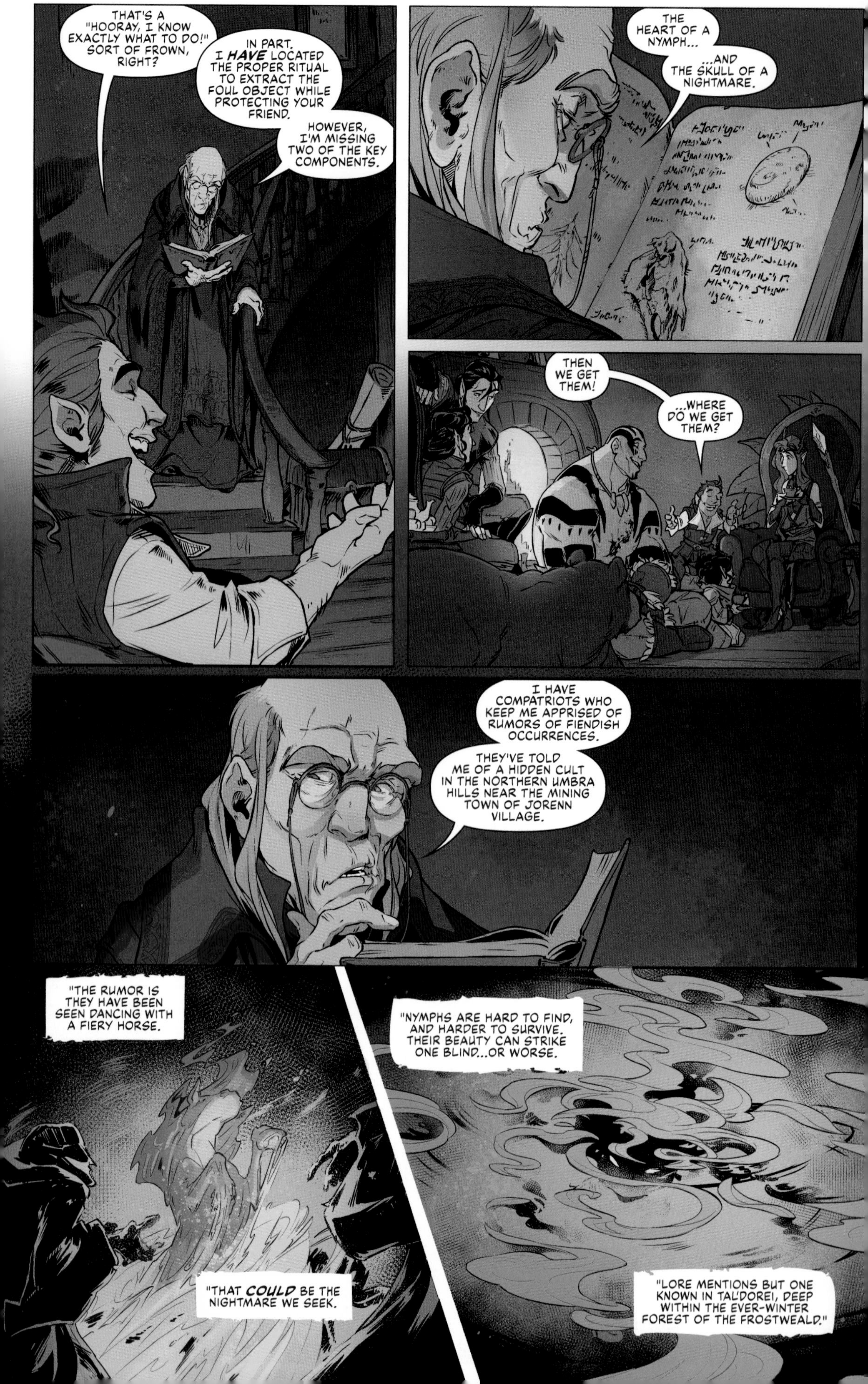
THAT'S A "HOORAY, I KNOW EXACTLY WHAT TO DO!" SORT OF FROWN, RIGHT?
IN PART. I HAVE LOCATED THE PROPER RITUAL TO EXTRACT THE FOUL OBJECT WHILE PROTECTING YOUR FRIEND.
HOWEVER, I'M MISSING TWO OF THE KEY COMPONENTS.
THE HEART OF A NYMPH...
...AND THE SKULL OF A NIGHTMARE.
THEN WE GET THEM!
...WHERE DO WE GET THEM?
I HAVE COMPATRIOTS WHO KEEP ME APPRISED OF RUMORS OF FIENDISH OCCURRENCES.
THEY'VE TOLD ME OF A HIDDEN CULT IN THE NORTHERN UMBRA HILLS NEAR THE MINING TOWN OF JORENN VILLAGE.
"THE RUMOR IS THEY HAVE BEEN SEEN DANCING WITH A FIERY HORSE.
"THAT COULD BE THE NIGHTMARE WE SEEK.
"NYMPHS ARE HARD TO FIND, AND HARDER TO SURVIVE. THEIR BEAUTY CAN STRIKE ONE BLIND...OR WORSE.
"LORE MENTIONS BUT ONE KNOWN IN TAL'DOREI, DEEP WITHIN THE EVER-WINTER FOREST OF THE FROSTWEALD."

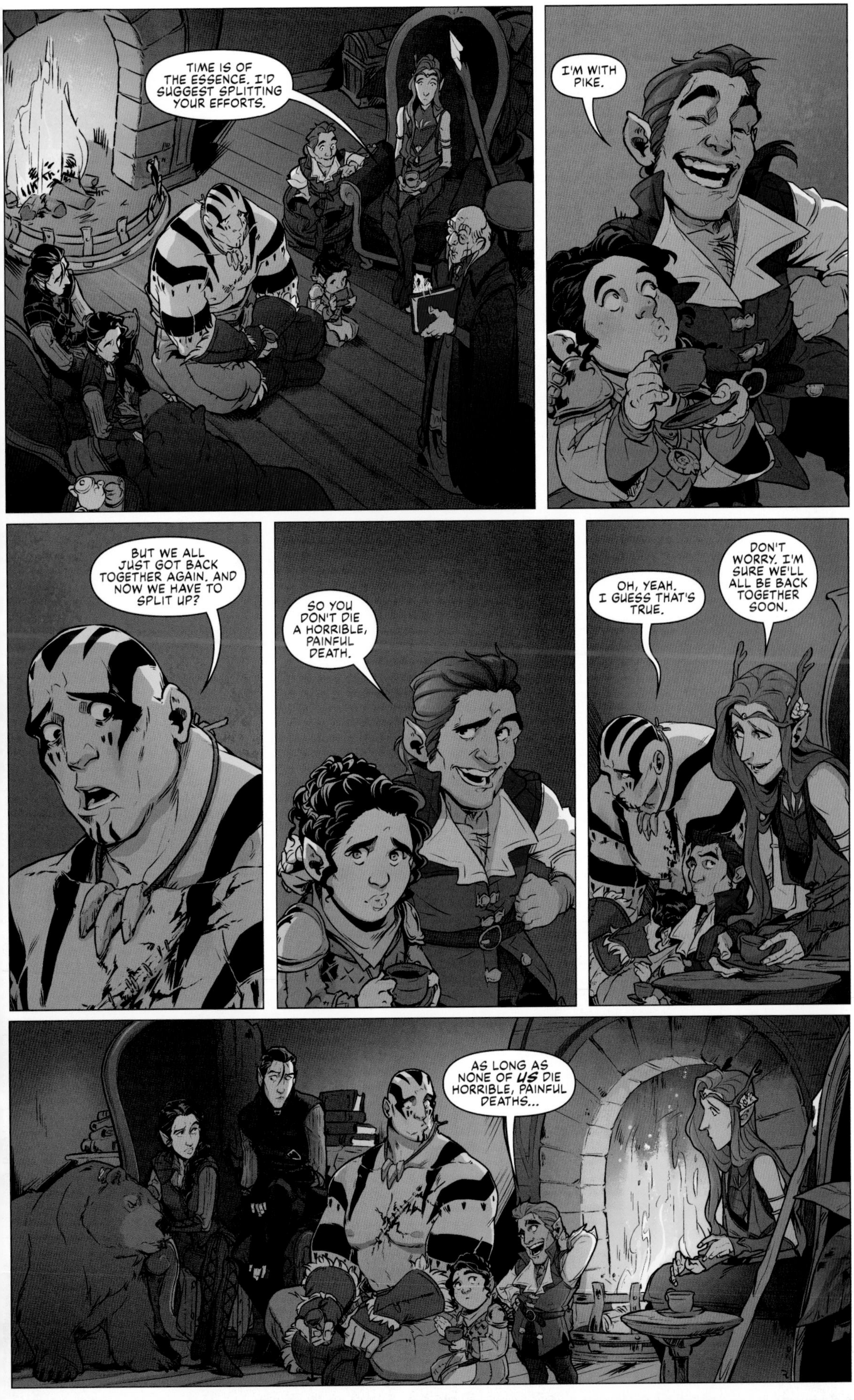
TIME IS OF THE ESSENCE. I'D SUGGEST SPLITTING YOUR EFFORTS.
I'M WITH PIKE.
BUT WE ALL JUST GOT BACK TOGETHER AGAIN. AND NOW WE HAVE TO SPLIT UP?
SO YOU DON'T DIE A HORRIBLE, PAINFUL DEATH.
OH, YEAH. I GUESS THAT'S TRUE.
DON'T WORRY. I'M SURE WE'LL ALL BE BACK TOGETHER SOON.
AS LONG AS NONE OF US DIE HORRIBLE, PAINFUL DEATHS...

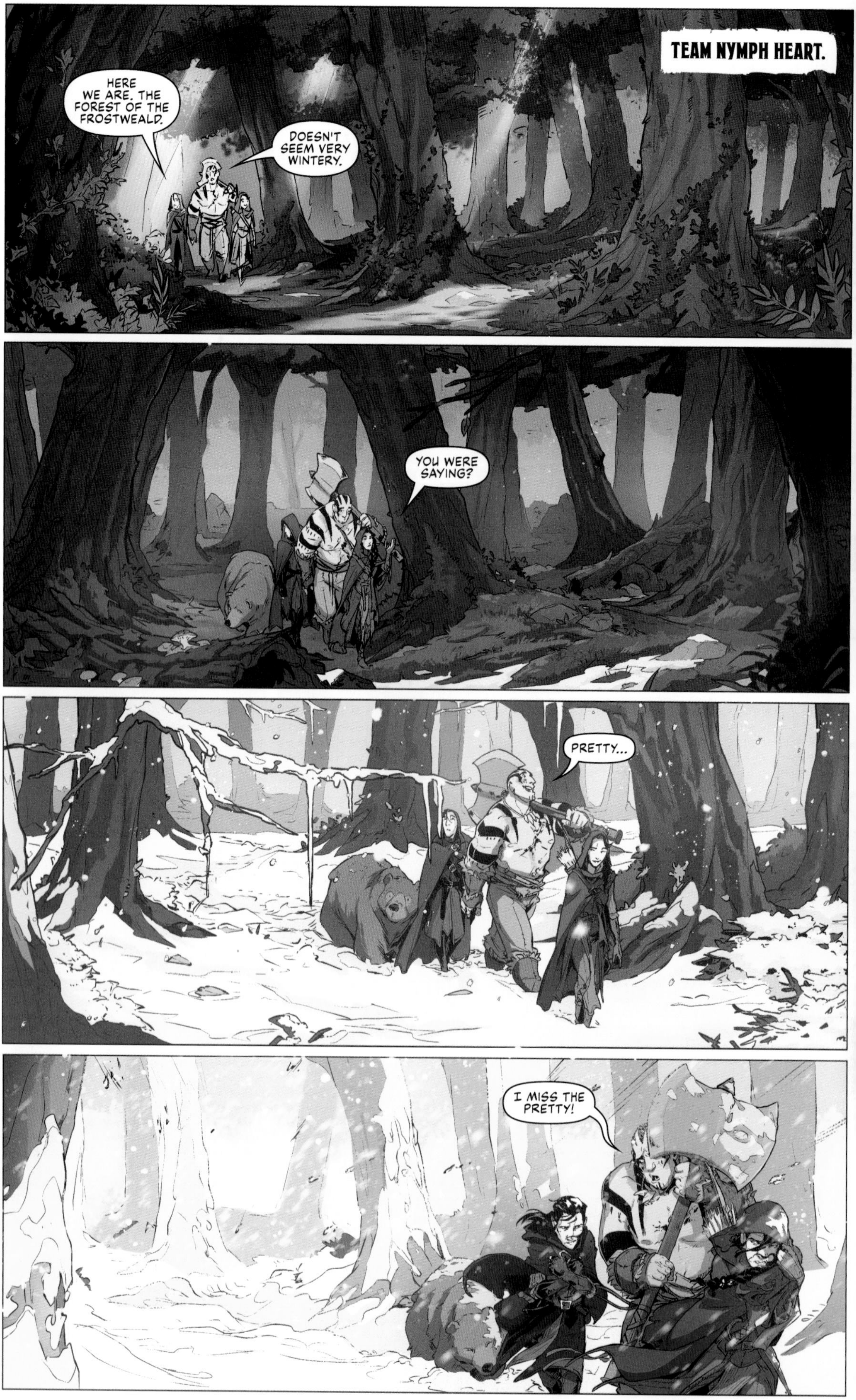
TEAM NYMPH HEART.
HERE WE ARE. THE FOREST OF THE FROSTWEALD.
DOESN'T SEEM VERY WINTERY.
YOU WERE SAYING?
PRETTY...
I MISS THE PRETTY!

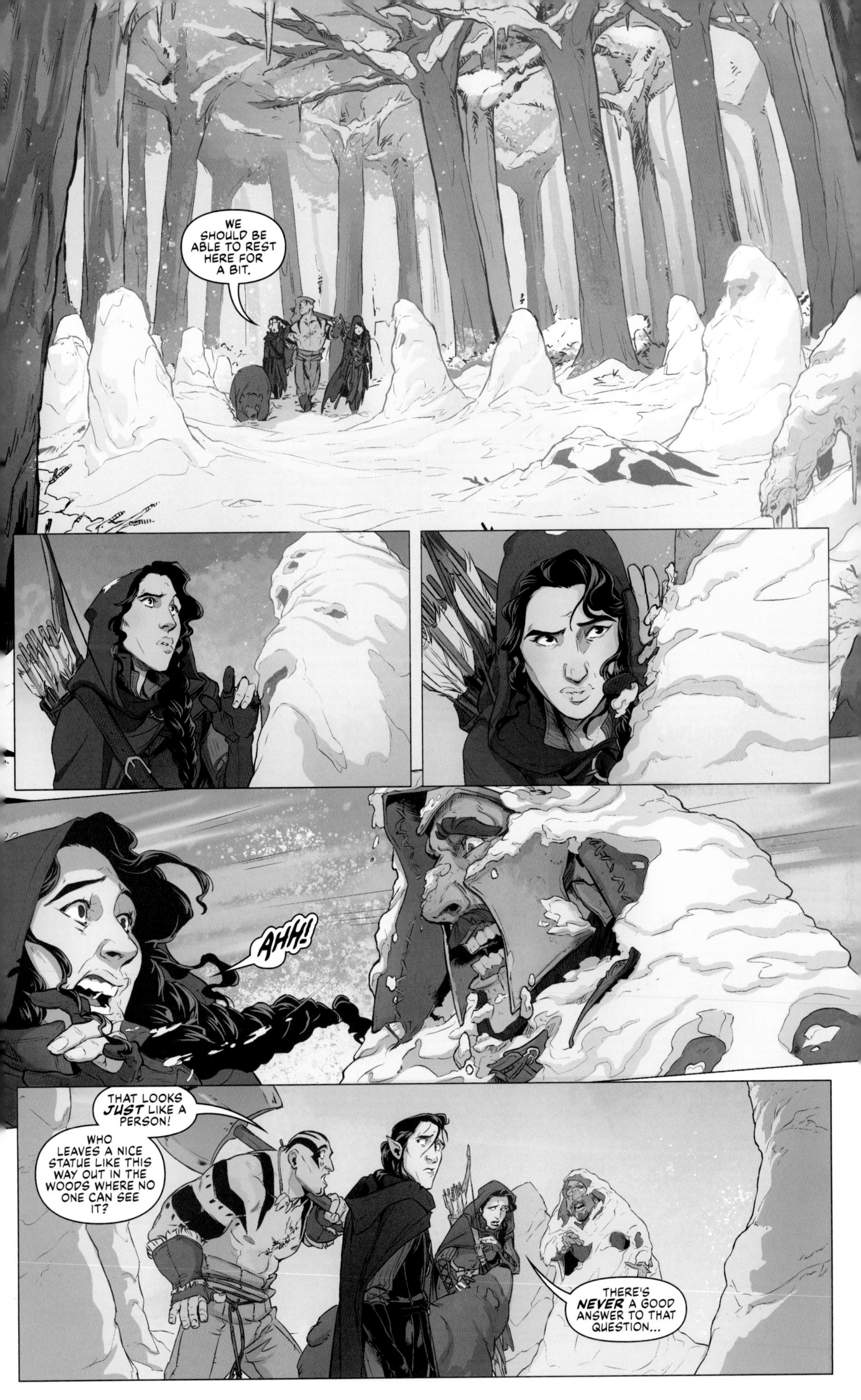
WE SHOULD BE ABLE TO REST HERE FOR A BIT.
AHH!
THAT LOOKS JUST LIKE A PERSON!
WHO LEAVES A NICE STATUE LIKE THIS WAY OUT IN THE WOODS WHERE NO ONE CAN SEE IT?
THERE'S NEVER A GOOD ANSWER TO THAT QUESTION...

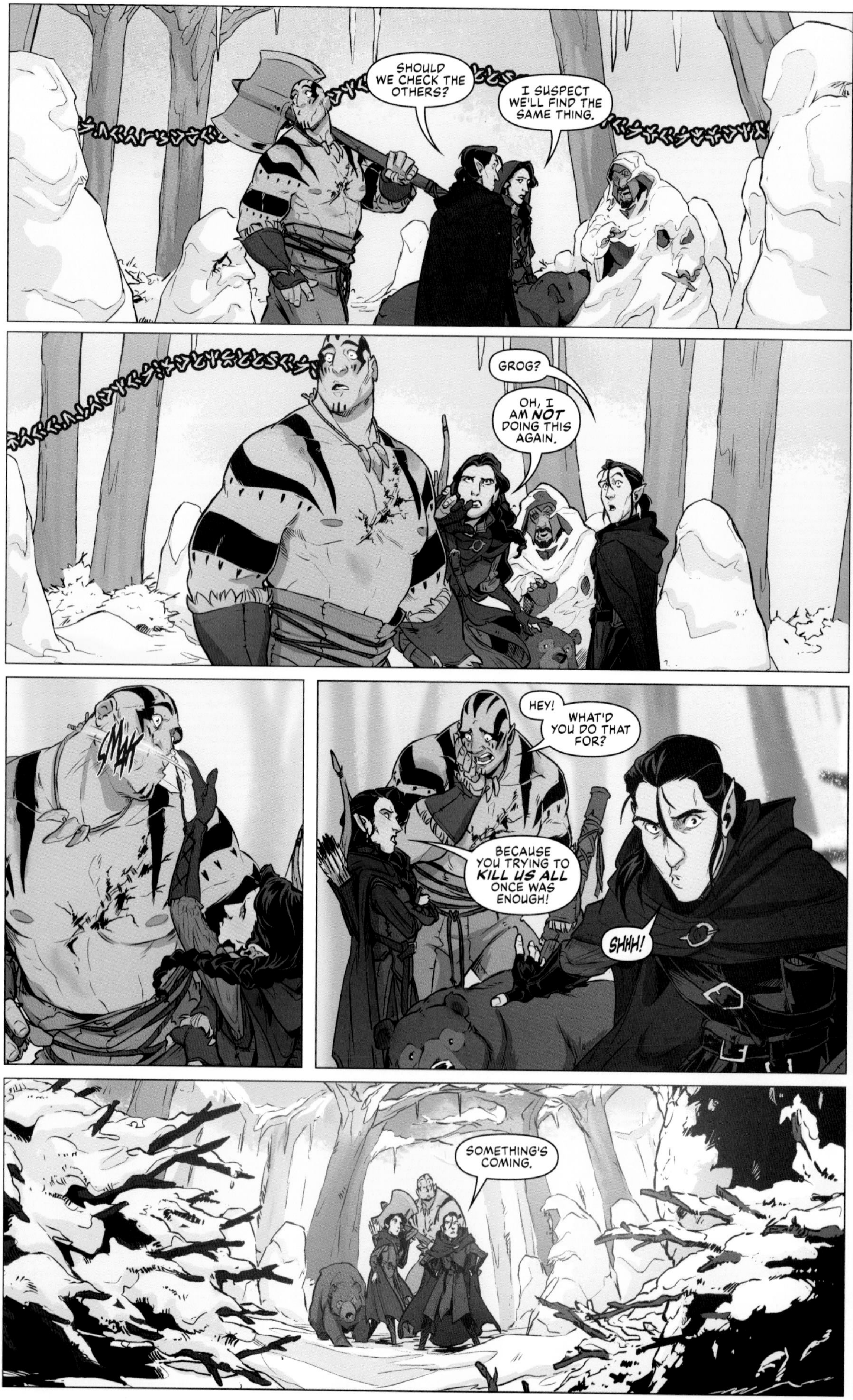
SHOULD WE CHECK THE OTHERS?
I SUSPECT WE'LL FIND THE SAME THING.
GROG?
OH, I AM NOT DOING THIS AGAIN.
SMAK
HEY! WHAT'D YOU DO THAT FOR?
BECAUSE YOU TRYING TO KILL US ALL ONCE WAS ENOUGH!
SHHH!
SOMETHING'S COMING.

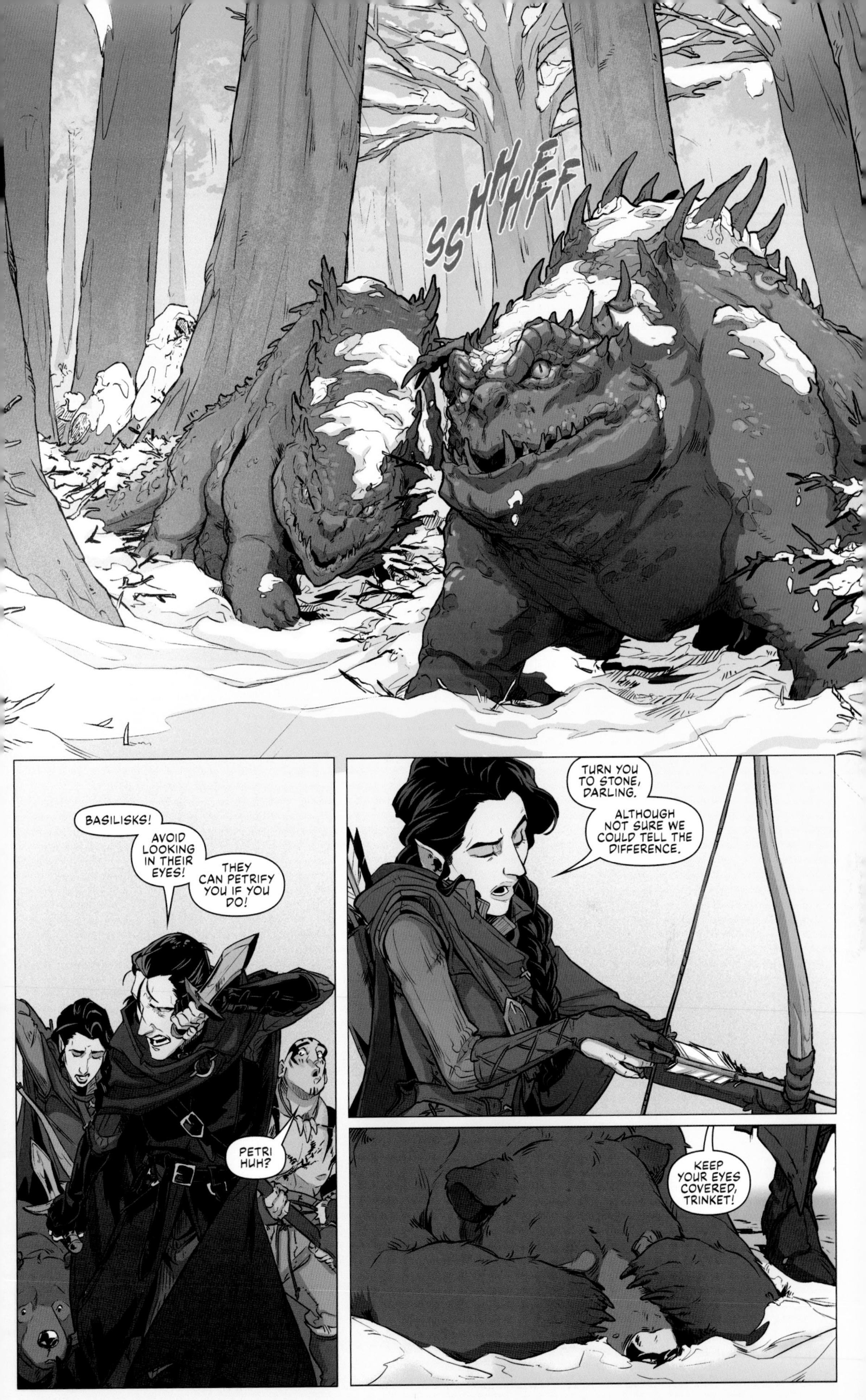
SSHHHFFF
BASILISKS!
AVOID LOOKING IN THEIR EYES!
THEY CAN PETRIFY YOU IF YOU DO!
PETRI HUH?
TURN YOU TO STONE, DARLING.
ALTHOUGH NOT SURE WE COULD TELL THE DIFFERENCE.
KEEP YOUR EYES COVERED, TRINKET!

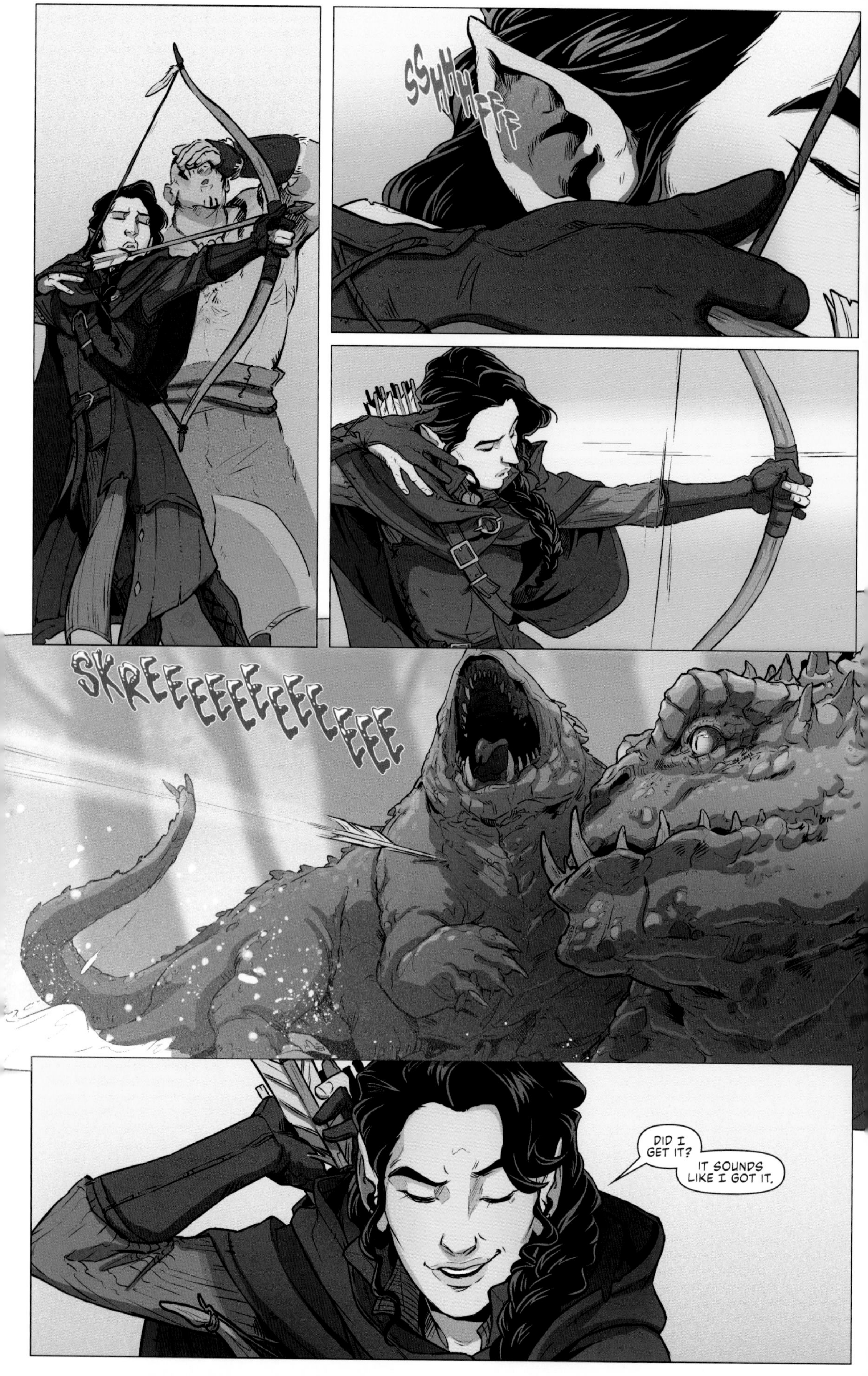
SSHHHFFF
SKREEEEEEEEEEEEEE
DID I GET IT?
IT SOUNDS LIKE I GOT IT.

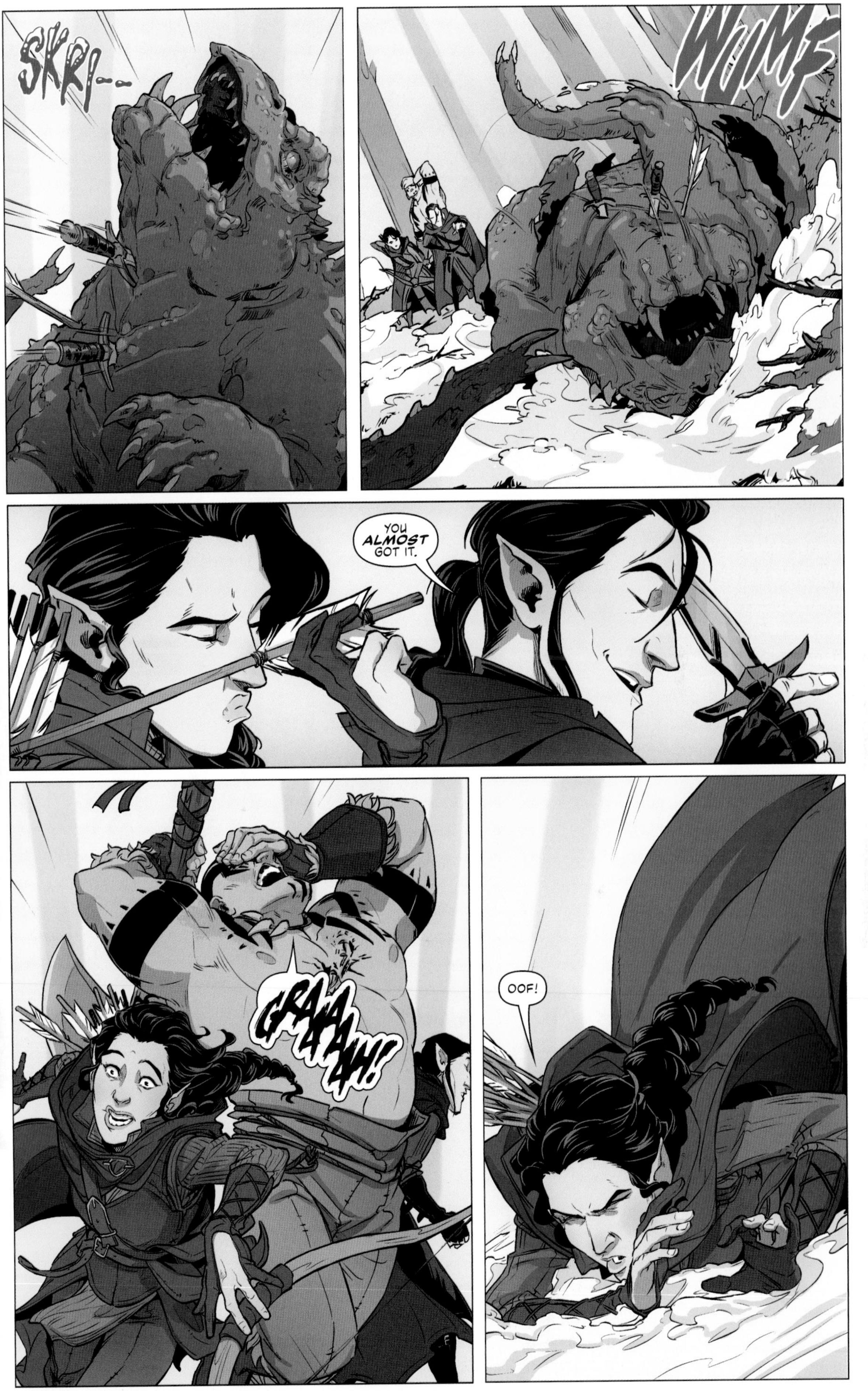
SKRI--
WUMF
YOU ALMOST GOT IT.
GRAAAAAH!
OOF!

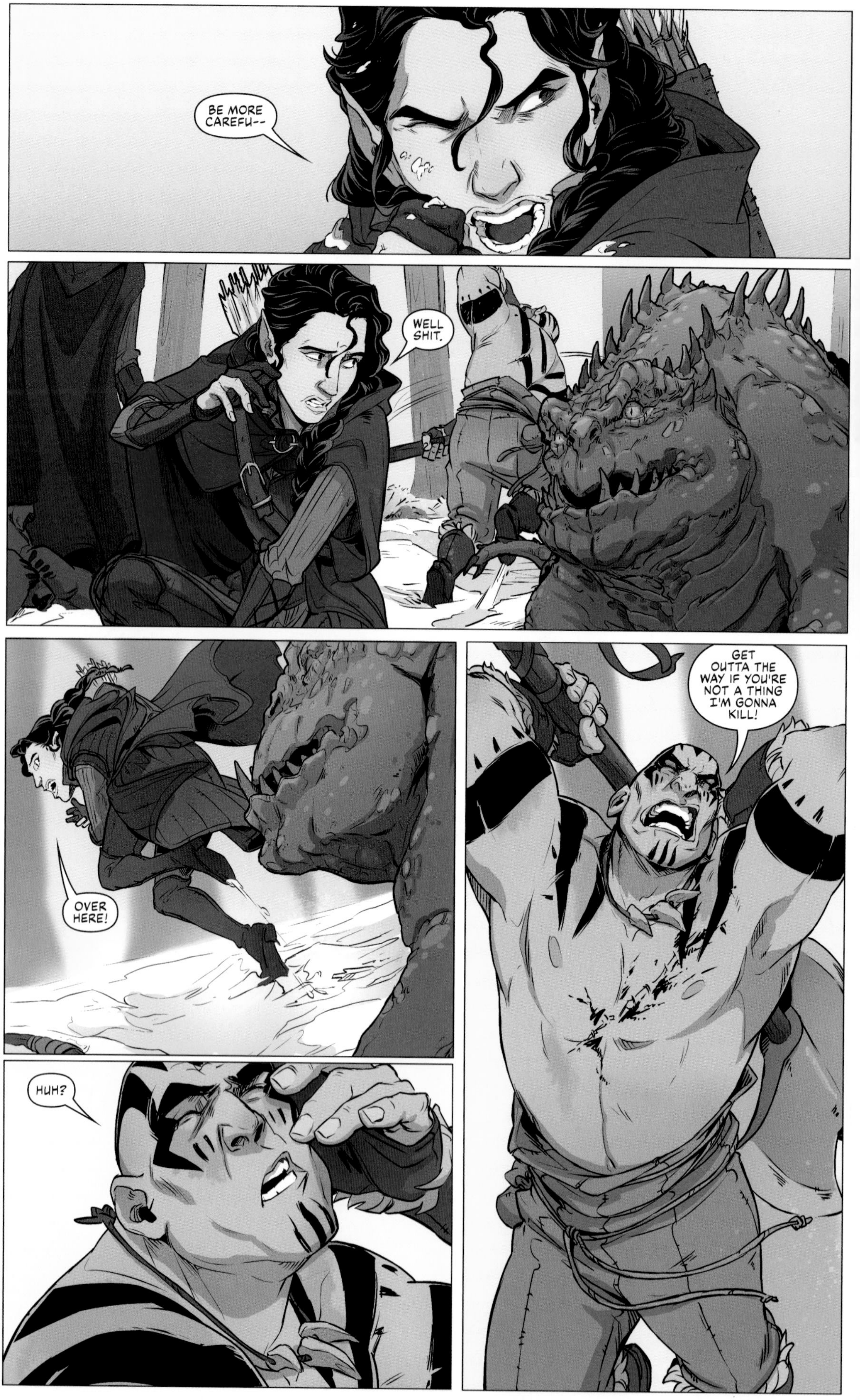
BE MORE CAREFU--
WELL SHIT.
OVER HERE!
GET OUTTA THE WAY IF YOU'RE NOT A THING I'M GONNA KILL!
HUH?

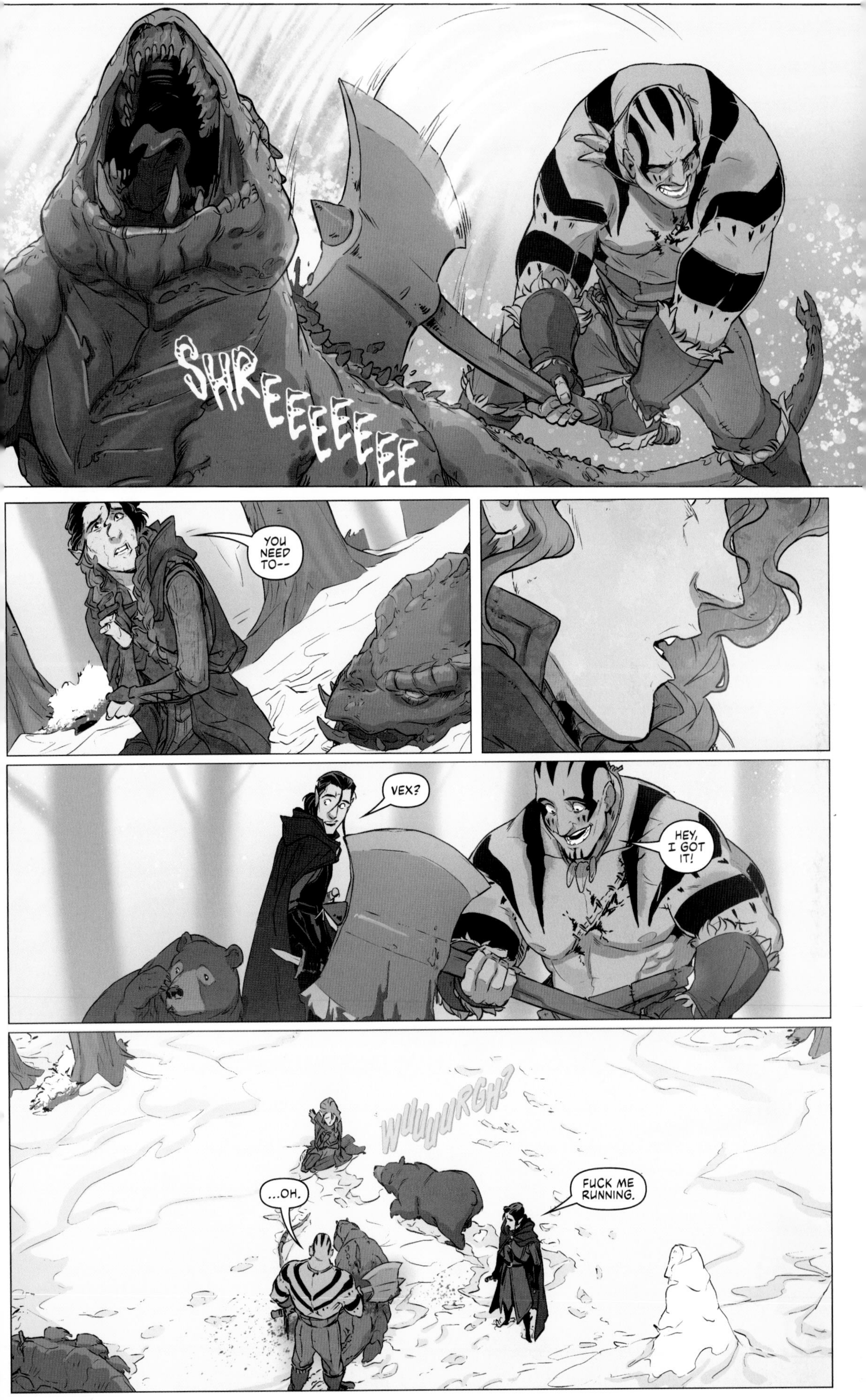
SHREEEEEEEE
YOU NEED TO--
VEX?
HEY, I GOT IT!
WUUUURGH?
...OH.
FUCK ME RUNNING.

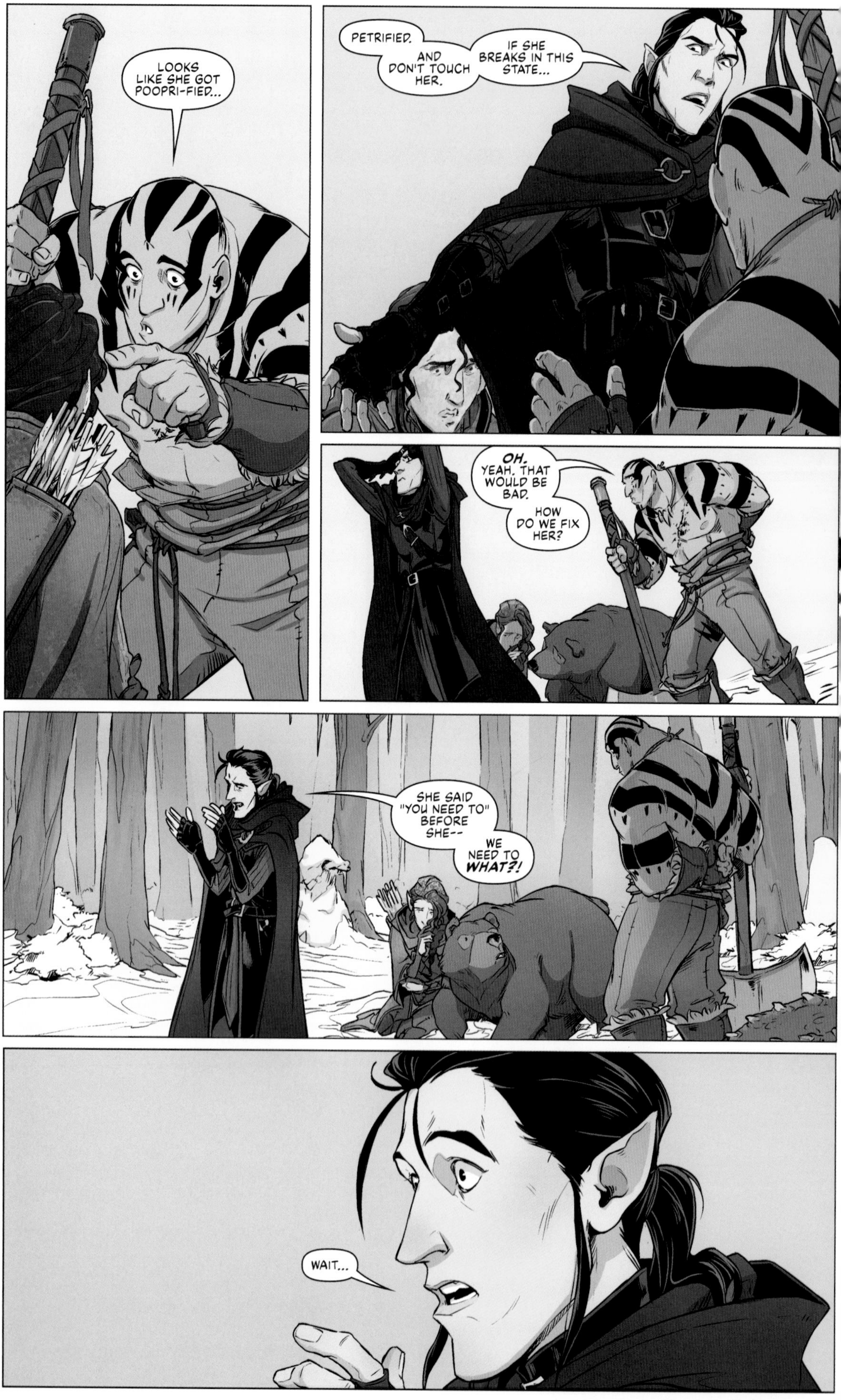
LOOKS LIKE SHE GOT POOPRI-FIED...
PETRIFIED.
AND DON'T TOUCH HER.
IF SHE BREAKS IN THIS STATE...
OH. YEAH. THAT WOULD BE BAD.
HOW DO WE FIX HER?
SHE SAID "YOU NEED TO" BEFORE SHE--
WE NEED TO WHAT?!
WAIT...

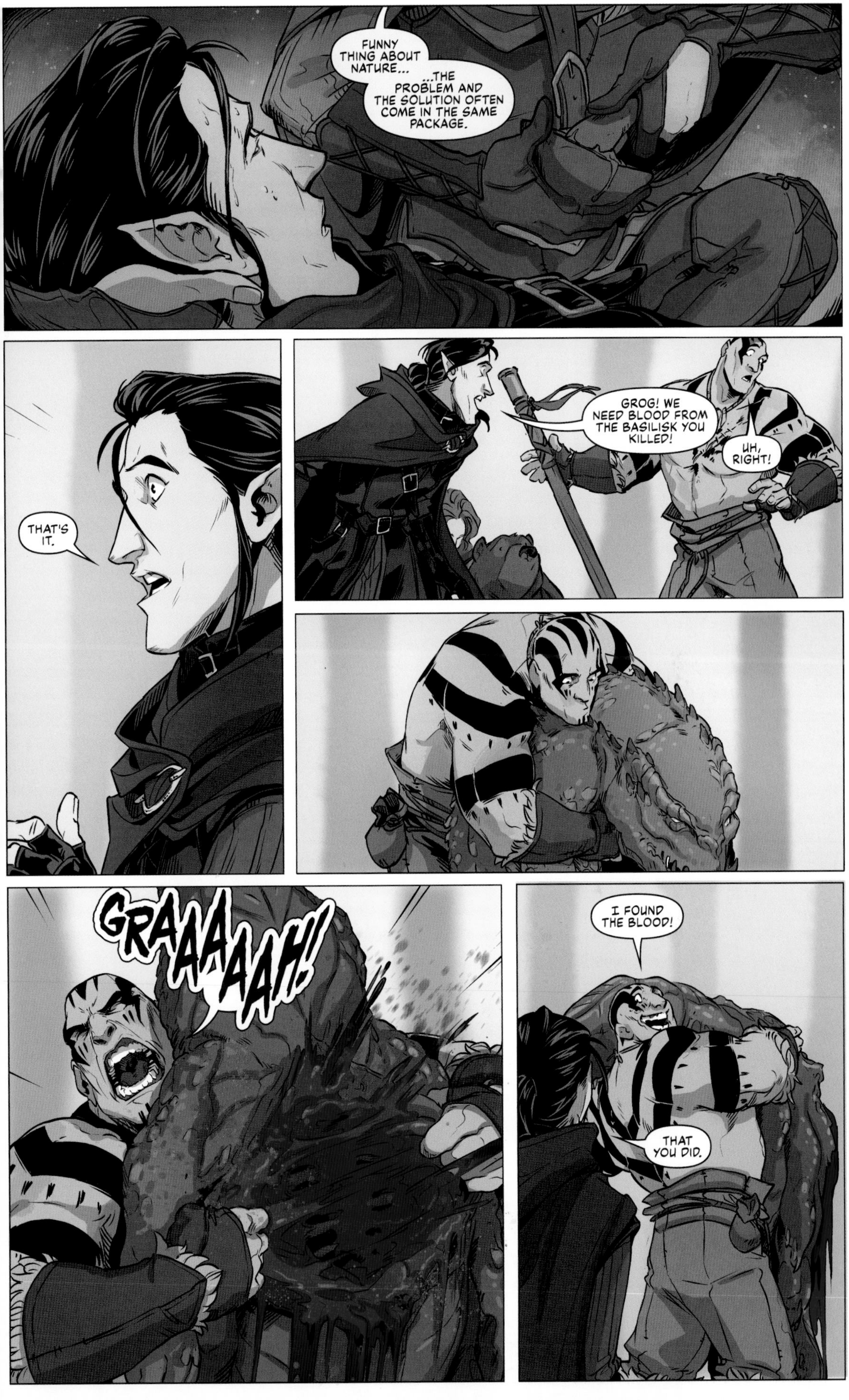
FUNNY THING ABOUT NATURE...
...THE PROBLEM AND THE SOLUTION OFTEN COME IN THE SAME PACKAGE.
THAT'S IT.
GROG! WE NEED BLOOD FROM THE BASILISK YOU KILLED!
UH, RIGHT!
GRAAAAAH!
I FOUND THE BLOOD!
THAT YOU DID.

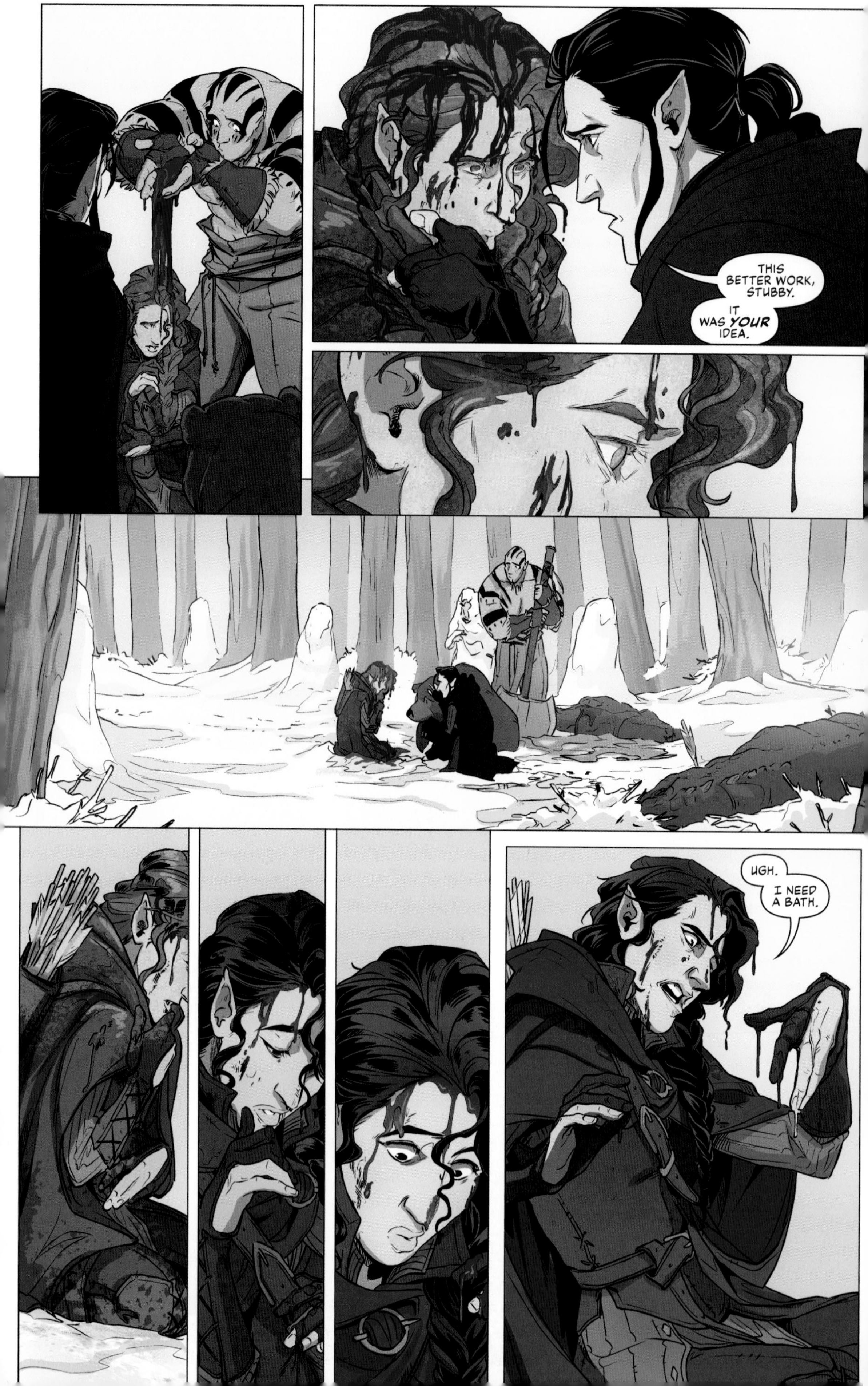
THIS BETTER WORK, STUBBY.
IT WAS YOUR IDEA.
UGH. I NEED A BATH.

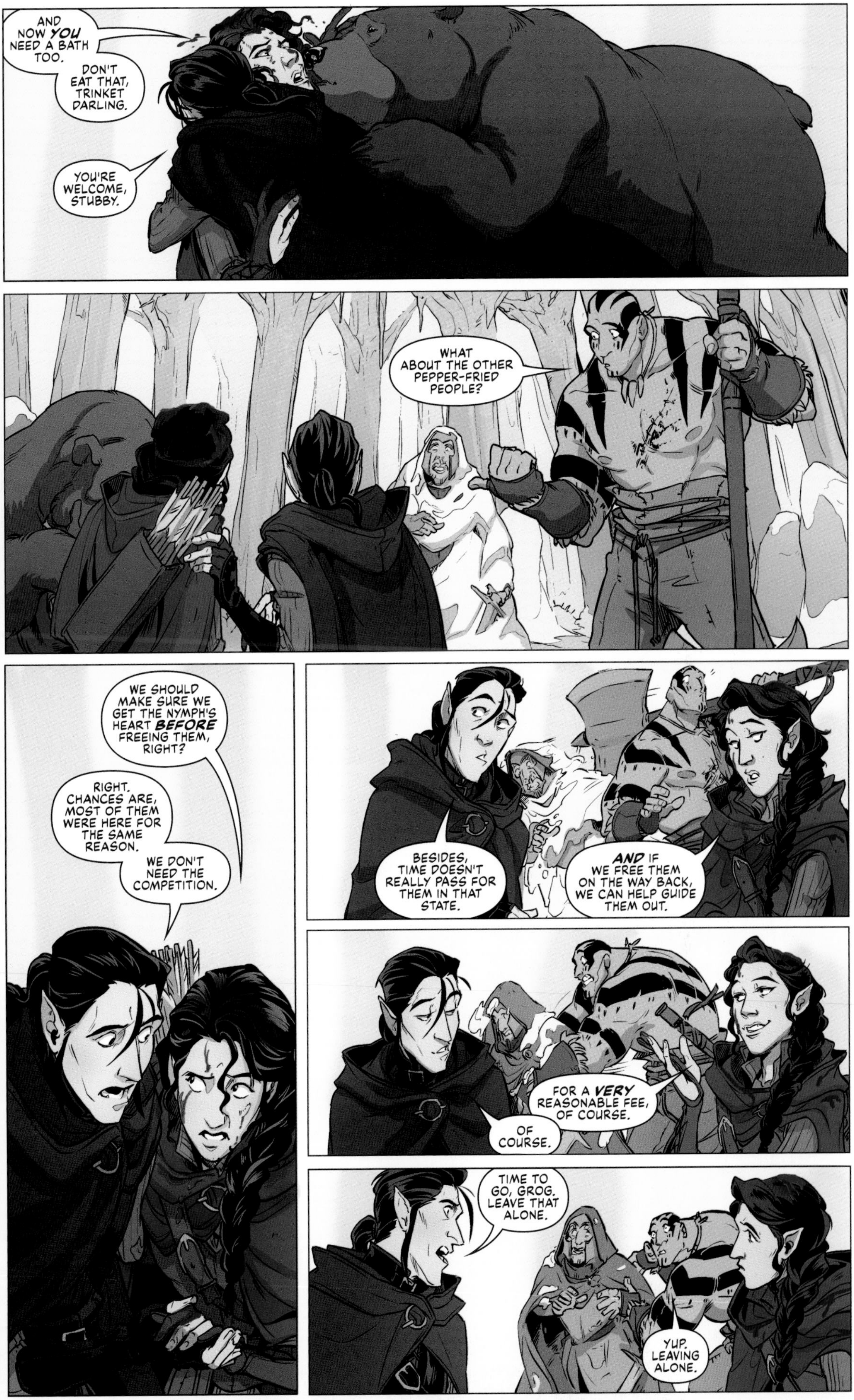
AND NOW *YOU* NEED A BATH TOO.
DON'T EAT THAT, TRINKET DARLING.
YOU'RE WELCOME, STUBBY.
WHAT ABOUT THE OTHER PEPPER-FRIED PEOPLE?
WE SHOULD MAKE SURE WE GET THE NYMPH'S HEART *BEFORE* FREEING THEM, RIGHT?
RIGHT. CHANCES ARE, MOST OF THEM WERE HERE FOR THE SAME REASON.
WE DON'T NEED THE COMPETITION.
BESIDES, TIME DOESN'T REALLY PASS FOR THEM IN THAT STATE.
AND IF WE FREE THEM ON THE WAY BACK, WE CAN HELP GUIDE THEM OUT.
FOR A *VERY* REASONABLE FEE, OF COURSE.
OF COURSE.
TIME TO GO, GROG. LEAVE THAT ALONE.
YUP. LEAVING ALONE.

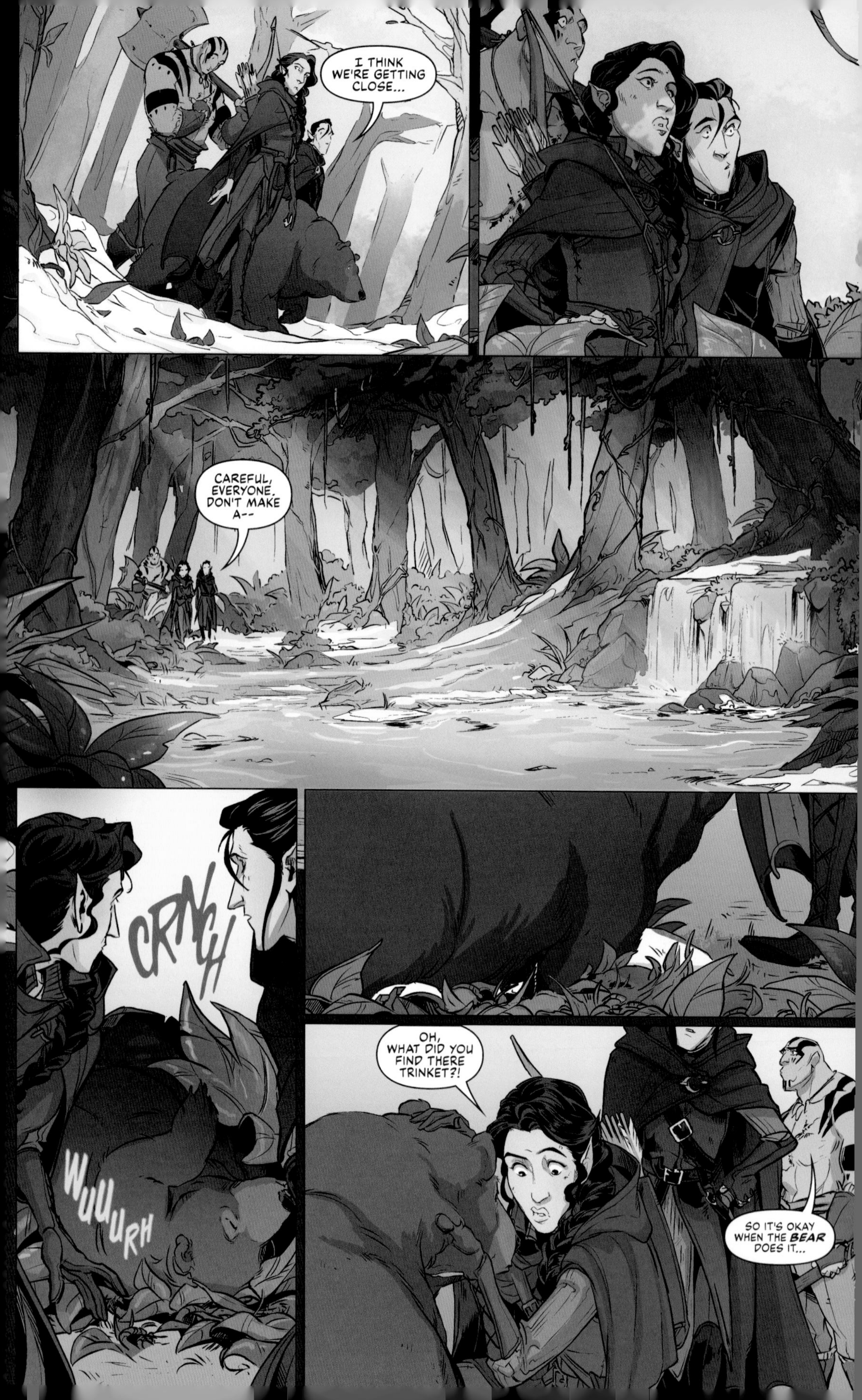

I THINK WE'RE GETTING CLOSE...
CAREFUL, EVERYONE. DON'T MAKE A--
CRNCH
WUUURH
OH, WHAT DID YOU FIND THERE TRINKET?!
SO IT'S OKAY WHEN THE BEAR DOES IT...

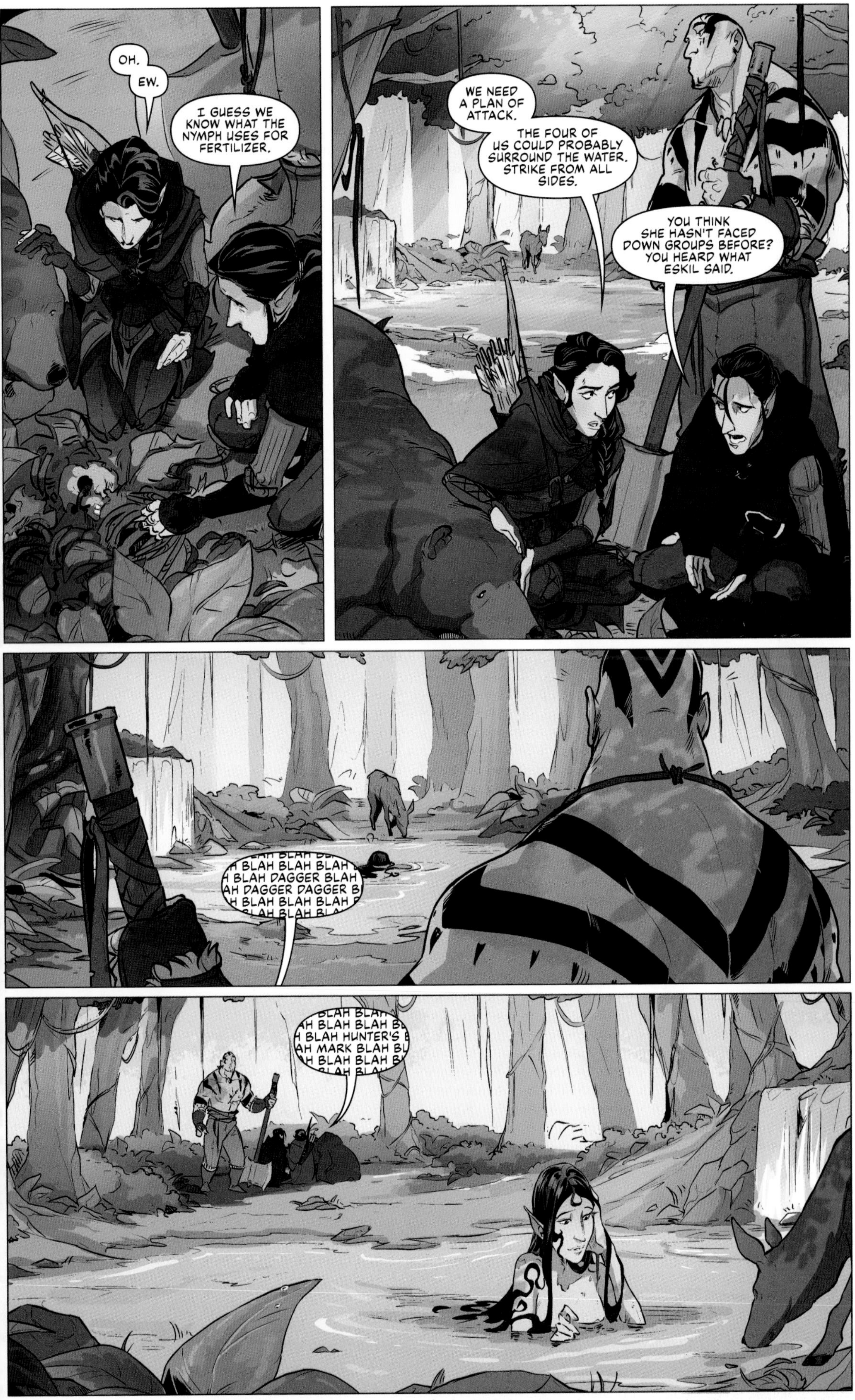
OH.
EW.
I GUESS WE KNOW WHAT THE NYMPH USES FOR FERTILIZER.
WE NEED A PLAN OF ATTACK.
THE FOUR OF US COULD PROBABLY SURROUND THE WATER. STRIKE FROM ALL SIDES.
YOU THINK SHE HASN'T FACED DOWN GROUPS BEFORE? YOU HEARD WHAT ESKIL SAID.
BLAH BLAH BLAH DAGGER BLAH DAGGER DAGGER BLAH BLAH BLAH
BLAH BLAH BLAH HUNTER'S MARK BLAH BLAH BLAH

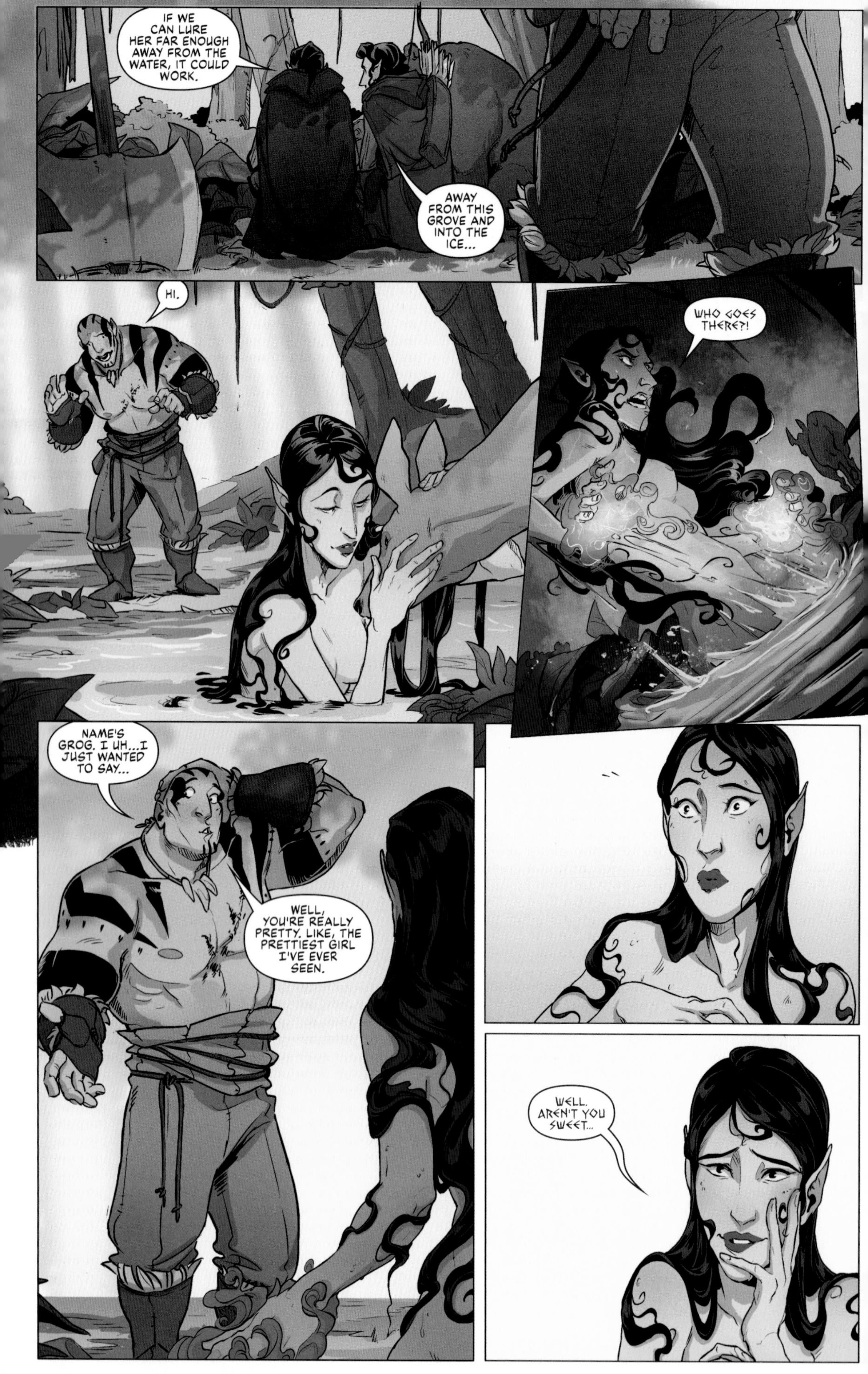
IF WE CAN LURE HER FAR ENOUGH AWAY FROM THE WATER, IT COULD WORK.
AWAY FROM THIS GROVE AND INTO THE ICE...
HI.
WHO GOES THERE?!
NAME'S GROG. I UH...I JUST WANTED TO SAY...
WELL, YOU'RE REALLY PRETTY. LIKE, THE PRETTIEST GIRL I'VE EVER SEEN.
WELL. AREN'T YOU SWEET...

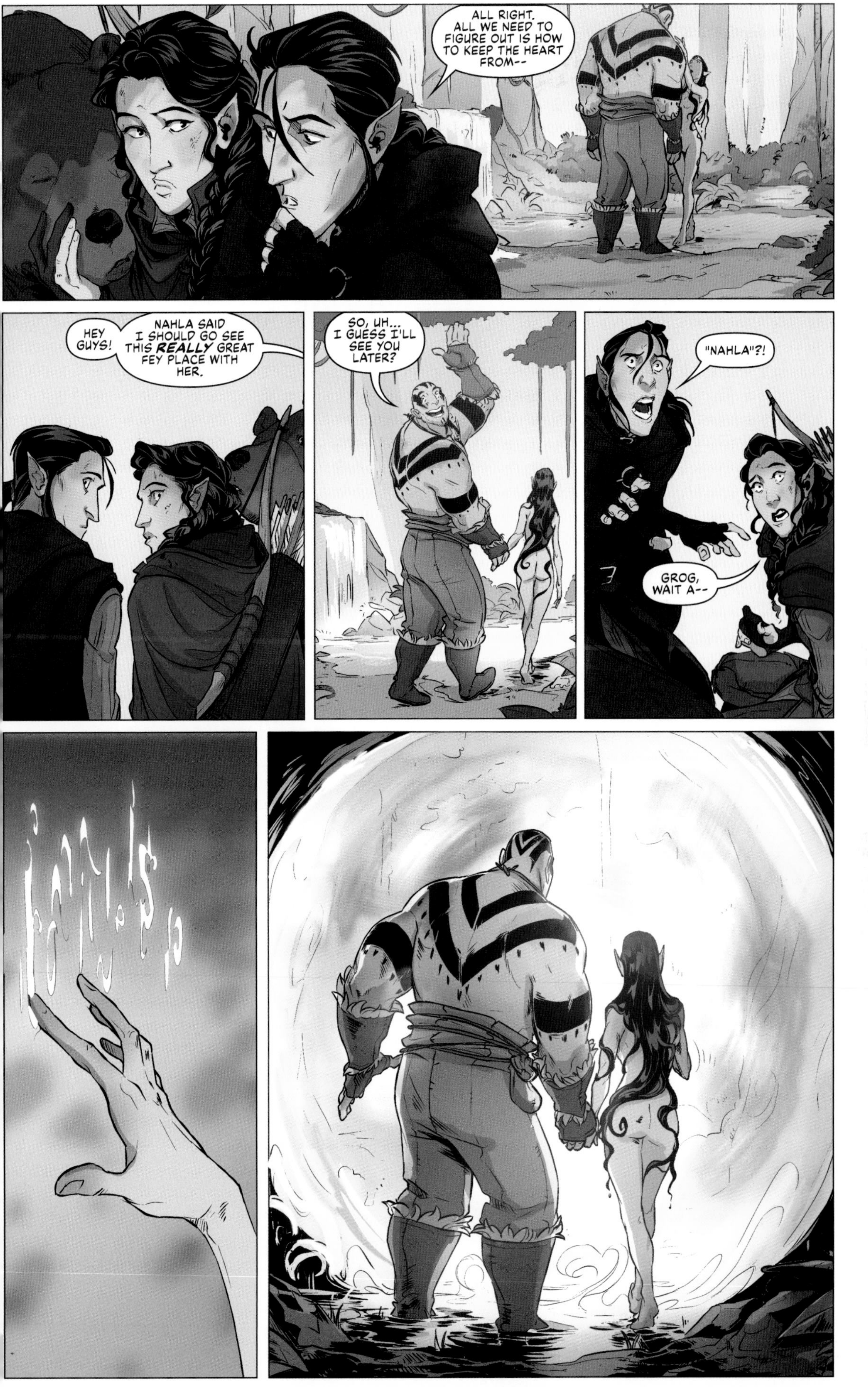
ALL RIGHT. ALL WE NEED TO FIGURE OUT IS HOW TO KEEP THE HEART FROM--
HEY GUYS!
NAHLA SAID I SHOULD GO SEE THIS REALLY GREAT FEY PLACE WITH HER.
SO, UH... I GUESS I'LL SEE YOU LATER?
"NAHLA"?!
GROG, WAIT A--

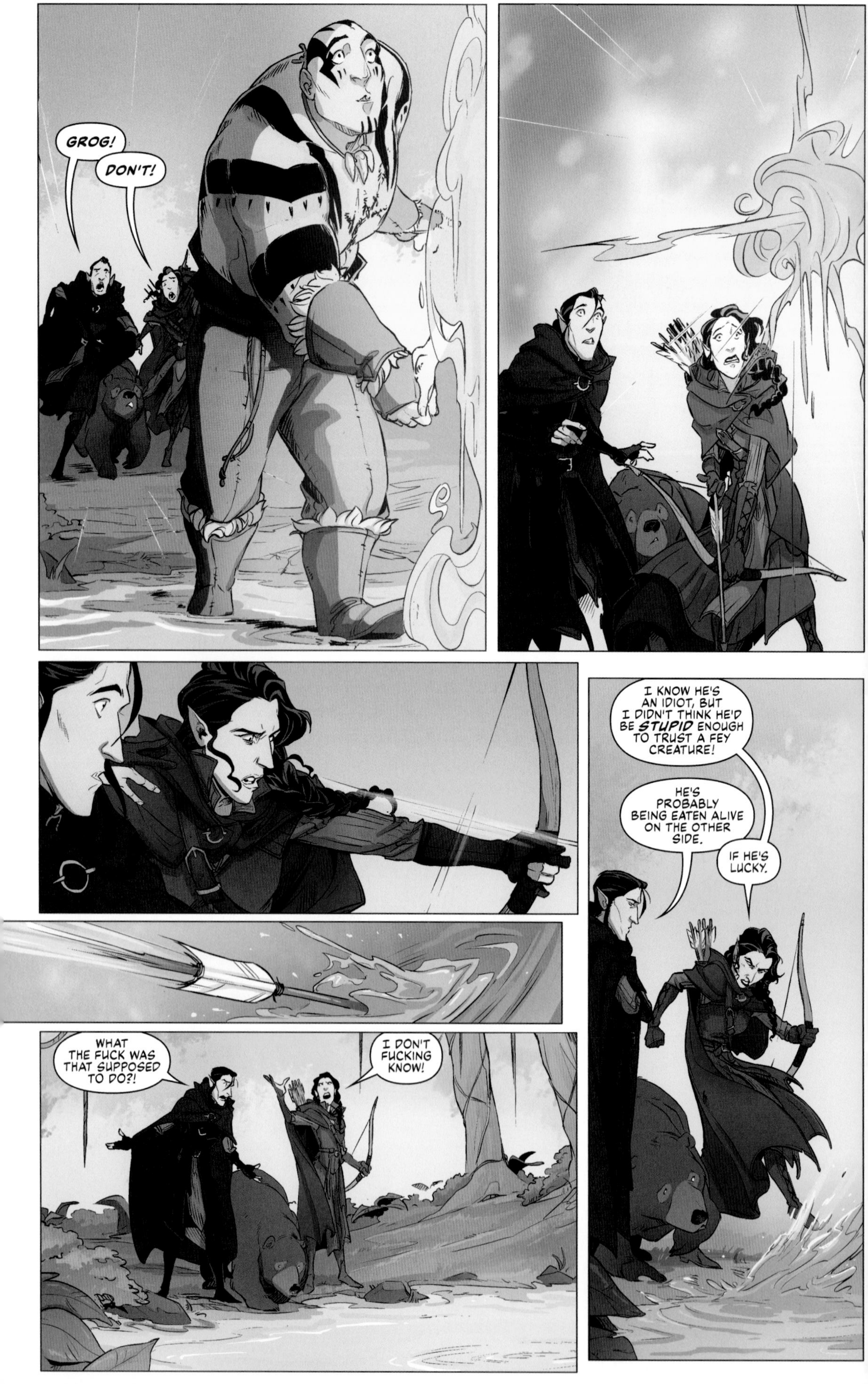
GROG!
DON'T!
I KNOW HE'S AN IDIOT, BUT I DIDN'T THINK HE'D BE STUPID ENOUGH TO TRUST A FEY CREATURE!
HE'S PROBABLY BEING EATEN ALIVE ON THE OTHER SIDE.
IF HE'S LUCKY.
WHAT THE FUCK WAS THAT SUPPOSED TO DO?!
I DON'T FUCKING KNOW!

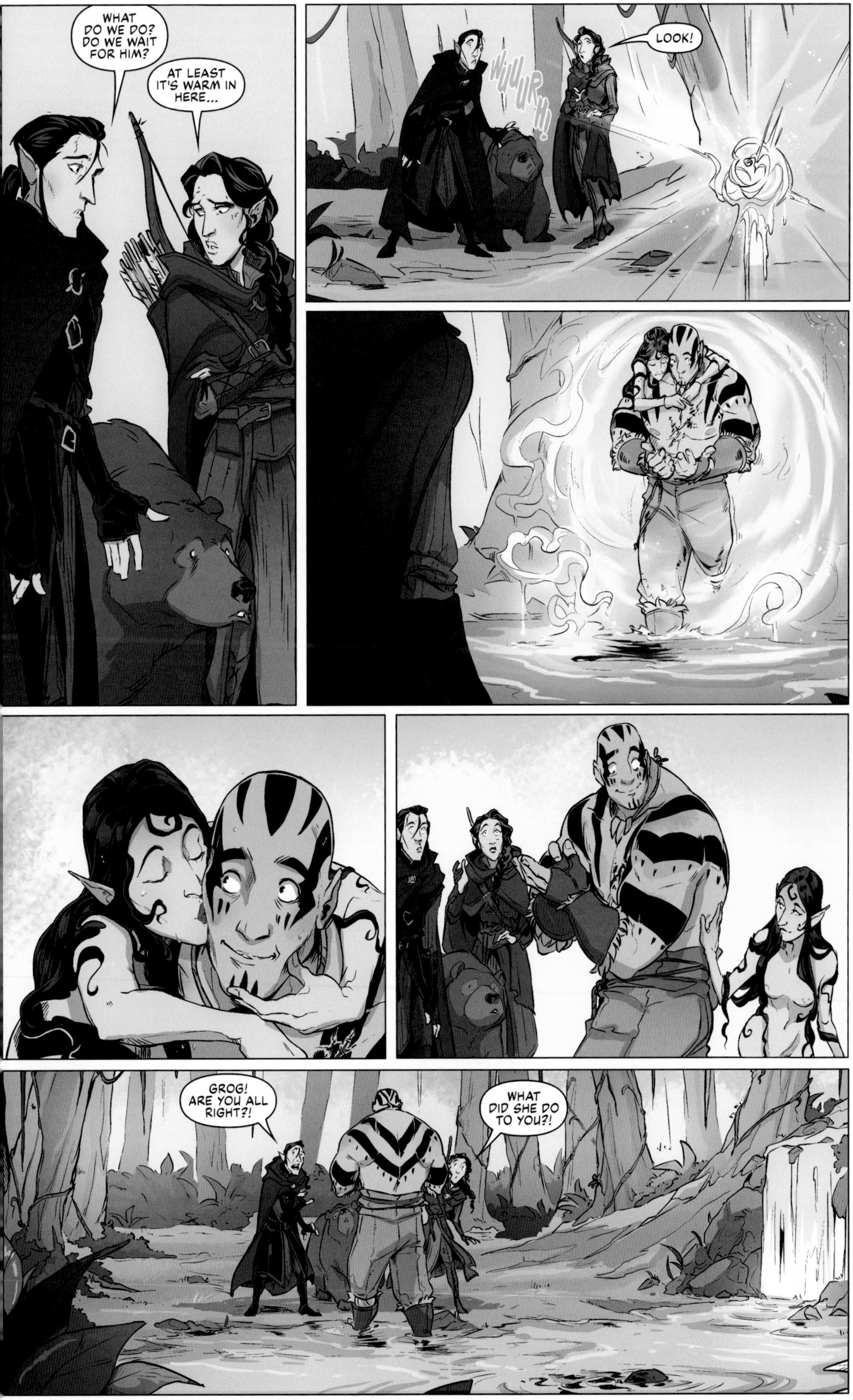
WHAT DO WE DO? DO WE WAIT FOR HIM?
AT LEAST IT'S WARM IN HERE...
LOOK!
WUUURHH!
GROG! ARE YOU ALL RIGHT?!
WHAT DID SHE DO TO YOU?!

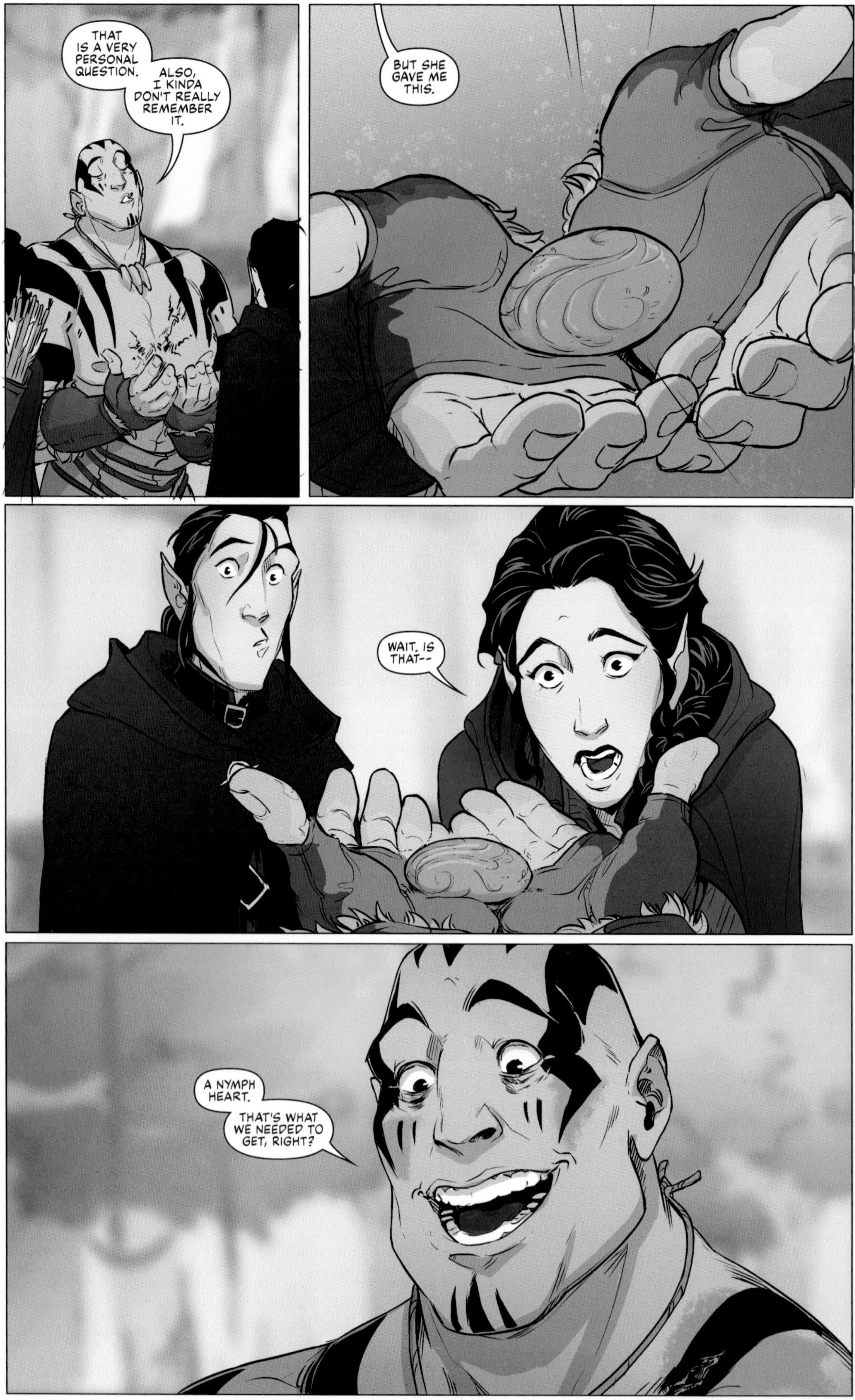
THAT IS A VERY PERSONAL QUESTION.
ALSO, I KINDA DON'T REALLY REMEMBER IT.
BUT SHE GAVE ME THIS.
WAIT. IS THAT--
A NYMPH HEART.
THAT'S WHAT WE NEEDED TO GET, RIGHT?

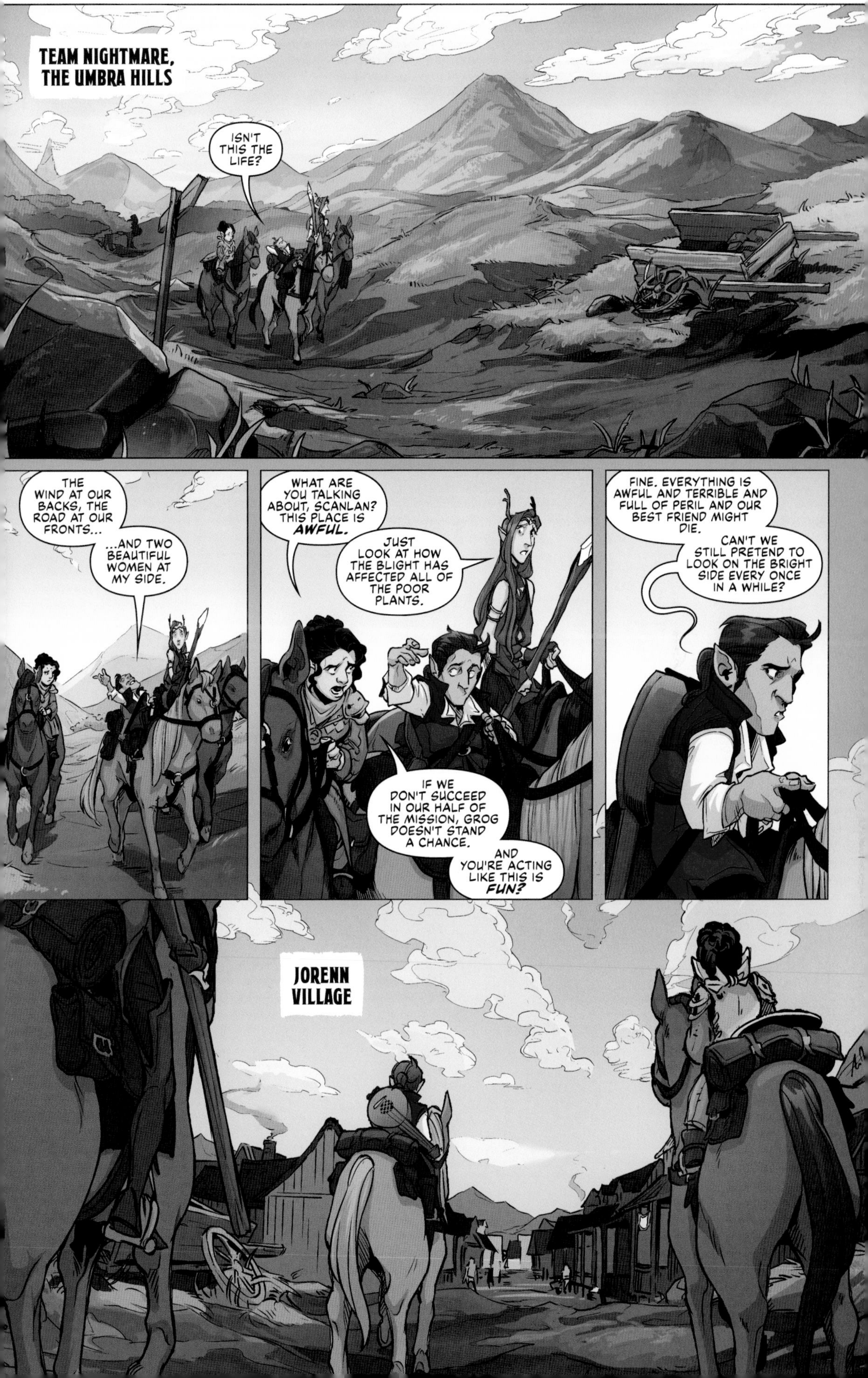
TEAM NIGHTMARE, THE UMBRA HILLS
ISN'T THIS THE LIFE?
THE WIND AT OUR BACKS, THE ROAD AT OUR FRONTS...
...AND TWO BEAUTIFUL WOMEN AT MY SIDE.
WHAT ARE YOU TALKING ABOUT, SCANLAN? THIS PLACE IS AWFUL.
JUST LOOK AT HOW THE BLIGHT HAS AFFECTED ALL OF THE POOR PLANTS.
IF WE DON'T SUCCEED IN OUR HALF OF THE MISSION, GROG DOESN'T STAND A CHANCE.
AND YOU'RE ACTING LIKE THIS IS FUN?
FINE. EVERYTHING IS AWFUL AND TERRIBLE AND FULL OF PERIL AND OUR BEST FRIEND MIGHT DIE.
CAN'T WE STILL PRETEND TO LOOK ON THE BRIGHT SIDE EVERY ONCE IN A WHILE?
JORENN VILLAGE

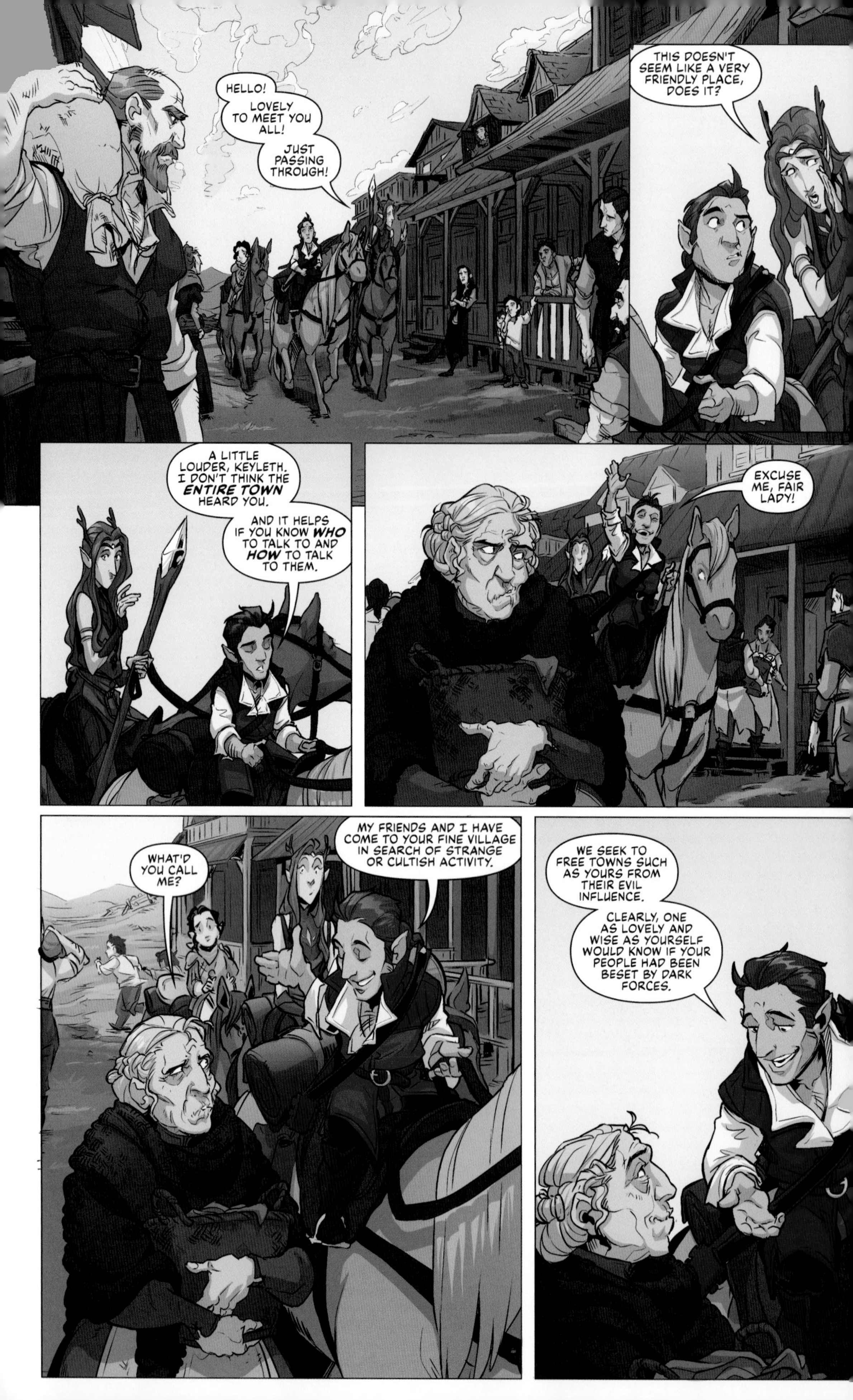
HELLO!
LOVELY TO MEET YOU ALL!
JUST PASSING THROUGH!
THIS DOESN'T SEEM LIKE A VERY FRIENDLY PLACE, DOES IT?
A LITTLE LOUDER, KEYLETH. I DON'T THINK THE ***ENTIRE TOWN*** HEARD YOU.
AND IT HELPS IF YOU KNOW ***WHO*** TO TALK TO AND ***HOW*** TO TALK TO THEM.
EXCUSE ME, FAIR LADY!
WHAT'D YOU CALL ME?
MY FRIENDS AND I HAVE COME TO YOUR FINE VILLAGE IN SEARCH OF STRANGE OR CULTISH ACTIVITY.
WE SEEK TO FREE TOWNS SUCH AS YOURS FROM THEIR EVIL INFLUENCE.
CLEARLY, ONE AS LOVELY AND WISE AS YOURSELF WOULD KNOW IF YOUR PEOPLE HAD BEEN BESET BY DARK FORCES.

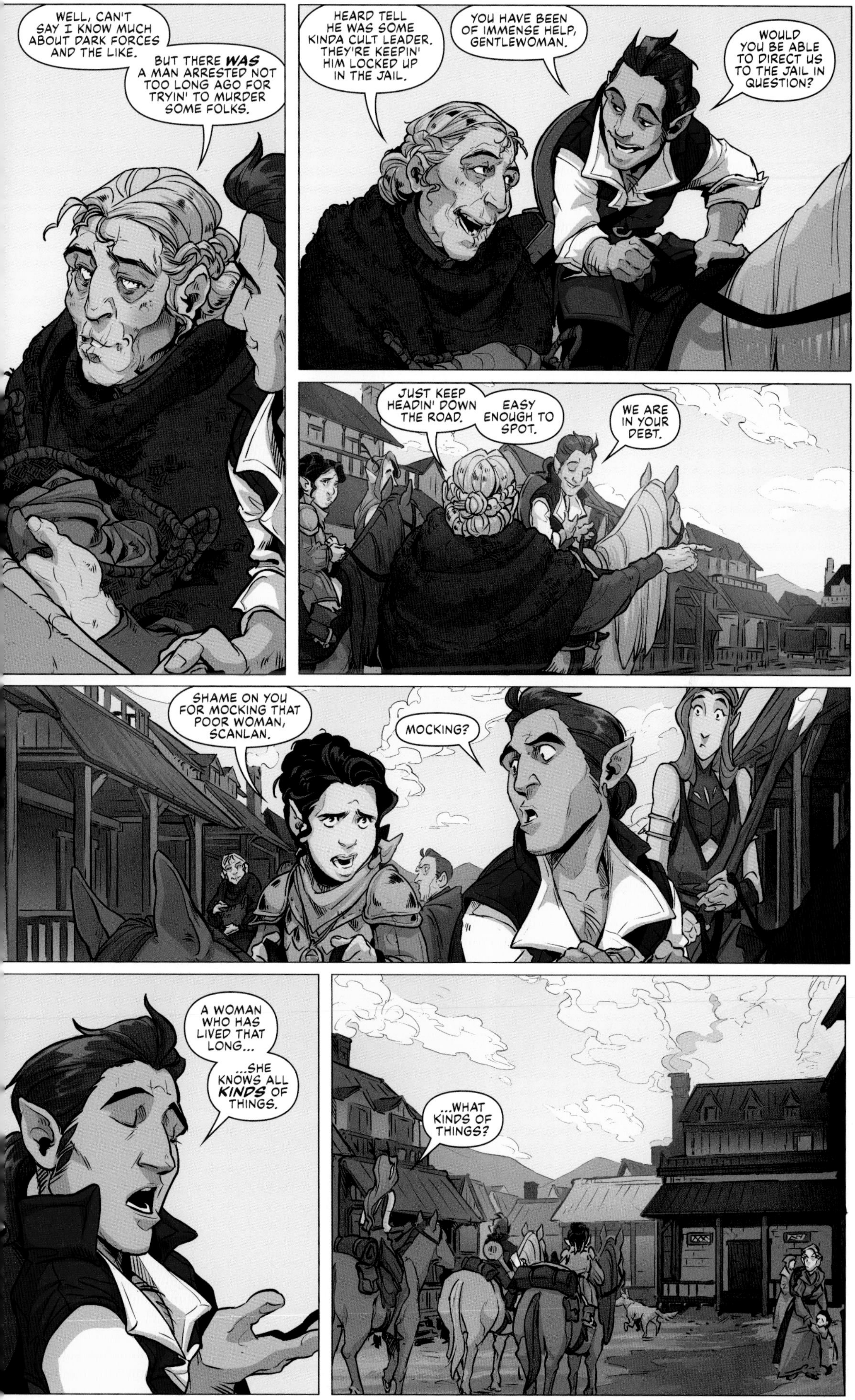
WELL, CAN'T SAY I KNOW MUCH ABOUT DARK FORCES AND THE LIKE.
BUT THERE WAS A MAN ARRESTED NOT TOO LONG AGO FOR TRYIN' TO MURDER SOME FOLKS.
HEARD TELL HE WAS SOME KINDA CULT LEADER. THEY'RE KEEPIN' HIM LOCKED UP IN THE JAIL.
YOU HAVE BEEN OF IMMENSE HELP, GENTLEWOMAN.
WOULD YOU BE ABLE TO DIRECT US TO THE JAIL IN QUESTION?
JUST KEEP HEADIN' DOWN THE ROAD.
EASY ENOUGH TO SPOT.
WE ARE IN YOUR DEBT.
SHAME ON YOU FOR MOCKING THAT POOR WOMAN, SCANLAN.
MOCKING?
A WOMAN WHO HAS LIVED THAT LONG...
...SHE KNOWS ALL KINDS OF THINGS.
...WHAT KINDS OF THINGS?

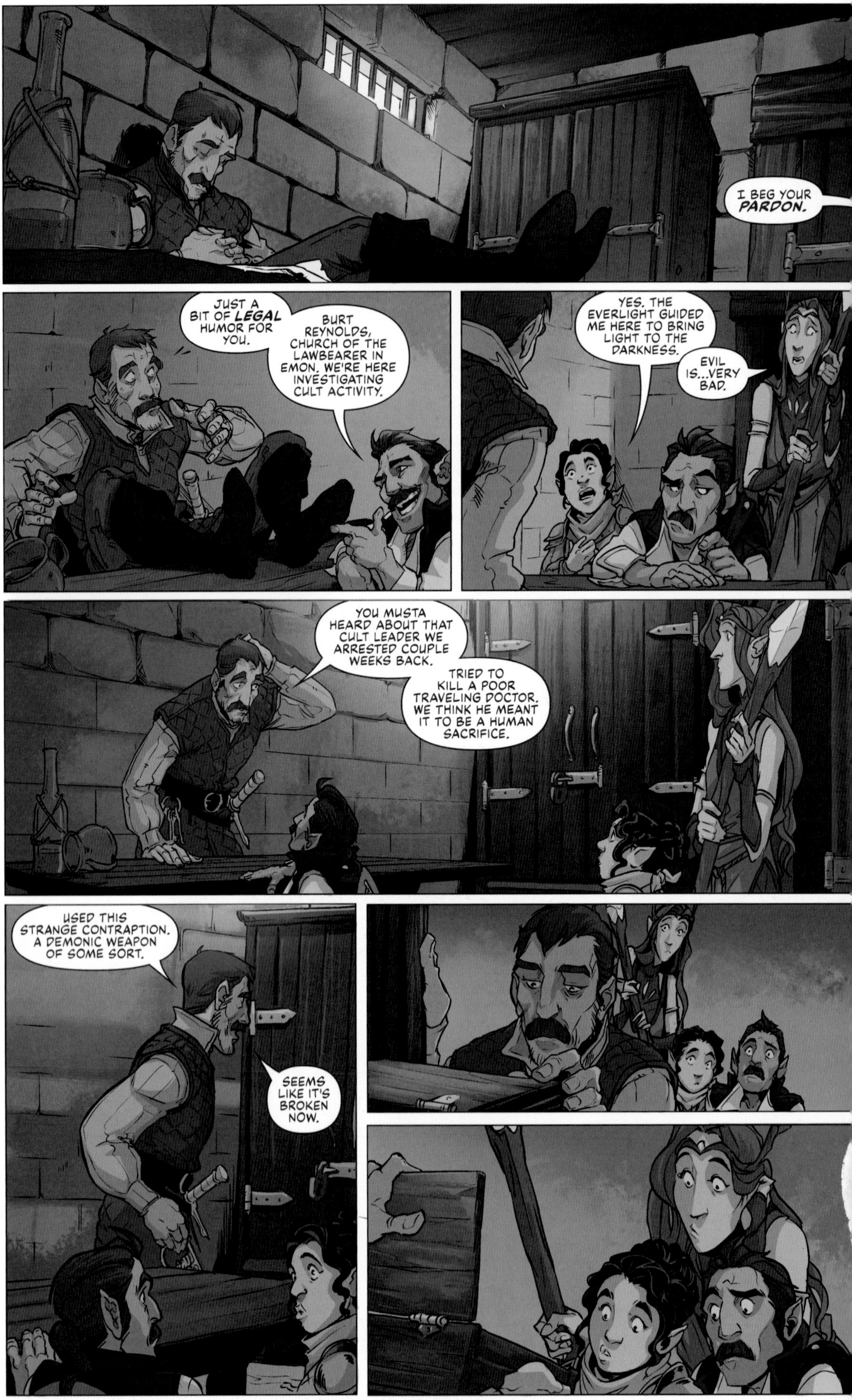
I BEG YOUR *PARDON.*
JUST A BIT OF *LEGAL* HUMOR FOR YOU.
BURT REYNOLDS, CHURCH OF THE LAWBEARER IN EMON. WE'RE HERE INVESTIGATING CULT ACTIVITY.
YES. THE EVERLIGHT GUIDED ME HERE TO BRING LIGHT TO THE DARKNESS.
EVIL IS...VERY BAD.
YOU MUSTA HEARD ABOUT THAT CULT LEADER WE ARRESTED COUPLE WEEKS BACK.
TRIED TO KILL A POOR TRAVELING DOCTOR. WE THINK HE MEANT IT TO BE A HUMAN SACRIFICE.
USED THIS STRANGE CONTRAPTION. A DEMONIC WEAPON OF SOME SORT.
SEEMS LIKE IT'S BROKEN NOW.

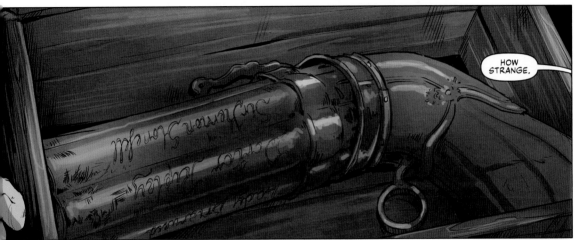

HOW STRANGE.

OBVIOUSLY, WE'LL NEED TO KNOW *ALL* THE DETAILS ABOUT HIS...

...CULTINESS.

YOU CAN QUESTION HIM YOURSELF IF YOU WANT.

HE'S BACK THERE.

EASY ENOUGH TO FIND. ONLY PRISONER WE HAVE AT THE MOMENT.

THANK YOU FOR YOUR HELP.

DOWN WITH EVIL!

HAVE YOU EVER SEEN ANYTHING LIKE THAT DEVICE?

NO. BUT HOW DANGEROUS CAN THIS CULT GUY BE IF THE PEOPLE *HERE* WERE ABLE TO CAPTURE HIM?

WELL, IF YOU THREE ARE SUPPOSED TO BE MY LEGAL COUNSEL...

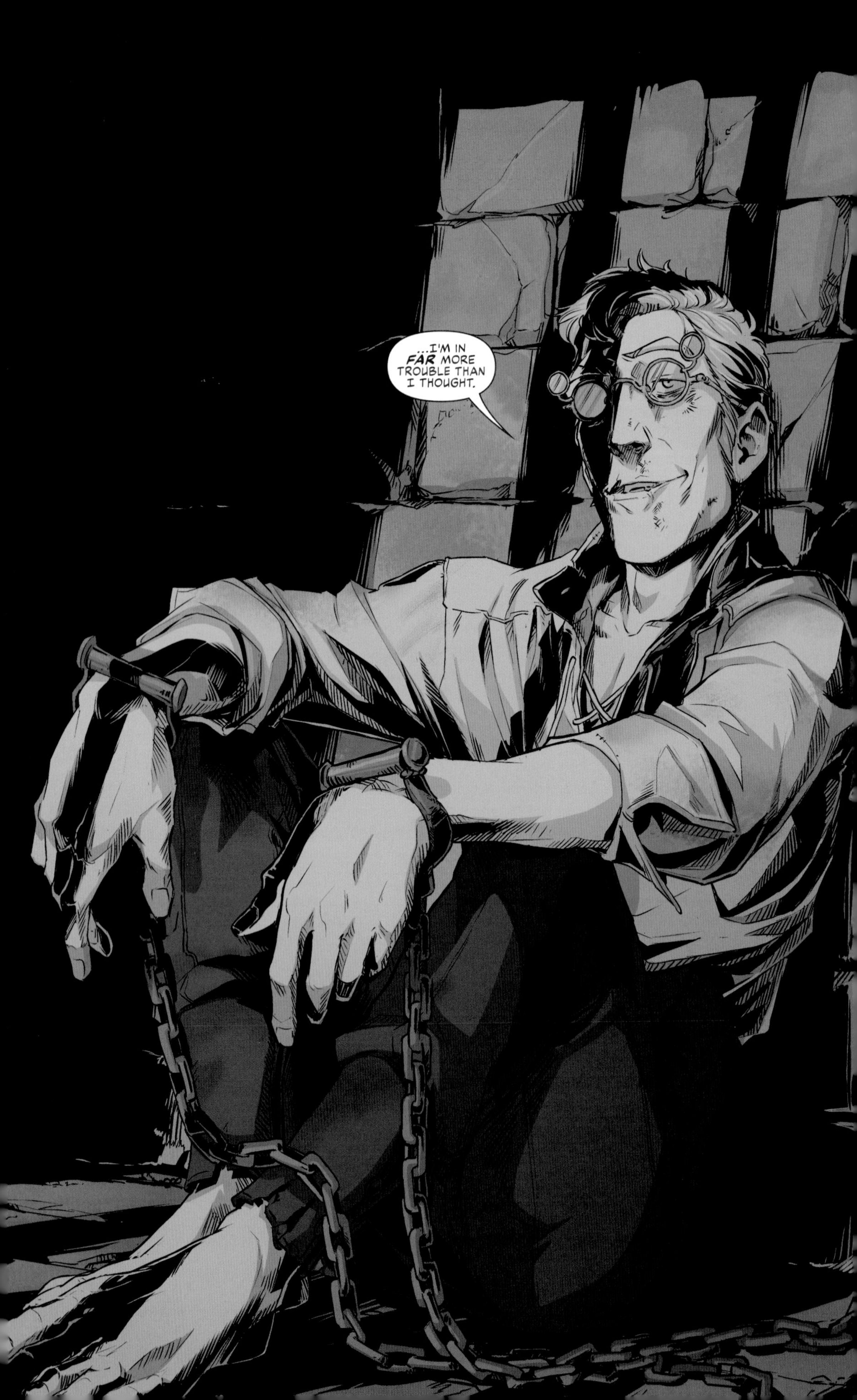
...I'M IN FAR MORE TROUBLE THAN I THOUGHT.

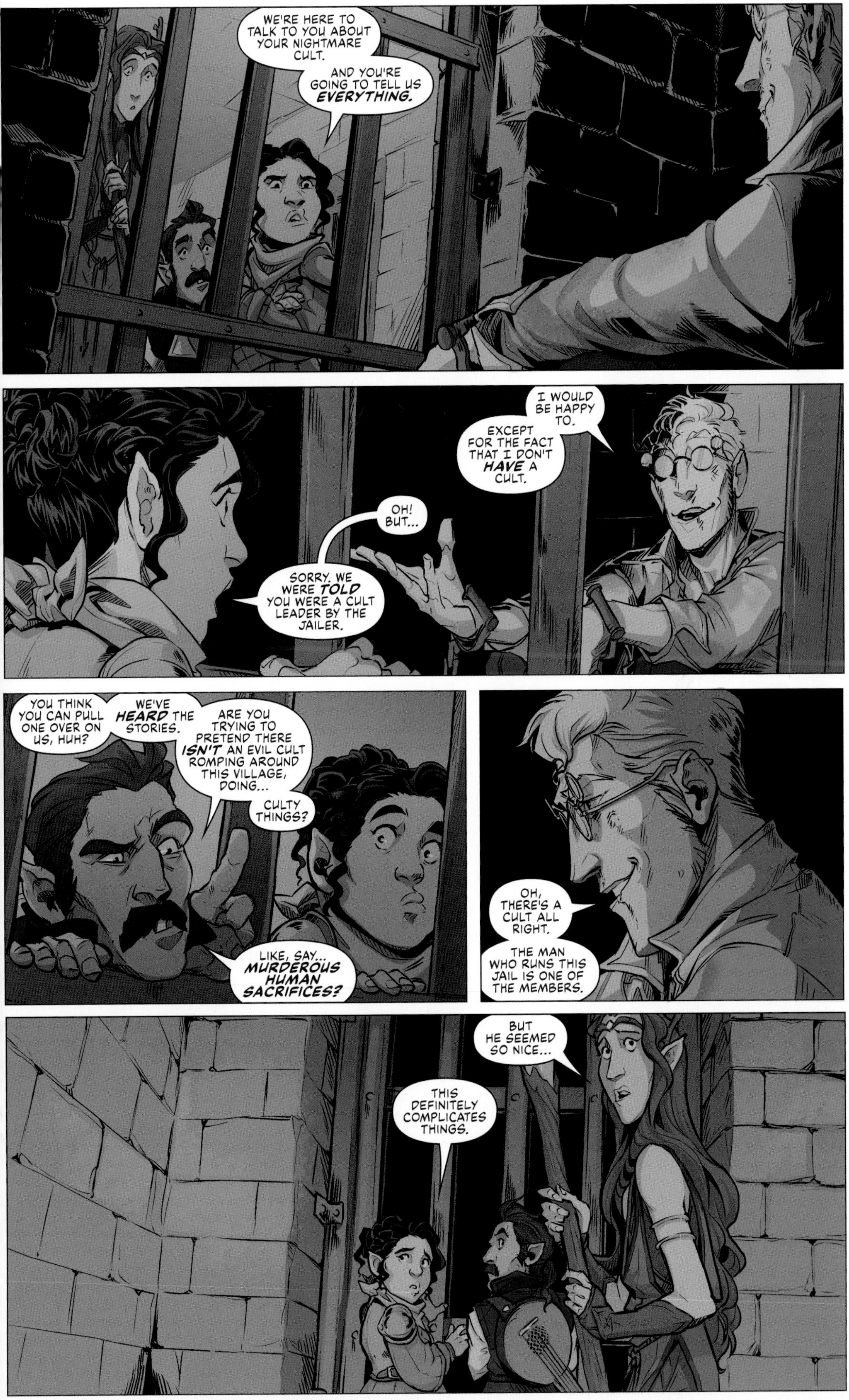
WE'RE HERE TO TALK TO YOU ABOUT YOUR NIGHTMARE CULT.
AND YOU'RE GOING TO TELL US *EVERYTHING.*
I WOULD BE HAPPY TO.
EXCEPT FOR THE FACT THAT I DON'T *HAVE* A CULT.
OH! BUT...
SORRY. WE WERE *TOLD* YOU WERE A CULT LEADER BY THE JAILER.
YOU THINK YOU CAN PULL ONE OVER ON US, HUH?
WE'VE *HEARD* THE STORIES.
ARE YOU TRYING TO PRETEND THERE *ISN'T* AN EVIL CULT ROMPING AROUND THIS VILLAGE, DOING...
CULTY THINGS?
LIKE, SAY... *MURDEROUS HUMAN SACRIFICES?*
OH, THERE'S A CULT ALL RIGHT.
THE MAN WHO RUNS THIS JAIL IS ONE OF THE MEMBERS.
BUT HE SEEMED SO NICE...
THIS DEFINITELY COMPLICATES THINGS.

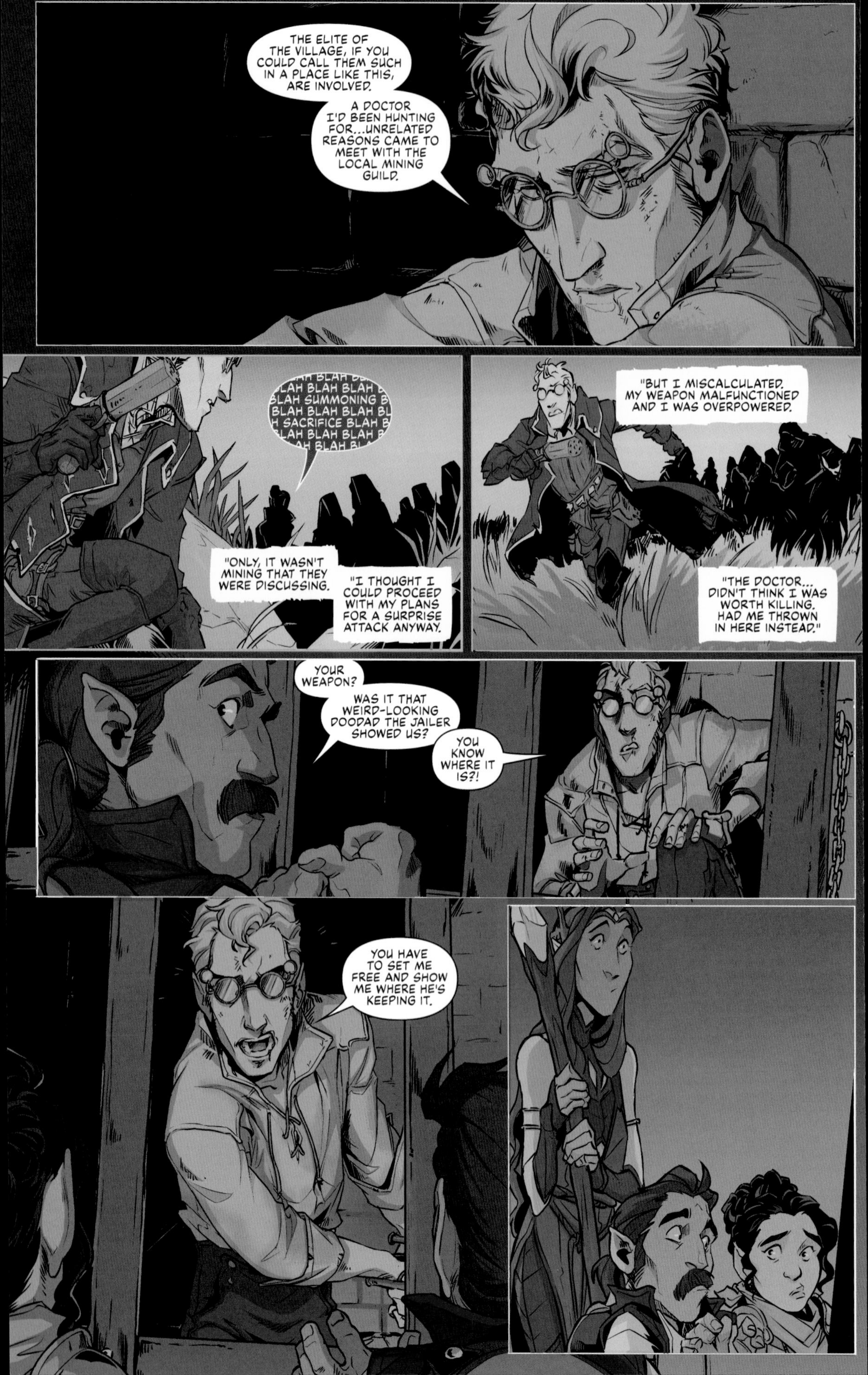
THE ELITE OF THE VILLAGE, IF YOU COULD CALL THEM SUCH IN A PLACE LIKE THIS, ARE INVOLVED.
A DOCTOR I'D BEEN HUNTING FOR...UNRELATED REASONS CAME TO MEET WITH THE LOCAL MINING GUILD.
BLAH BLAH BLAH SUMMONING BLAH BLAH BLAH SACRIFICE BLAH BLAH BLAH
"ONLY, IT WASN'T MINING THAT THEY WERE DISCUSSING.
"I THOUGHT I COULD PROCEED WITH MY PLANS FOR A SURPRISE ATTACK ANYWAY.
"BUT I MISCALCULATED. MY WEAPON MALFUNCTIONED AND I WAS OVERPOWERED.
"THE DOCTOR... DIDN'T THINK I WAS WORTH KILLING. HAD ME THROWN IN HERE INSTEAD."
YOUR WEAPON?
WAS IT THAT WEIRD-LOOKING DOODAD THE JAILER SHOWED US?
YOU KNOW WHERE IT IS?!
YOU HAVE TO SET ME FREE AND SHOW ME WHERE HE'S KEEPING IT.

LOOK, BUDDY. I DON'T KNOW WHAT KIND OF SCAM YOU'RE TRYING TO PULL ON US.

BUT IT'S PRETTY CONVENIENT THAT THE GUY WHO WANTS OUT OF JAIL IS CLAIMING EVERYONE *ELSE* HERE IS EVIL.

YOU COULD ALSO BE A PERFECTLY NICE PERSON!

BUT... SCANLAN DOES HAVE A POINT.

IT'S *BURT!* WHEN I'M WEARING THE MUSTACHE, IT'S BURT!

I'M SORRY... BURT.

YOU JUST... LOOK *SO* MUCH LIKE MY FRIEND SCANLAN. IT'S REALLY UNCANNY!

WE DIDN'T ACTUALLY COME HERE TO STOP THE NIGHTMARE CULT. WE CAME TO FIND THE NIGHTMARE.

WE NEED ITS SKULL FOR... A QUEST.

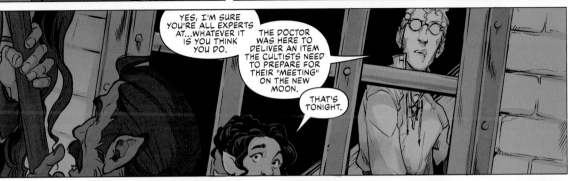

YES, I'M SURE YOU'RE ALL EXPERTS AT... WHATEVER IT IS YOU THINK YOU DO.

THE DOCTOR WAS HERE TO DELIVER AN ITEM THE CULTISTS NEED TO PREPARE FOR THEIR "MEETING" ON THE NEW MOON.

THAT'S TONIGHT.

INDEED IT IS. AND I CAN LEAD YOU TO WHERE THEY WILL BE SUMMONING THE NIGHTMARE.

BUT NOT IF I'M IN HERE. AND NOT IF I'M *UNARMED.*

I DON'T THINK WE HAVE MUCH OF A CHOICE.

WAIT, WHAT ARE WE DOING?

I SUPPOSE I'LL BE SEEING YOU LATER TONIGHT, THEN.

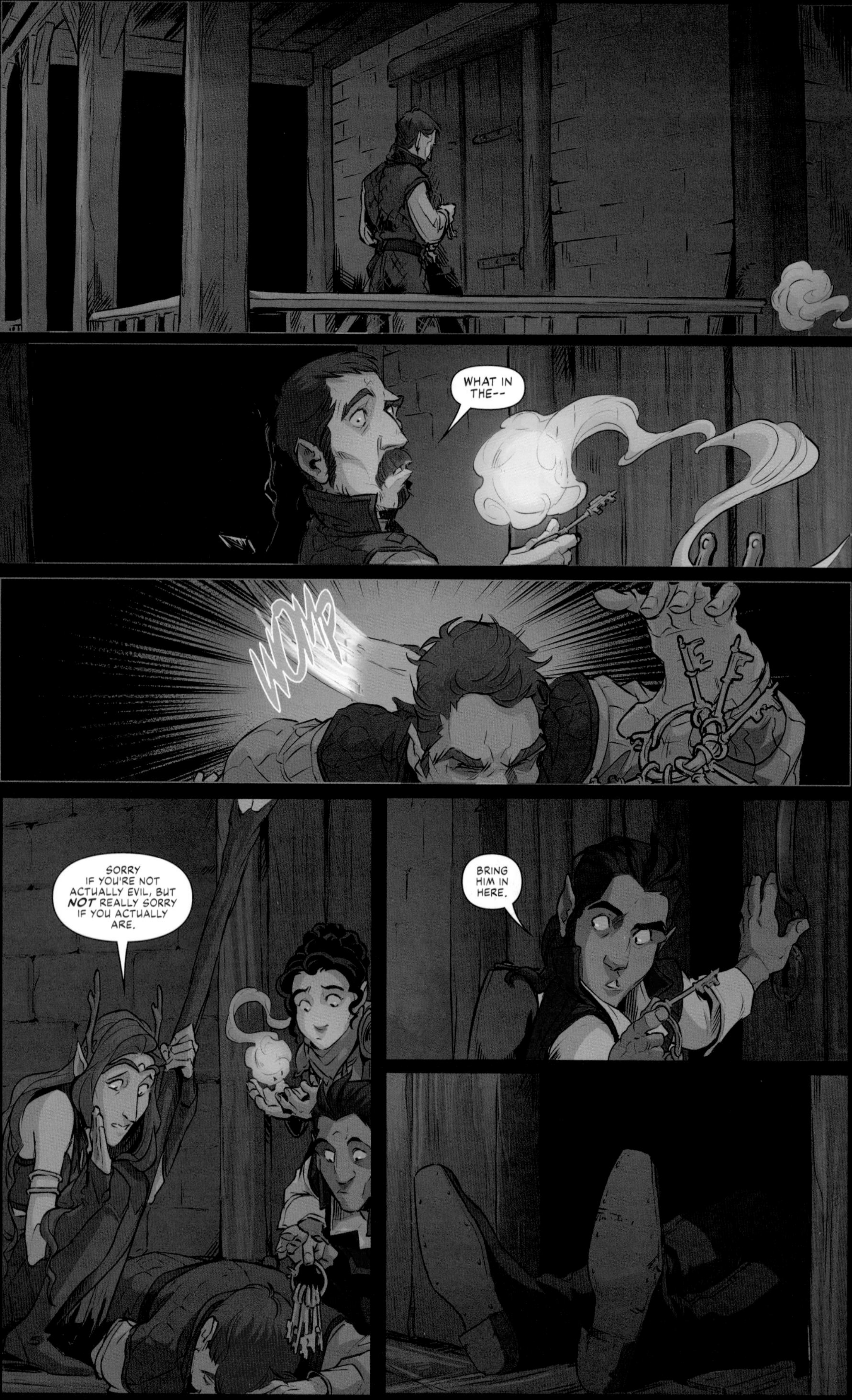
WHAT IN THE--
WOMP
SORRY IF YOU'RE NOT ACTUALLY EVIL, BUT **NOT** REALLY SORRY IF YOU ACTUALLY ARE.
BRING HIM IN HERE.

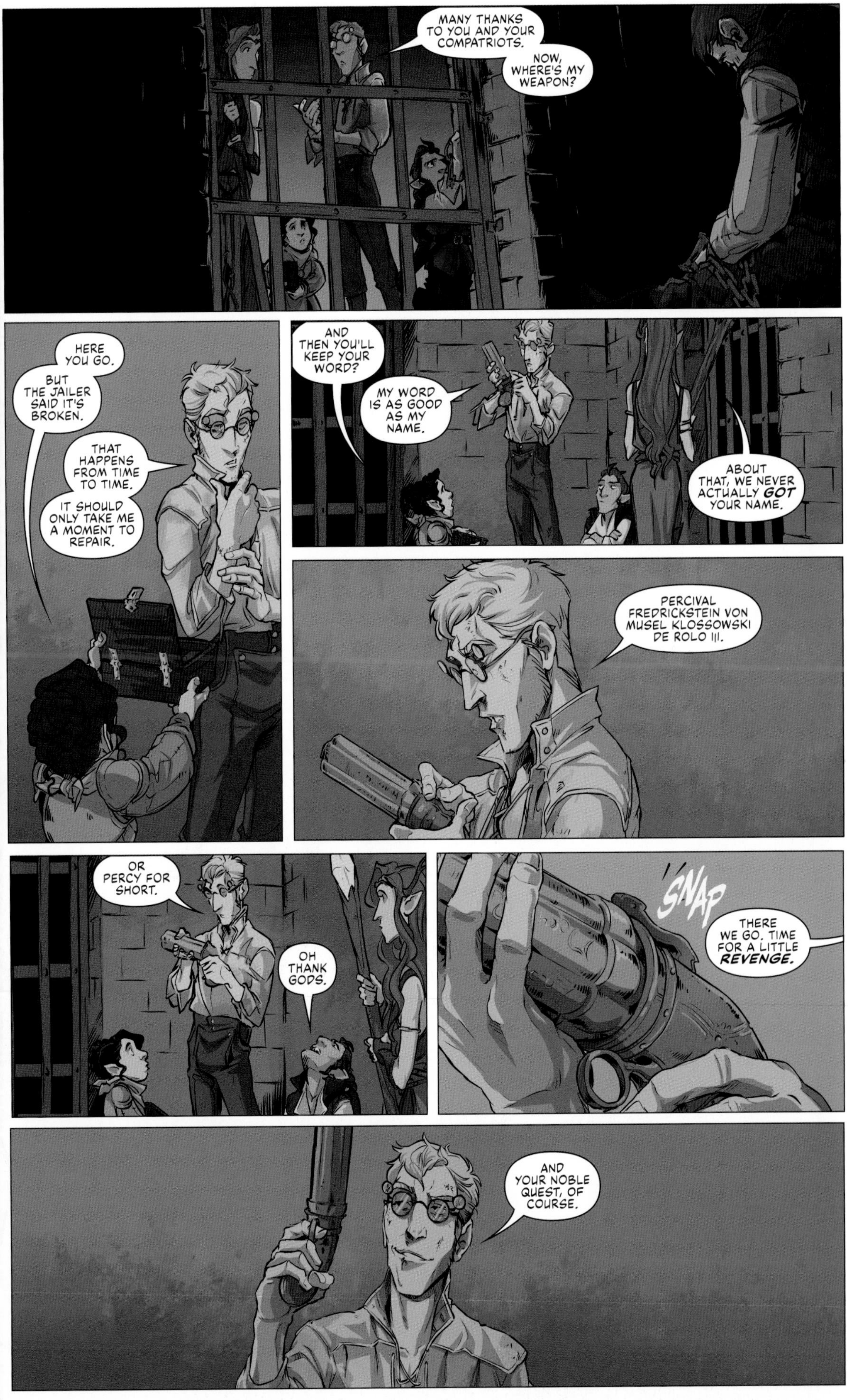
MANY THANKS TO YOU AND YOUR COMPATRIOTS.
NOW, WHERE'S MY WEAPON?
HERE YOU GO.
BUT THE JAILER SAID IT'S BROKEN.
THAT HAPPENS FROM TIME TO TIME.
IT SHOULD ONLY TAKE ME A MOMENT TO REPAIR.
AND THEN YOU'LL KEEP YOUR WORD?
MY WORD IS AS GOOD AS MY NAME.
ABOUT THAT, WE NEVER ACTUALLY **GOT** YOUR NAME.
PERCIVAL FREDRICKSTEIN VON MUSEL KLOSSOWSKI DE ROLO III.
OR PERCY FOR SHORT.
OH THANK GODS.
SNAP
THERE WE GO. TIME FOR A LITTLE ***REVENGE.***
AND YOUR NOBLE QUEST, OF COURSE.

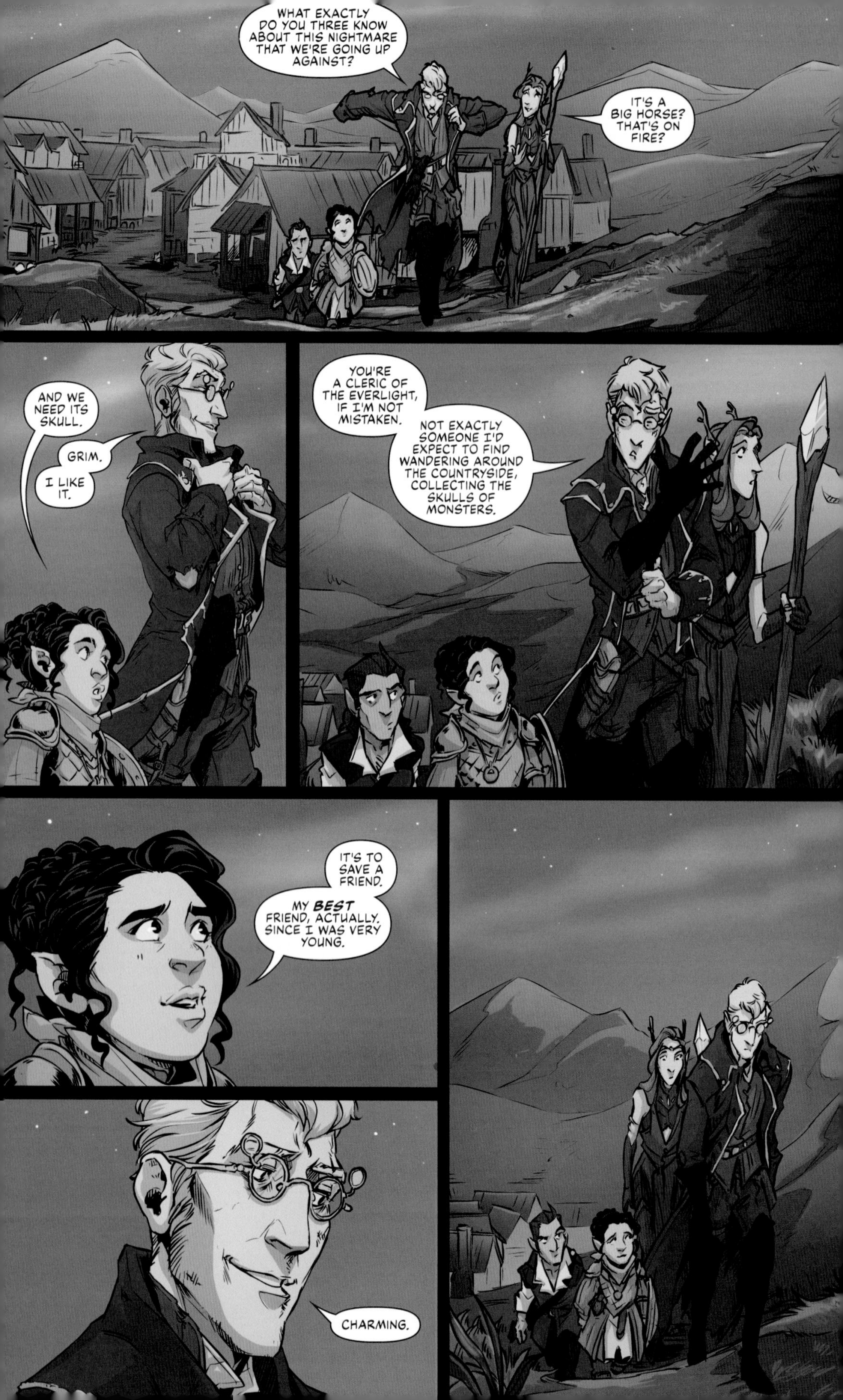
WHAT EXACTLY DO YOU THREE KNOW ABOUT THIS NIGHTMARE THAT WE'RE GOING UP AGAINST?
IT'S A BIG HORSE? THAT'S ON FIRE?
AND WE NEED ITS SKULL.
GRIM.
I LIKE IT.
YOU'RE A CLERIC OF THE EVERLIGHT, IF I'M NOT MISTAKEN.
NOT EXACTLY SOMEONE I'D EXPECT TO FIND WANDERING AROUND THE COUNTRYSIDE, COLLECTING THE SKULLS OF MONSTERS.
IT'S TO SAVE A FRIEND.
MY **BEST** FRIEND, ACTUALLY. SINCE I WAS VERY YOUNG.
CHARMING.

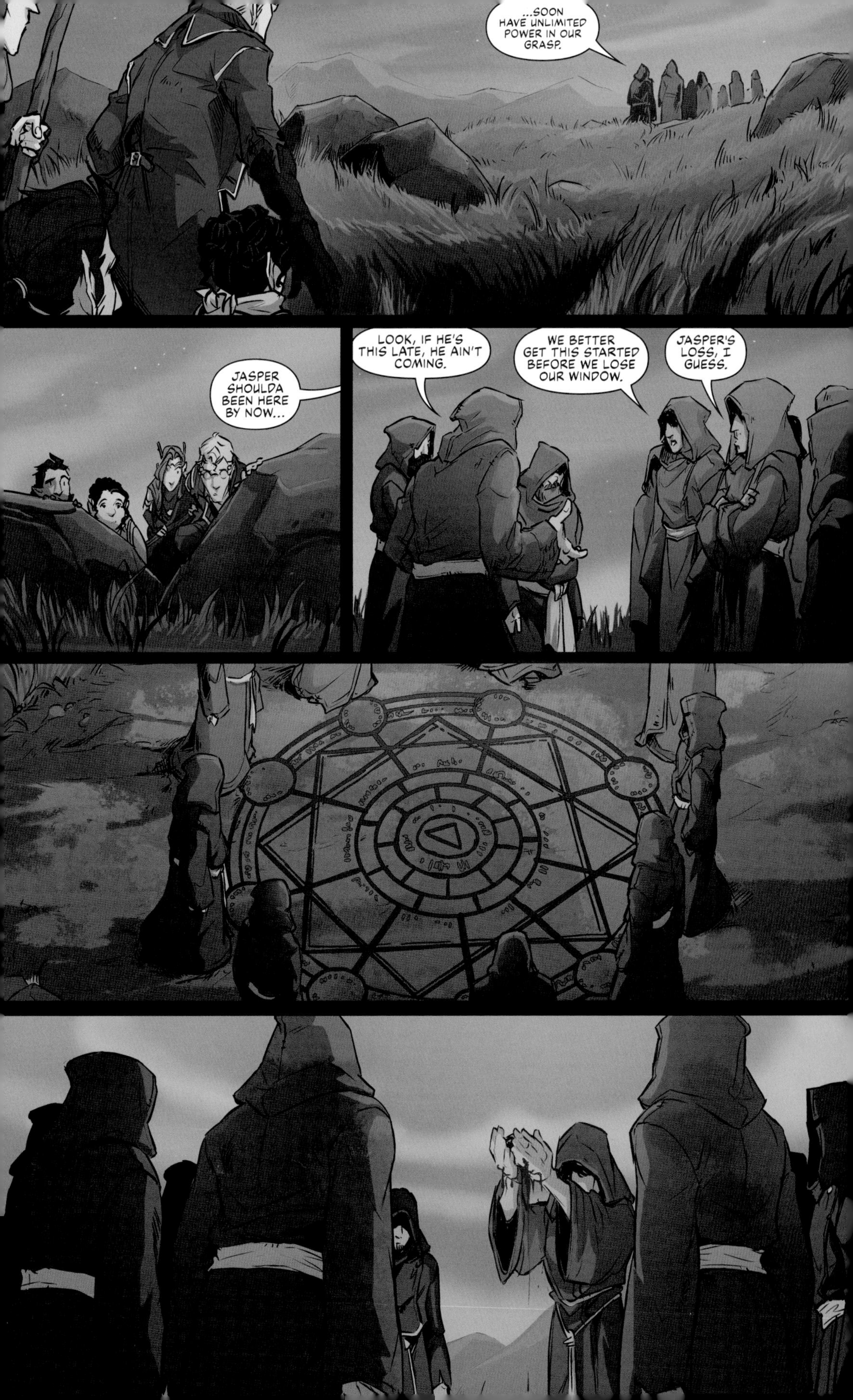
...SOON HAVE UNLIMITED POWER IN OUR GRASP.
JASPER SHOULDA BEEN HERE BY NOW...
LOOK, IF HE'S THIS LATE, HE AIN'T COMING.
WE BETTER GET THIS STARTED BEFORE WE LOSE OUR WINDOW.
JASPER'S LOSS, I GUESS.

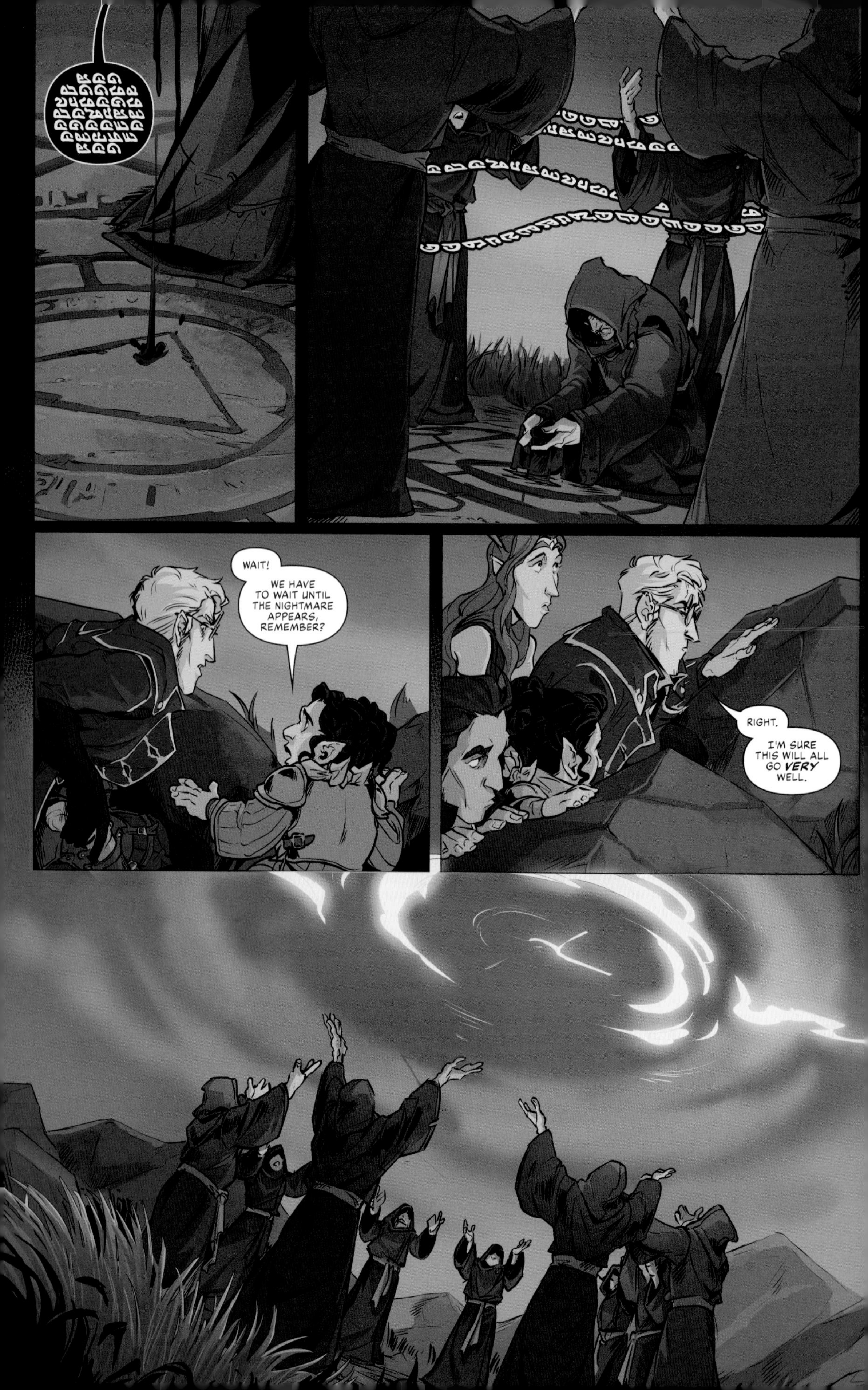
WAIT!
WE HAVE TO WAIT UNTIL THE NIGHTMARE APPEARS, REMEMBER?
RIGHT.
I'M SURE THIS WILL ALL GO **VERY** WELL.

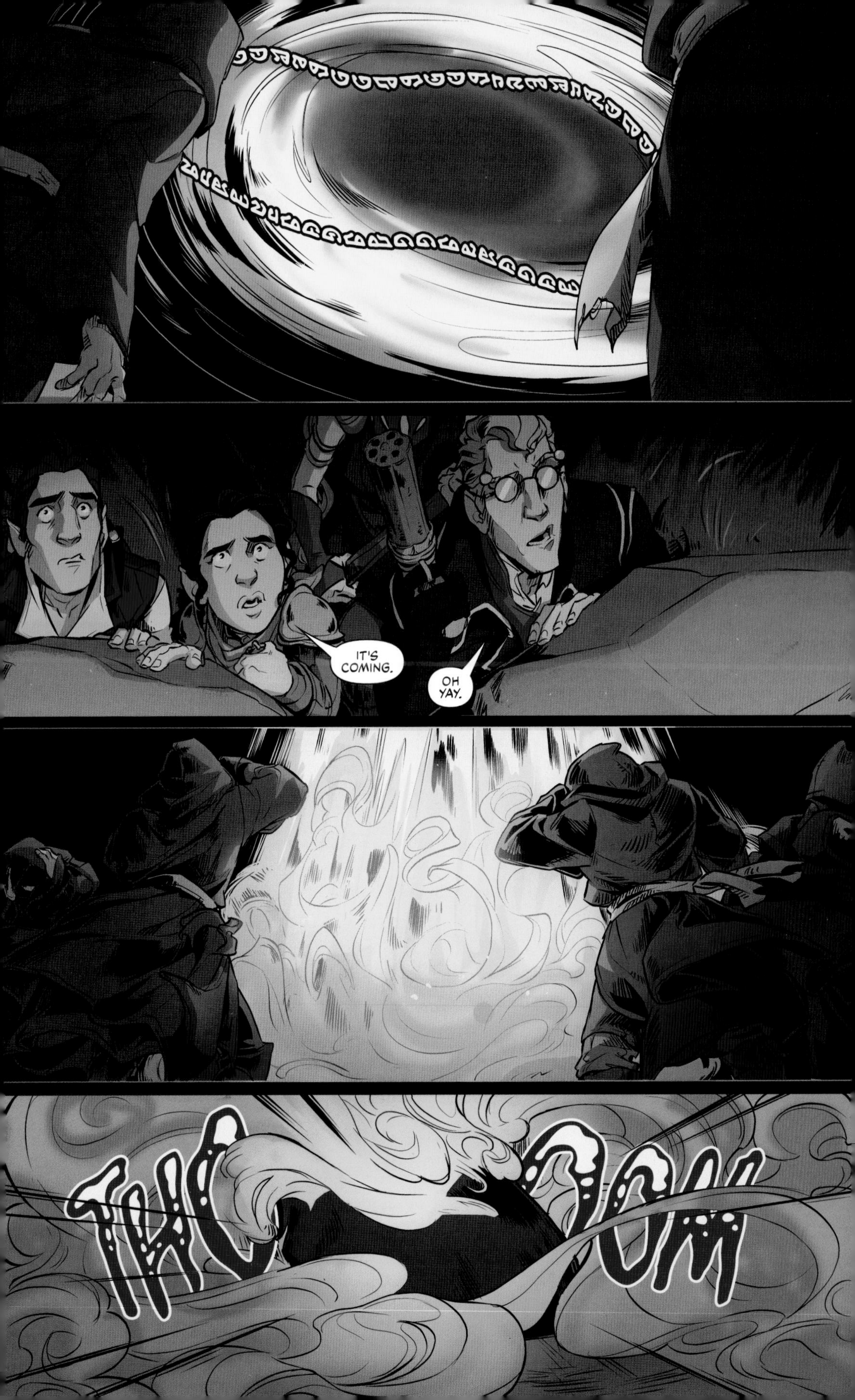
IT'S COMING.
OH YAY.
THOOOM

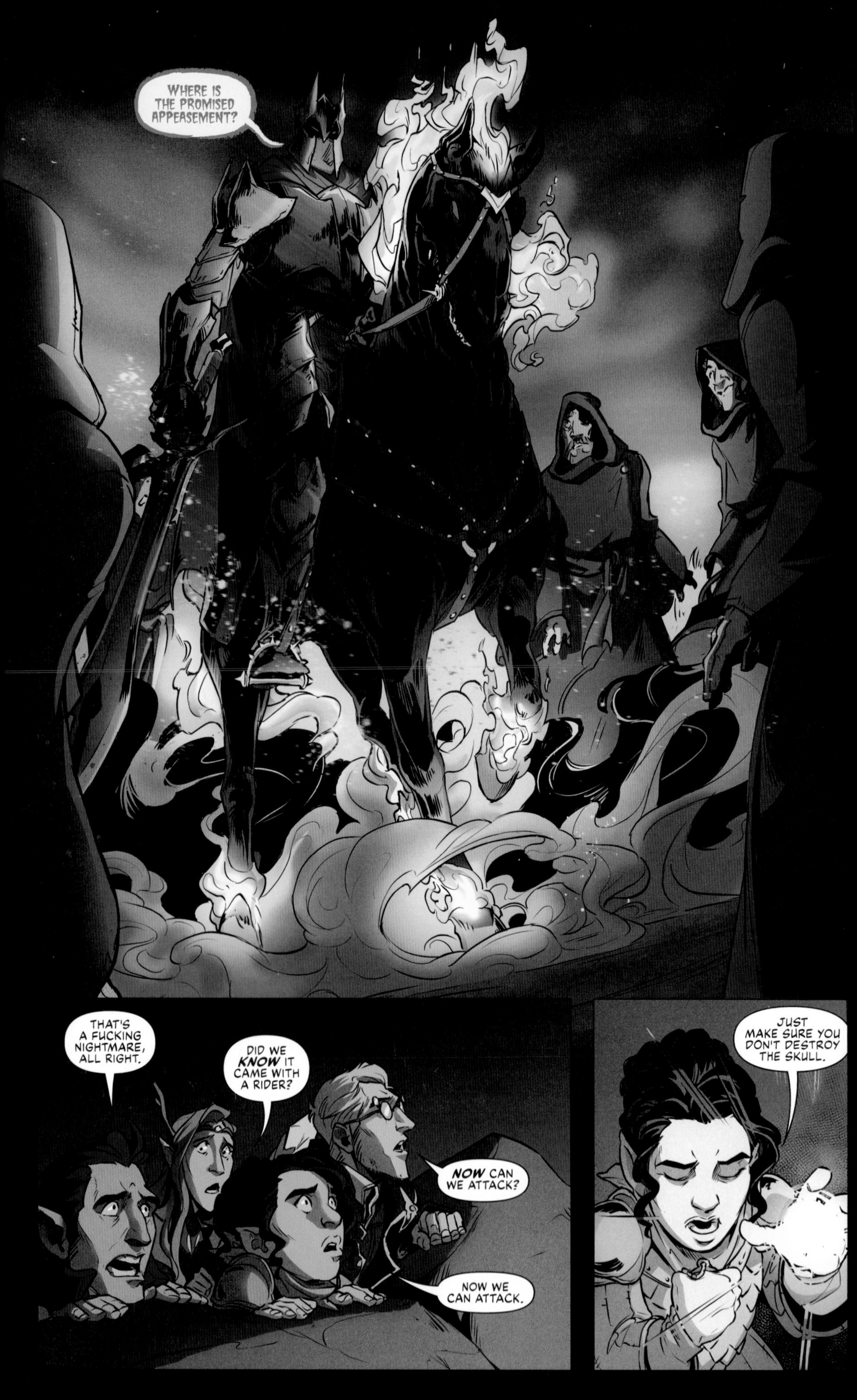
WHERE IS THE PROMISED APPEASEMENT?
THAT'S A FUCKING NIGHTMARE, ALL RIGHT.
DID WE KNOW IT CAME WITH A RIDER?
NOW CAN WE ATTACK?
NOW WE CAN ATTACK.
JUST MAKE SURE YOU DON'T DESTROY THE SKULL.

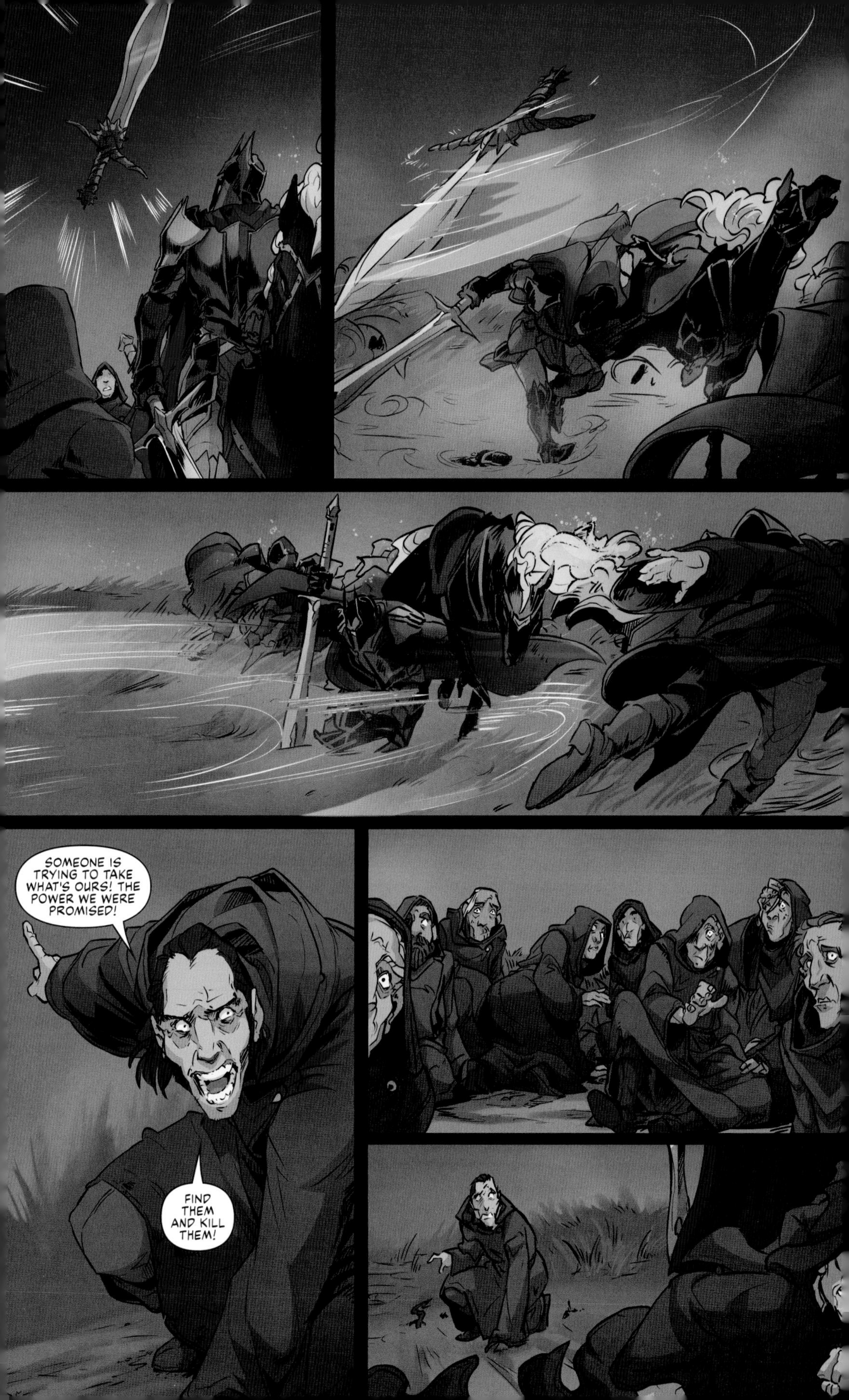
SOMEONE IS TRYING TO TAKE WHAT'S OURS! THE POWER WE WERE PROMISED!
FIND THEM AND KILL THEM!

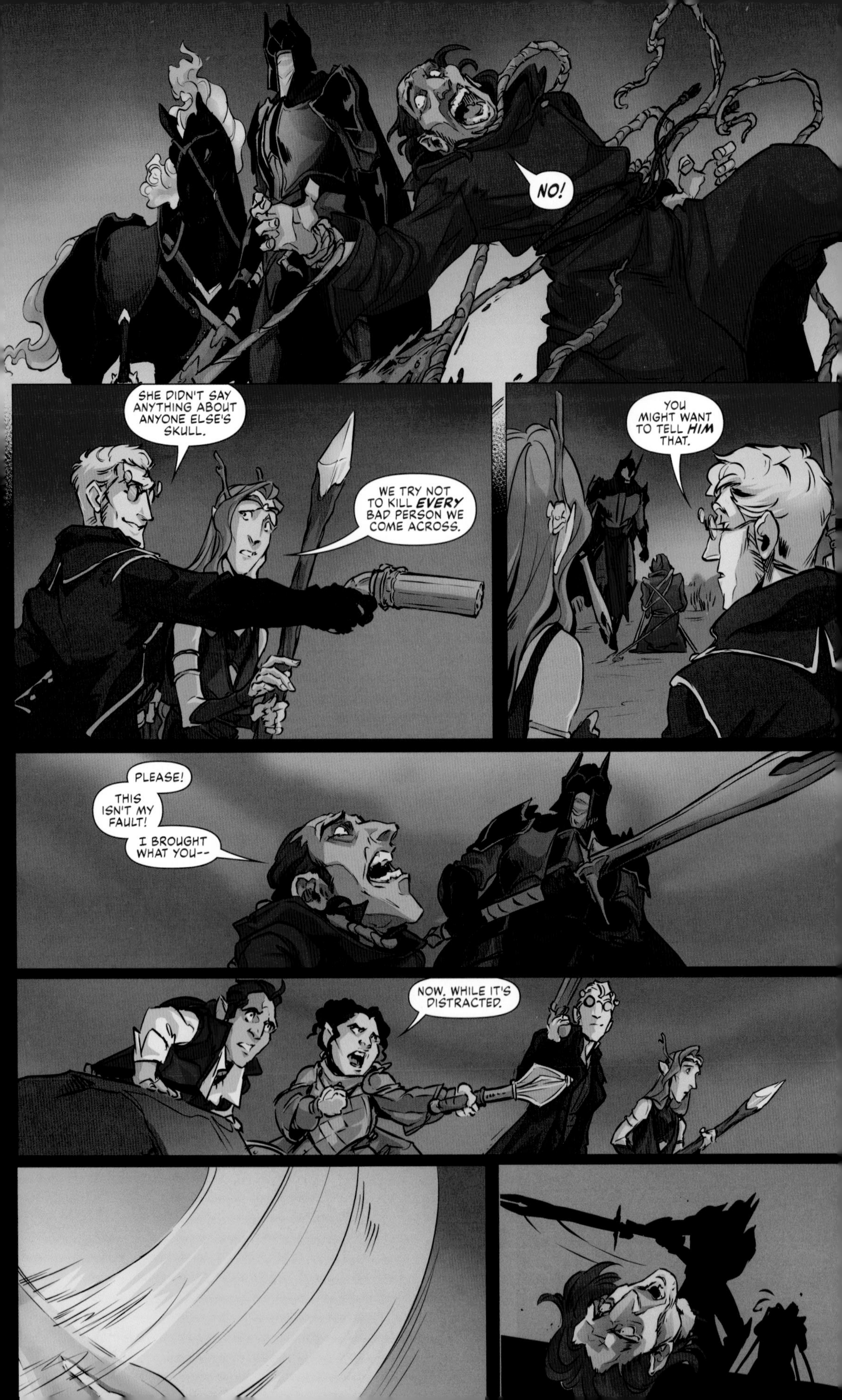
NO!
SHE DIDN'T SAY ANYTHING ABOUT ANYONE ELSE'S SKULL.
WE TRY NOT TO KILL EVERY BAD PERSON WE COME ACROSS.
YOU MIGHT WANT TO TELL HIM THAT.
PLEASE!
THIS ISN'T MY FAULT!
I BROUGHT WHAT YOU--
NOW. WHILE IT'S DISTRACTED.

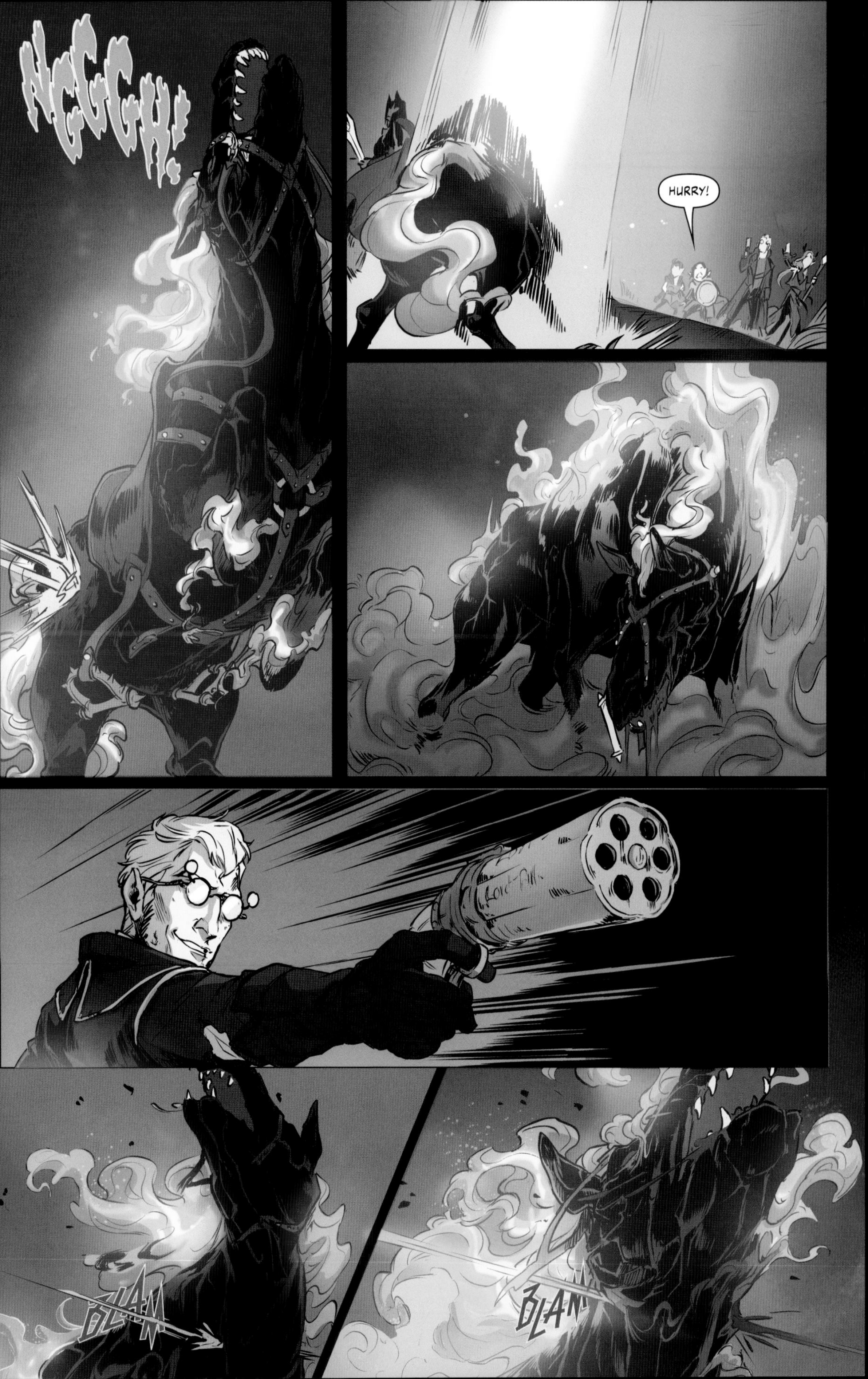
NGGGH!
HURRY!
BLAM
BLAM

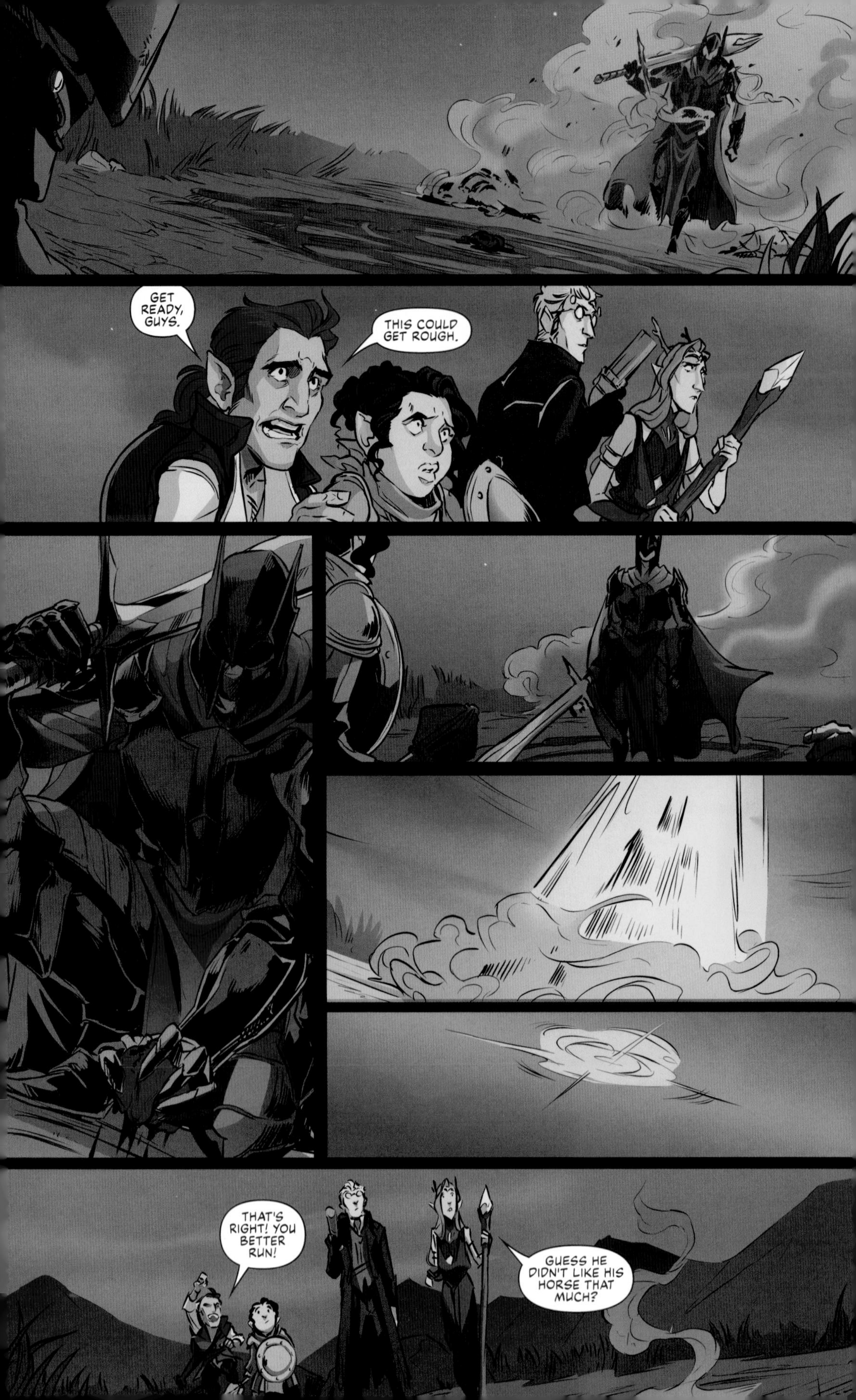
GET READY, GUYS.
THIS COULD GET ROUGH.
THAT'S RIGHT! YOU BETTER RUN!
GUESS HE DIDN'T LIKE HIS HORSE THAT MUCH?

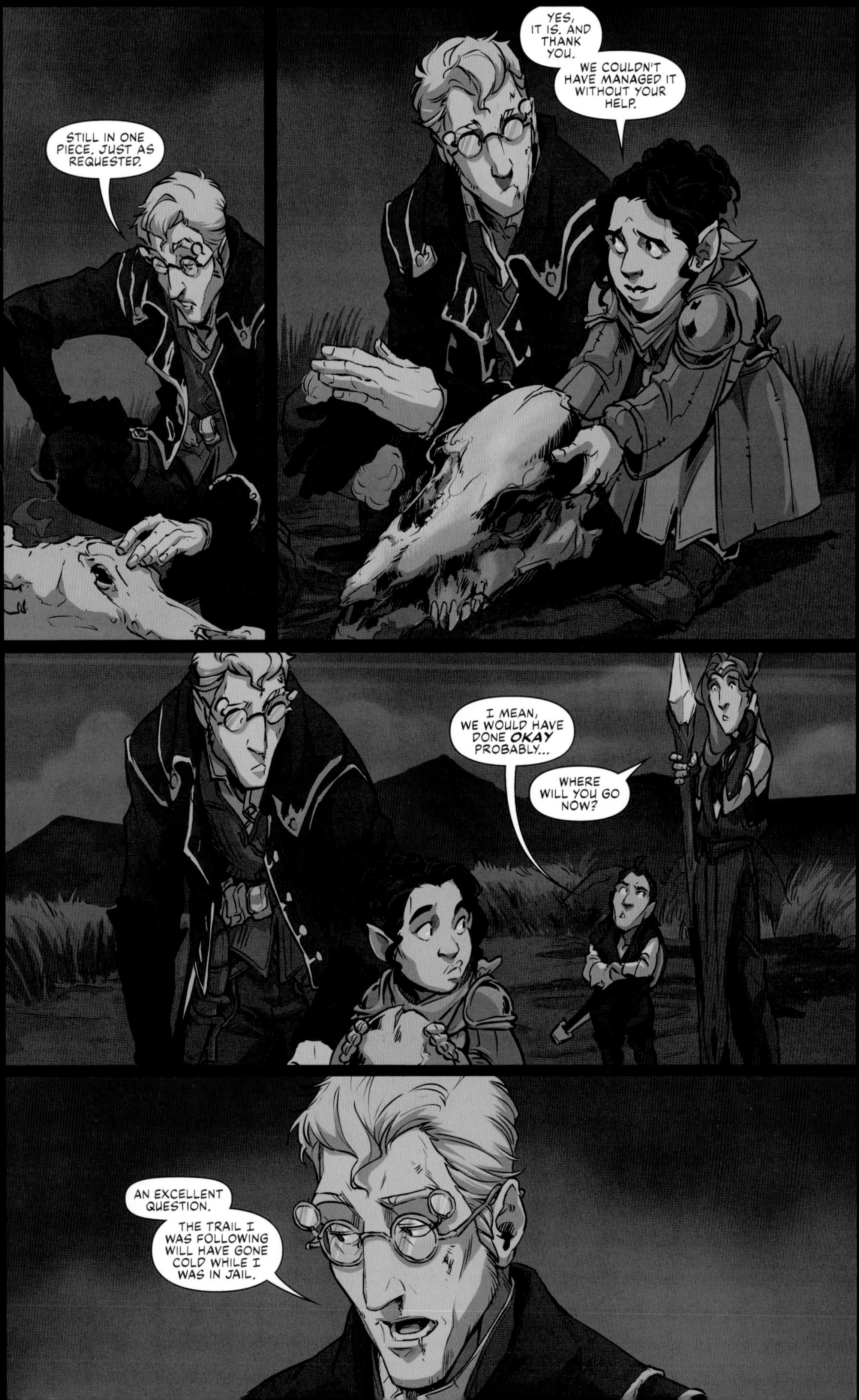
STILL IN ONE PIECE. JUST AS REQUESTED.
YES, IT IS. AND THANK YOU.
WE COULDN'T HAVE MANAGED IT WITHOUT YOUR HELP.
I MEAN, WE WOULD HAVE DONE **OKAY** PROBABLY...
WHERE WILL YOU GO NOW?
AN EXCELLENT QUESTION.
THE TRAIL I WAS FOLLOWING WILL HAVE GONE COLD WHILE I WAS IN JAIL.

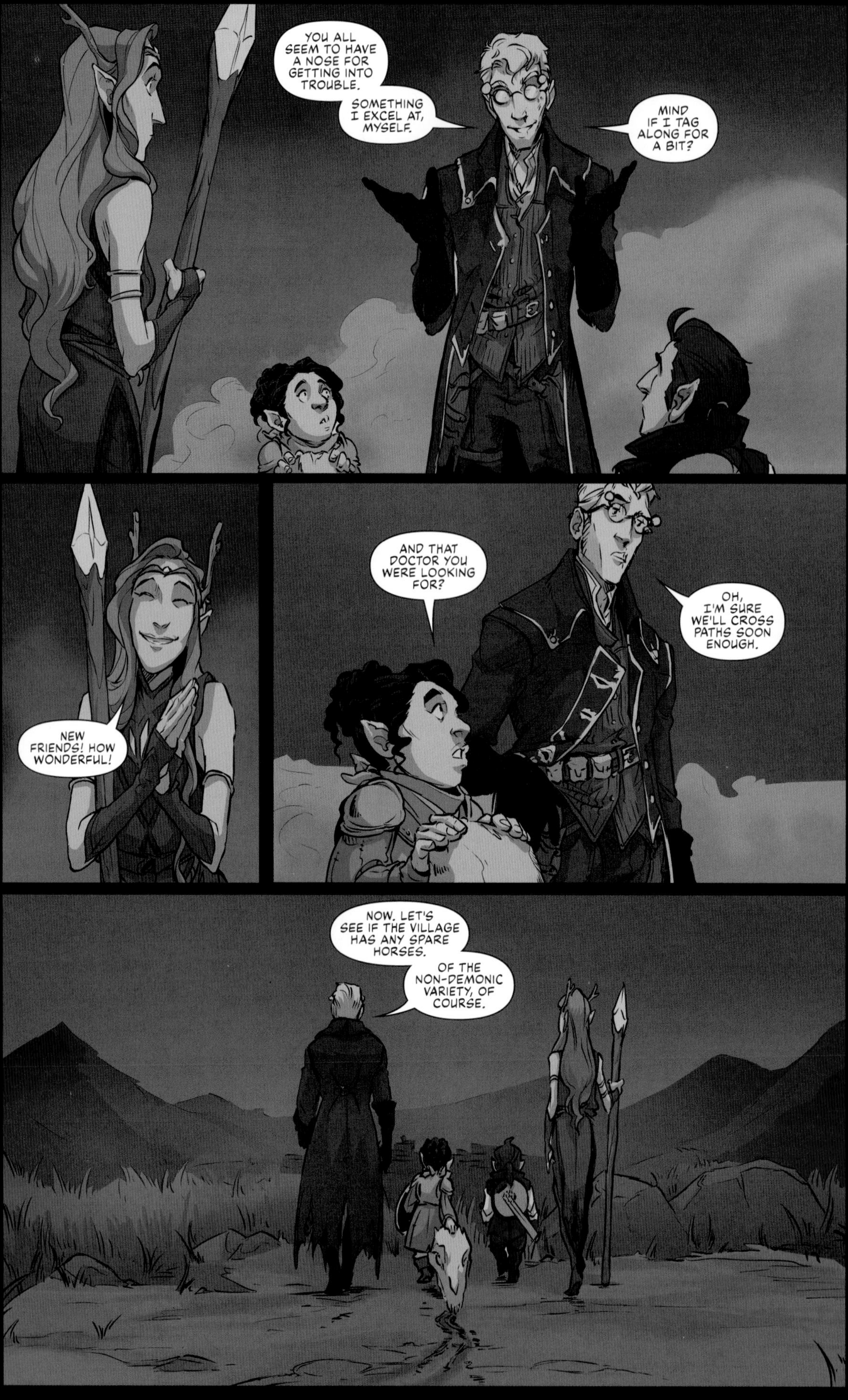
YOU ALL SEEM TO HAVE A NOSE FOR GETTING INTO TROUBLE.
SOMETHING I EXCEL AT, MYSELF.
MIND IF I TAG ALONG FOR A BIT?
NEW FRIENDS! HOW WONDERFUL!
AND THAT DOCTOR YOU WERE LOOKING FOR?
OH, I'M SURE WE'LL CROSS PATHS SOON ENOUGH.
NOW. LET'S SEE IF THE VILLAGE HAS ANY SPARE HORSES.
OF THE NON-DEMONIC VARIETY, OF COURSE.

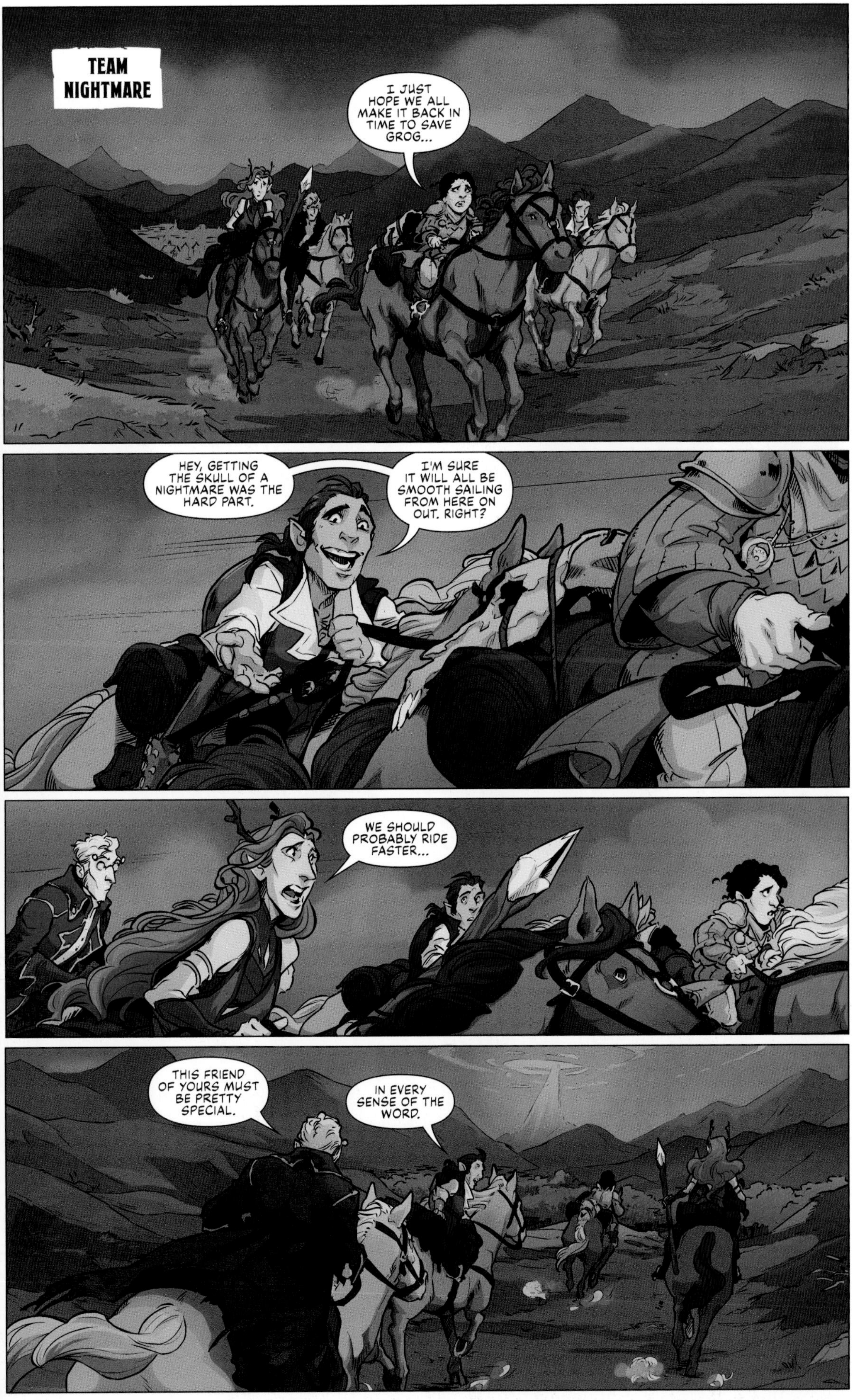
TEAM NIGHTMARE
I JUST HOPE WE ALL MAKE IT BACK IN TIME TO SAVE GROG...
HEY, GETTING THE SKULL OF A NIGHTMARE WAS THE HARD PART.
I'M SURE IT WILL ALL BE SMOOTH SAILING FROM HERE ON OUT. RIGHT?
WE SHOULD PROBABLY RIDE FASTER...
THIS FRIEND OF YOURS MUST BE PRETTY SPECIAL.
IN EVERY SENSE OF THE WORD.

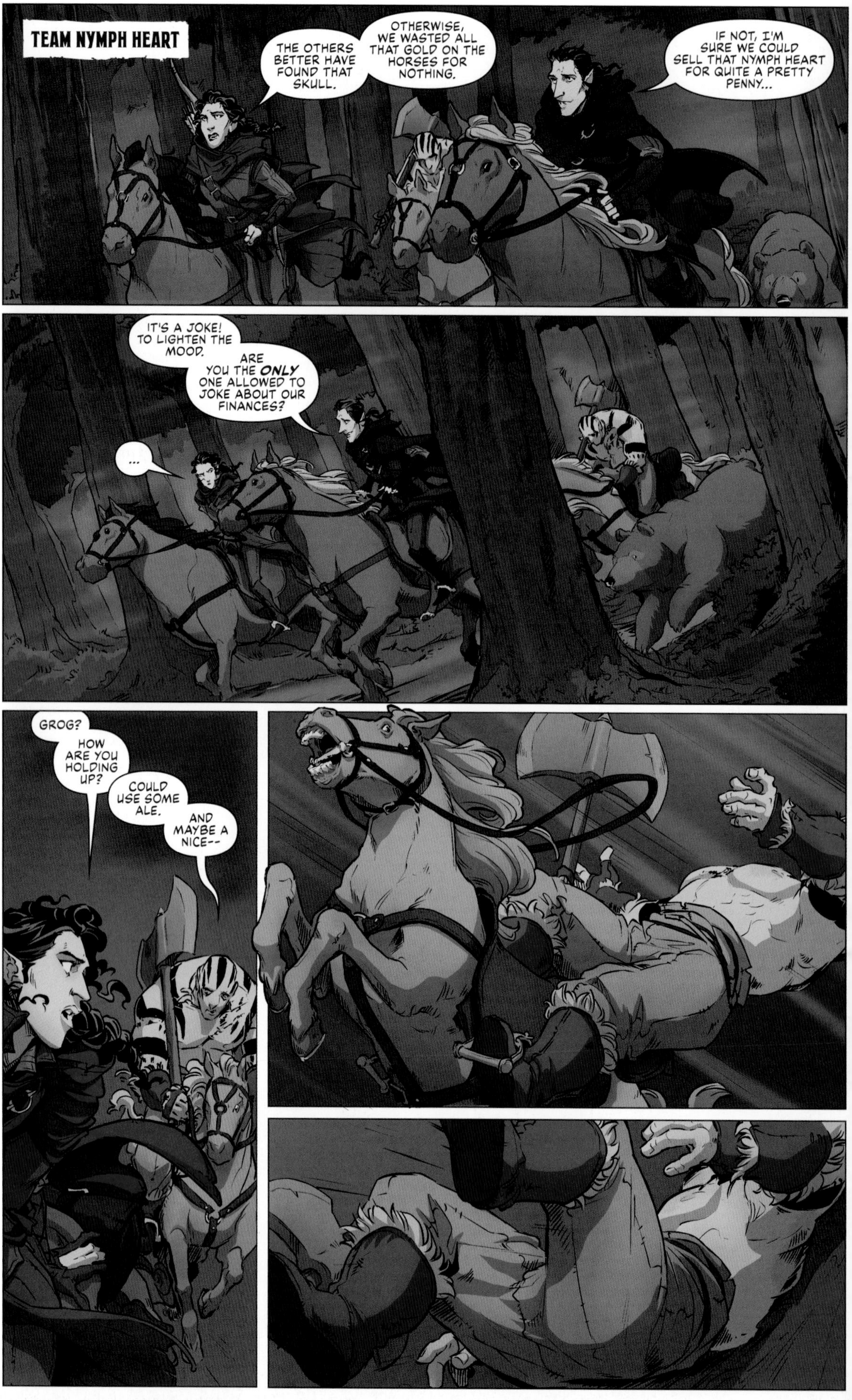
TEAM NYMPH HEART
THE OTHERS BETTER HAVE FOUND THAT SKULL...
OTHERWISE, WE WASTED ALL THAT GOLD ON THE HORSES FOR NOTHING.
IF NOT, I'M SURE WE COULD SELL THAT NYMPH HEART FOR QUITE A PRETTY PENNY...
IT'S A JOKE! TO LIGHTEN THE MOOD.
ARE YOU THE ONLY ONE ALLOWED TO JOKE ABOUT OUR FINANCES?
...
GROG?
HOW ARE YOU HOLDING UP?
COULD USE SOME ALE.
AND MAYBE A NICE--

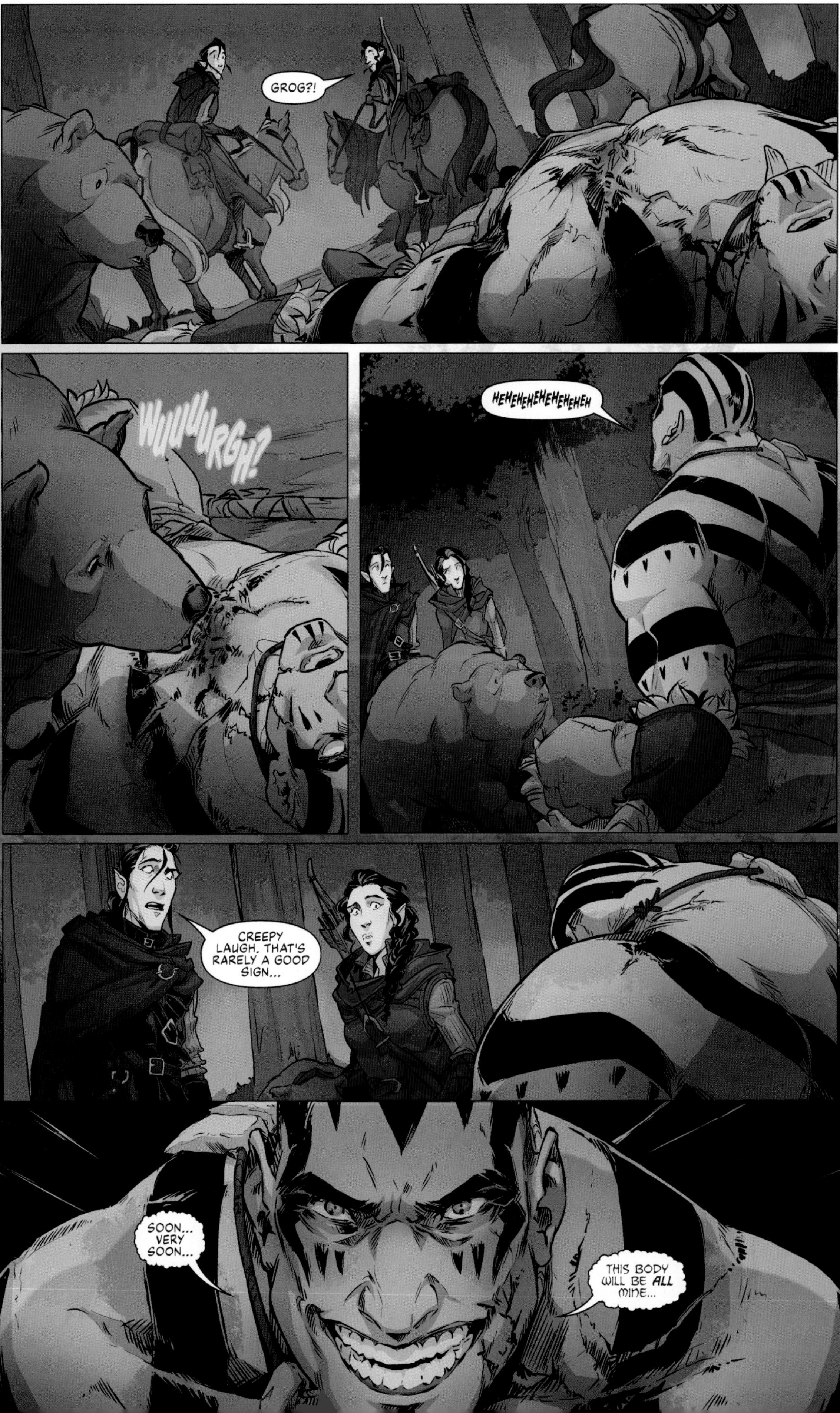
GROG?!
WUUUURGH?
HEHEHEHEHEHEHEHEH
CREEPY LAUGH. THAT'S RARELY A GOOD SIGN...
SOON... VERY SOON...
THIS BODY WILL BE **ALL** MINE...

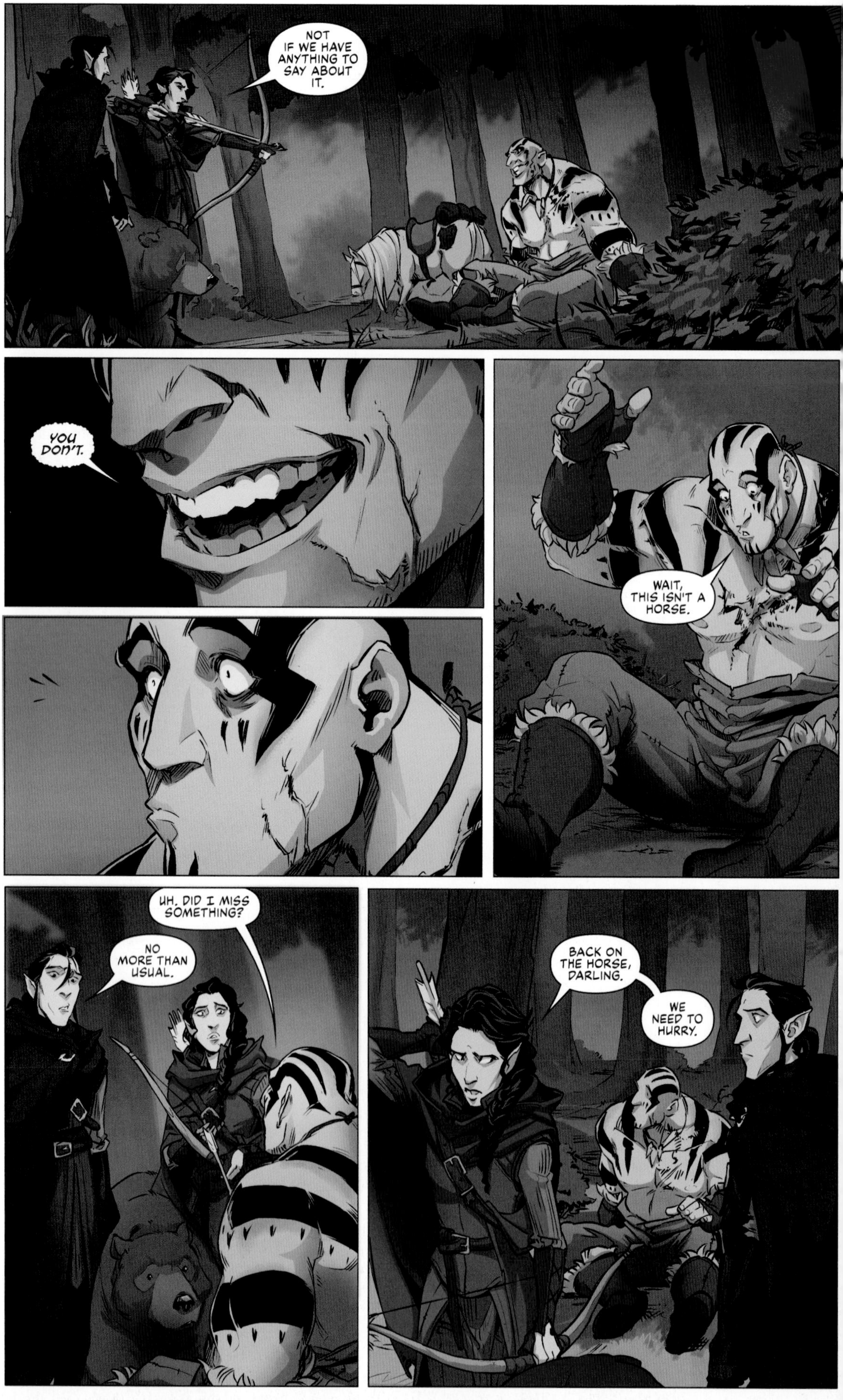
NOT IF WE HAVE ANYTHING TO SAY ABOUT IT.
YOU DON'T.
WAIT, THIS ISN'T A HORSE.
UH. DID I MISS SOMETHING?
NO MORE THAN USUAL.
BACK ON THE HORSE, DARLING.
WE NEED TO HURRY.

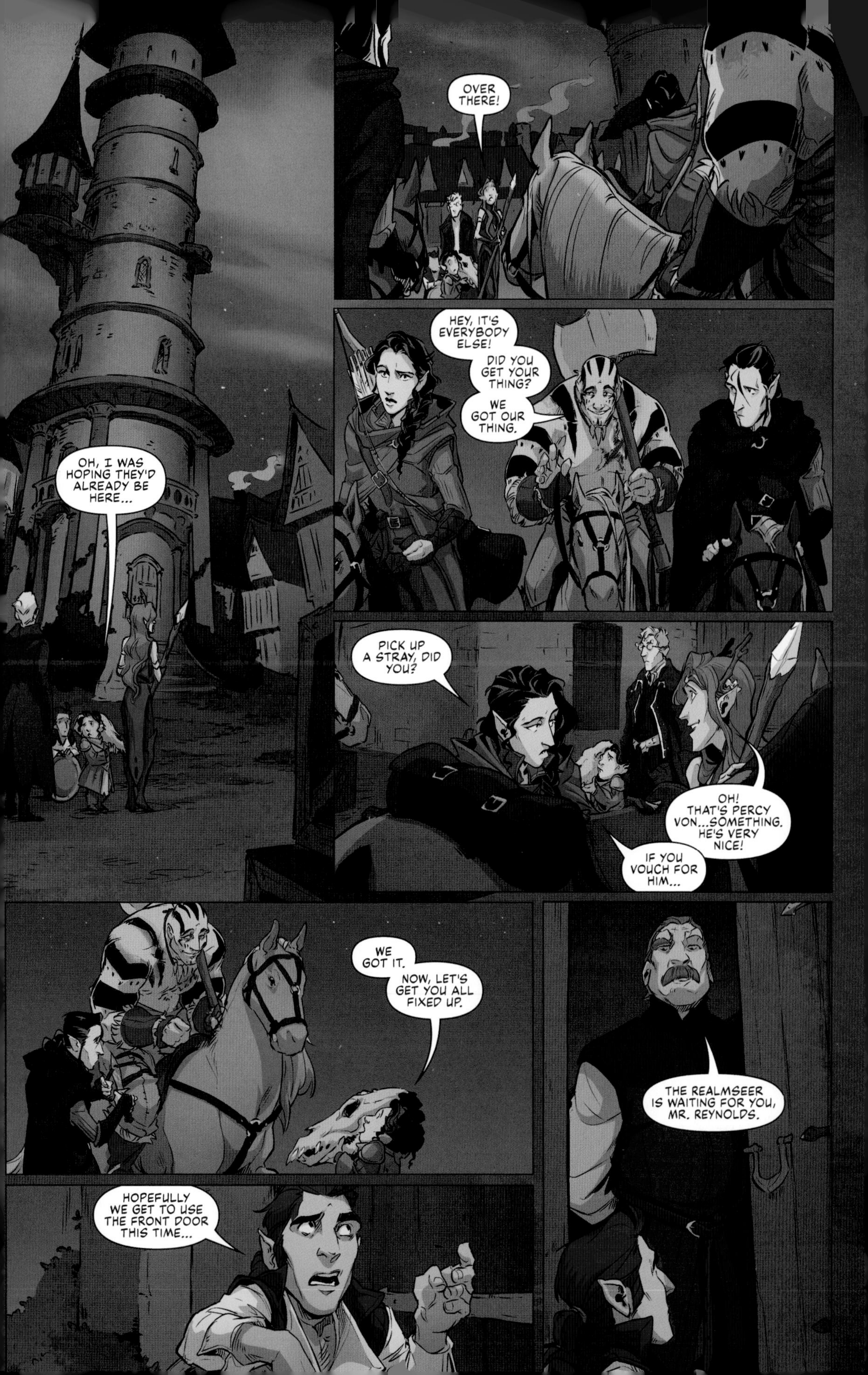
OH, I WAS HOPING THEY'D ALREADY BE HERE...
OVER THERE!
HEY, IT'S EVERYBODY ELSE!
DID YOU GET YOUR THING?
WE GOT OUR THING.
PICK UP A STRAY, DID YOU?
OH! THAT'S PERCY VON...SOMETHING. HE'S VERY NICE!
IF YOU VOUCH FOR HIM...
WE GOT IT.
NOW, LET'S GET YOU ALL FIXED UP.
HOPEFULLY WE GET TO USE THE FRONT DOOR THIS TIME...
THE REALMSEER IS WAITING FOR YOU, MR. REYNOLDS.

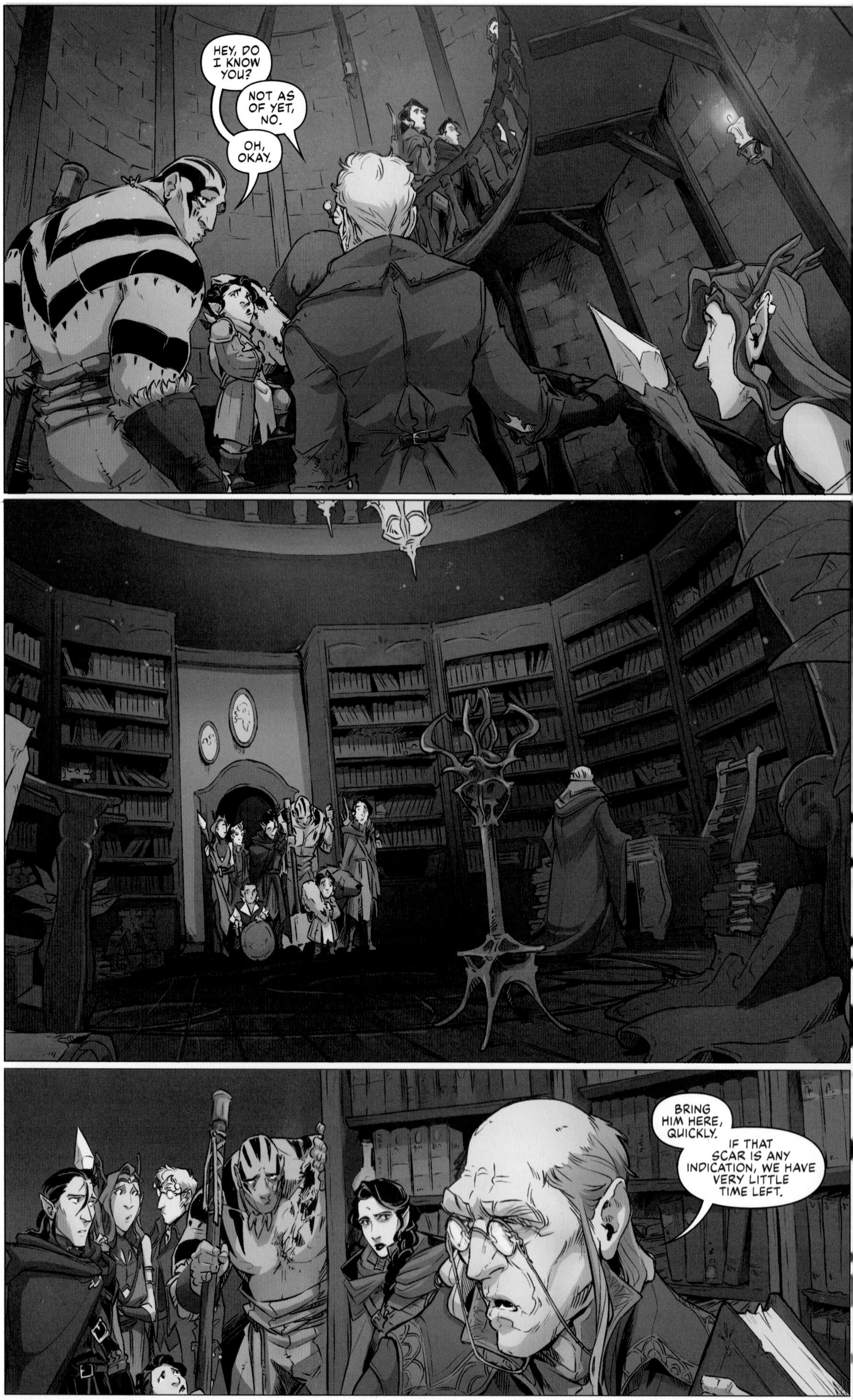
HEY, DO I KNOW YOU?
NOT AS OF YET, NO.
OH, OKAY.
BRING HIM HERE, QUICKLY.
IF THAT SCAR IS ANY INDICATION, WE HAVE VERY LITTLE TIME LEFT.

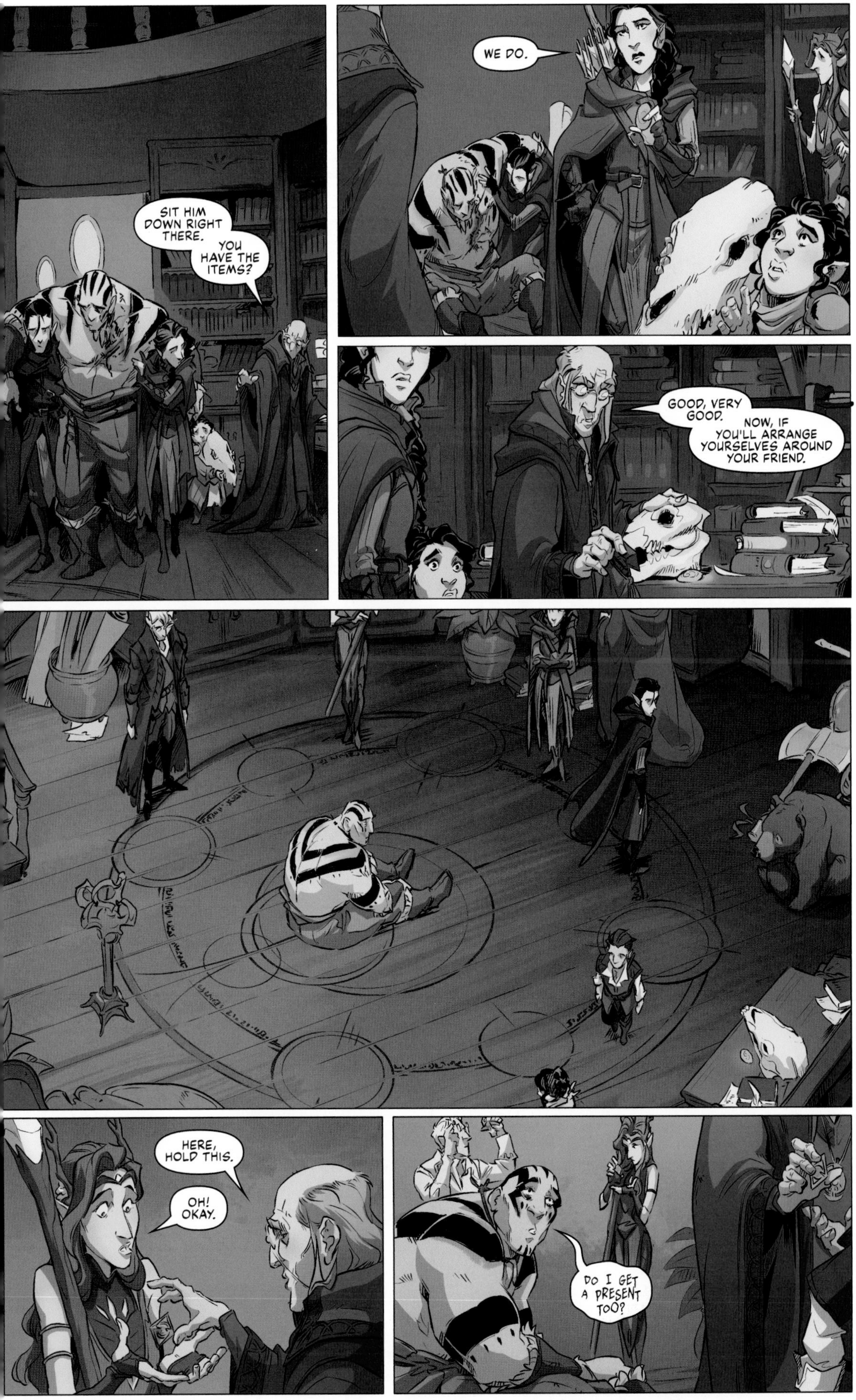
SIT HIM DOWN RIGHT THERE.
YOU HAVE THE ITEMS?
WE DO.
GOOD, VERY GOOD.
NOW, IF YOU'LL ARRANGE YOURSELVES AROUND YOUR FRIEND.
HERE, HOLD THIS.
OH! OKAY.
DO I GET A PRESENT TOO?

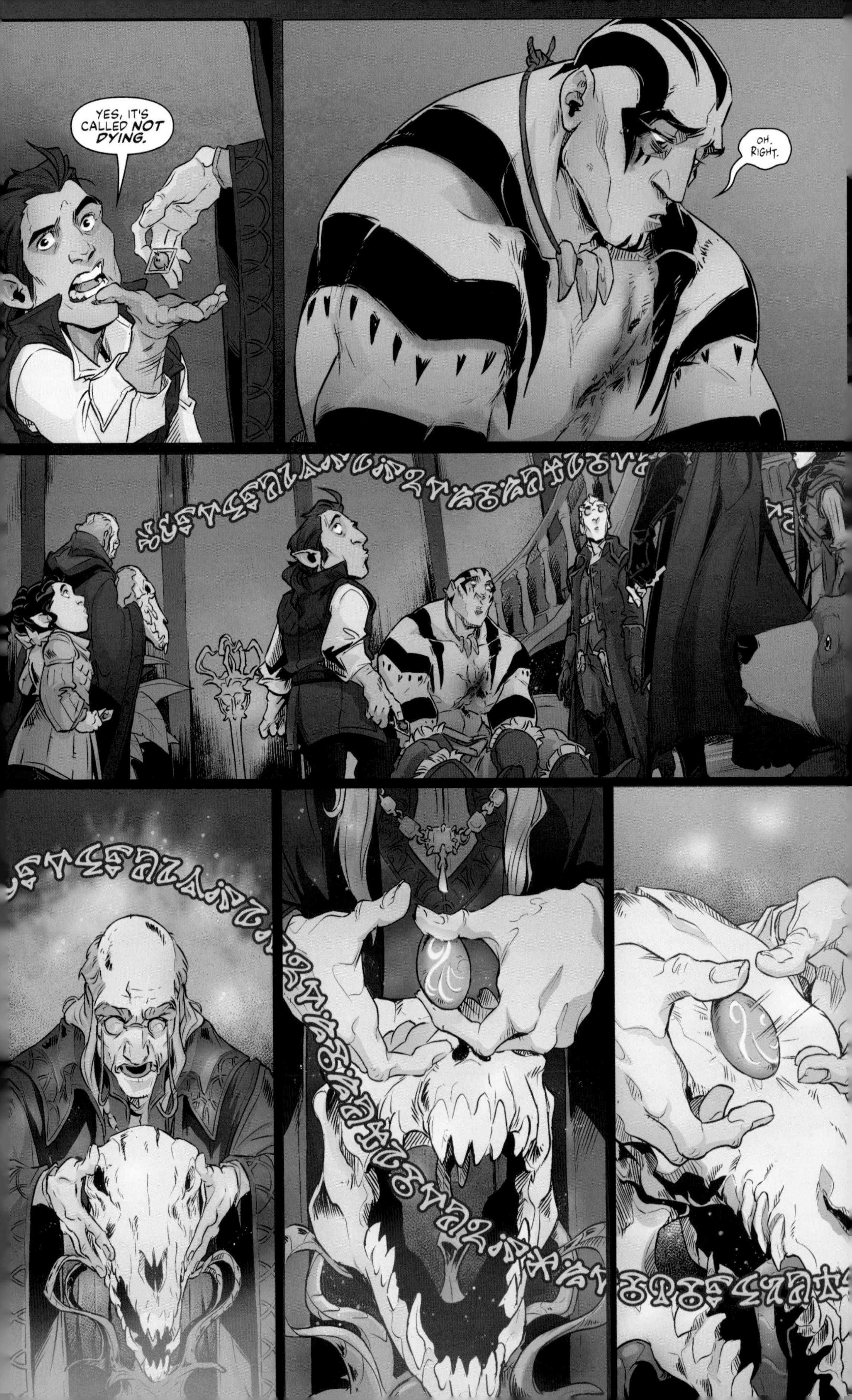
YES, IT'S CALLED **NOT DYING.**
OH. RIGHT.

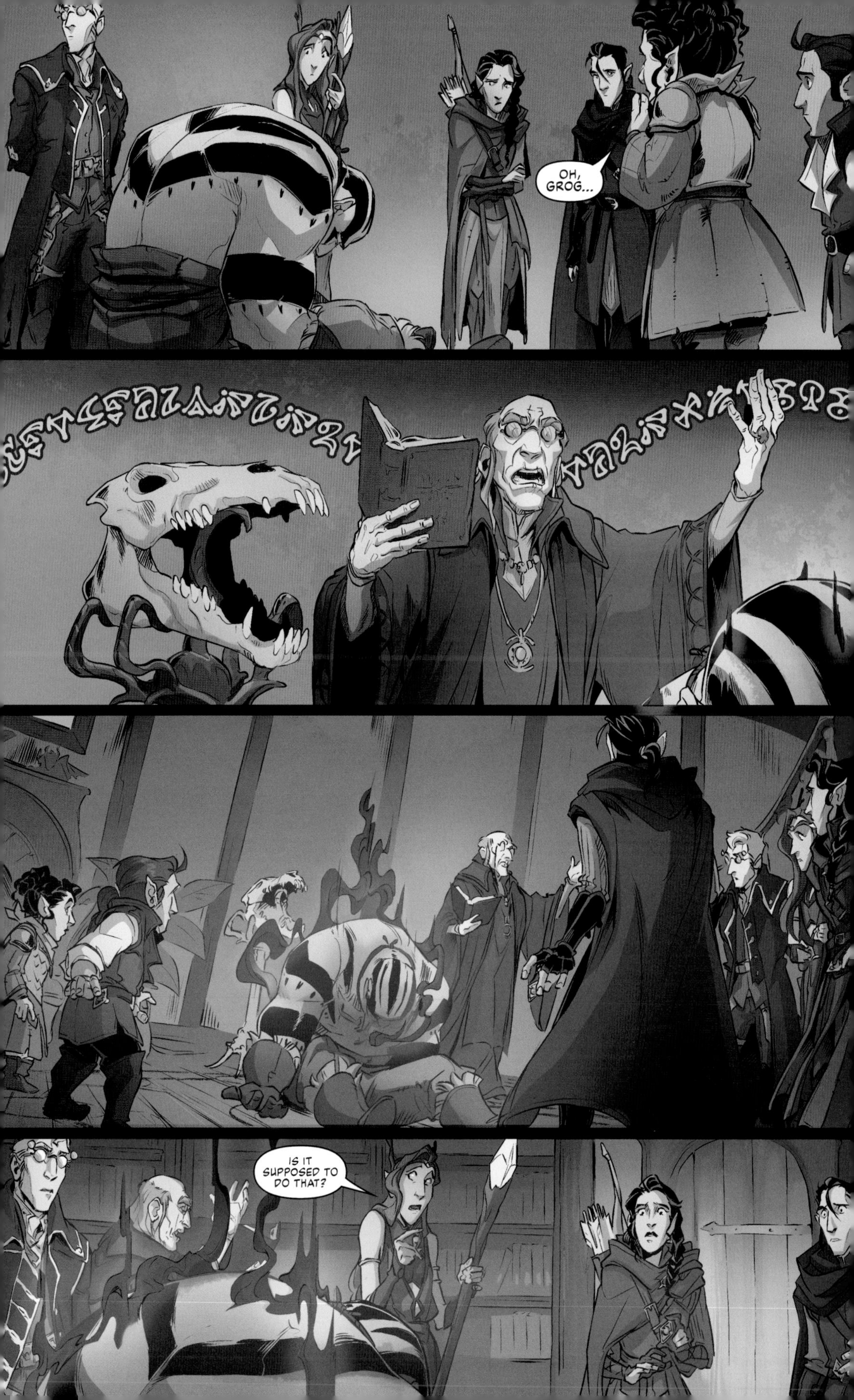
OH, GROG...
IS IT SUPPOSED TO DO THAT?

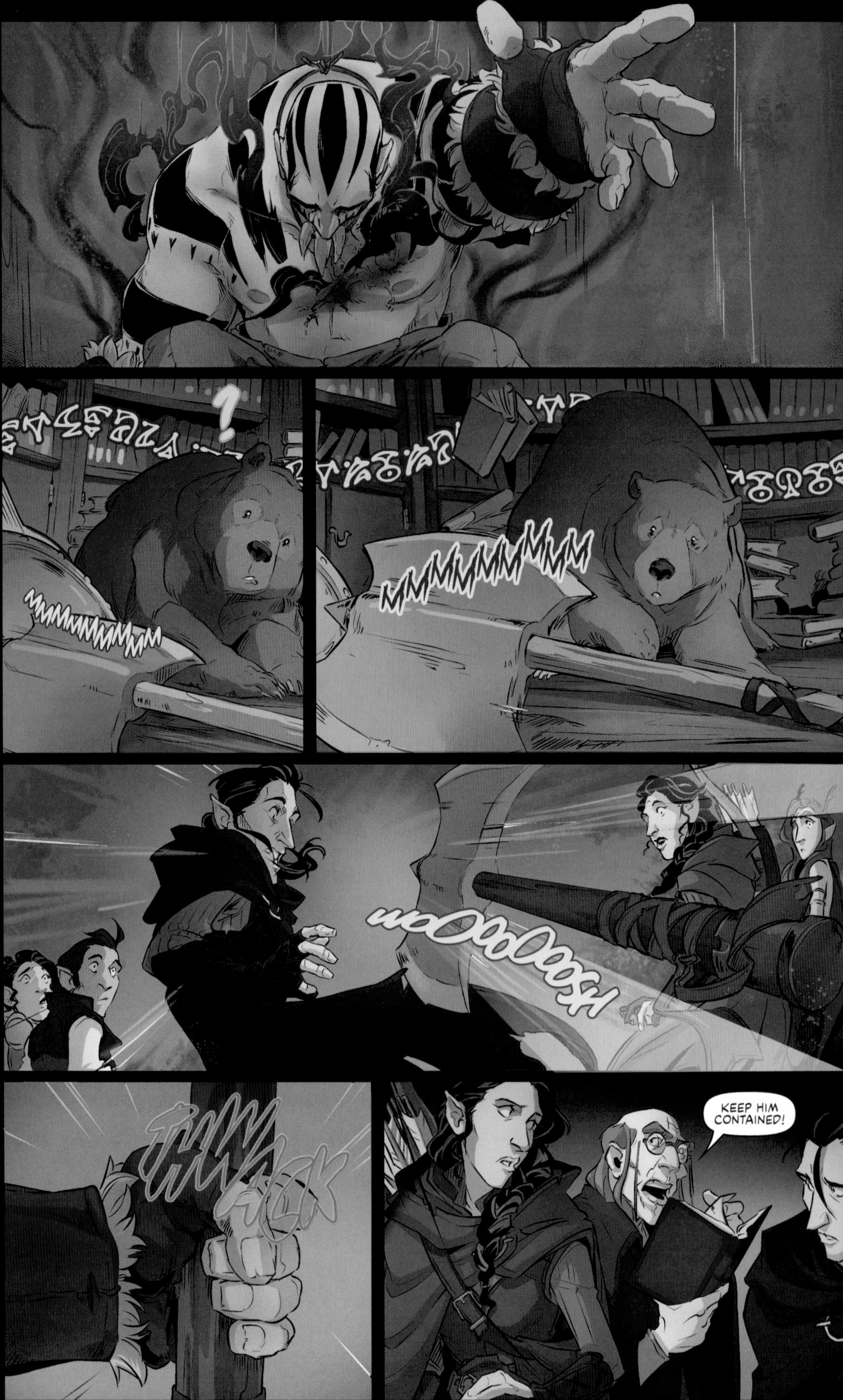
?
THWACK
KEEP HIM CONTAINED!

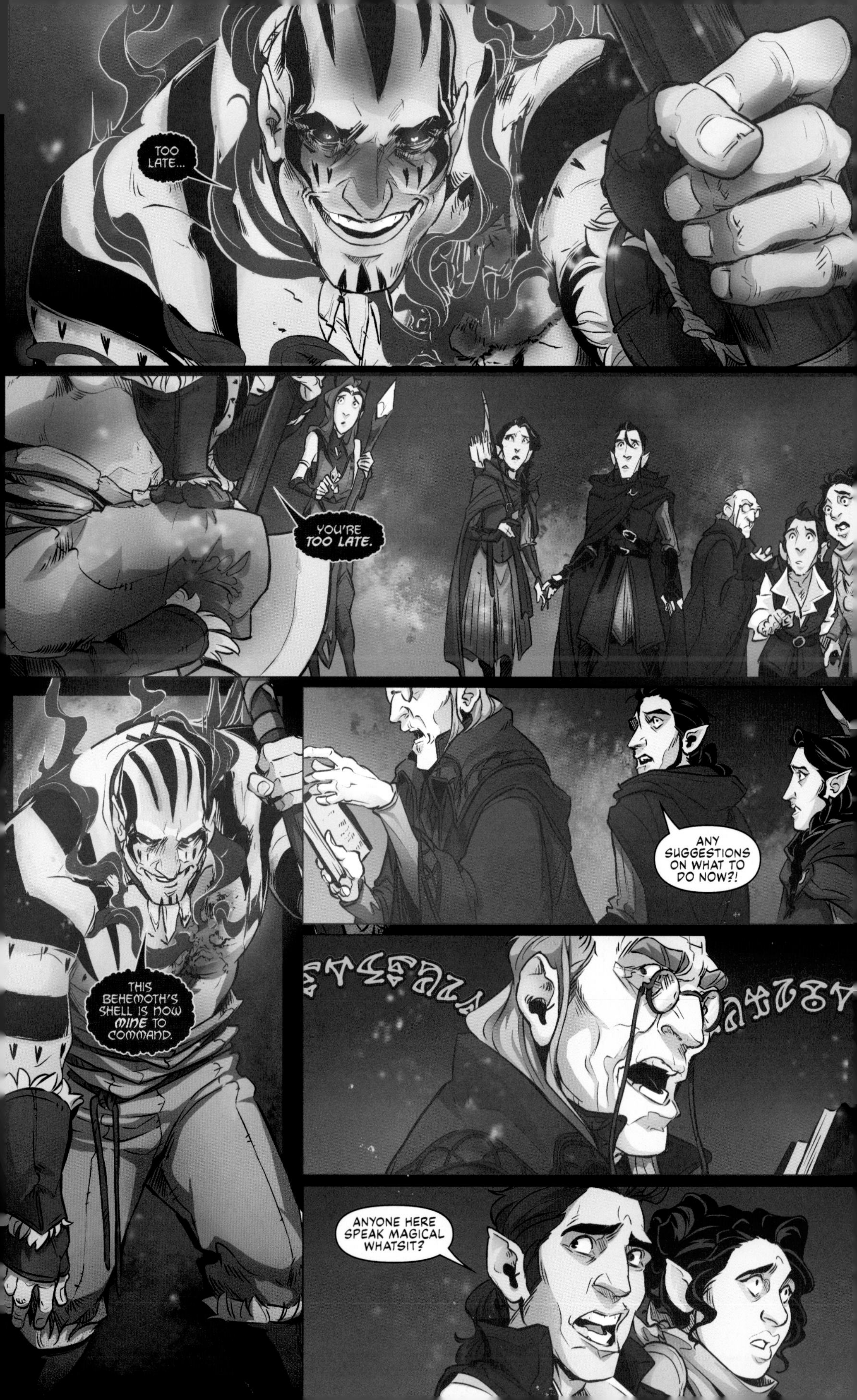
TOO LATE...
YOU'RE *TOO LATE.*
THIS BEHEMOTH'S SHELL IS NOW *MINE* TO COMMAND.
ANY SUGGESTIONS ON WHAT TO DO NOW?!
ANYONE HERE SPEAK MAGICAL WHATSIT?

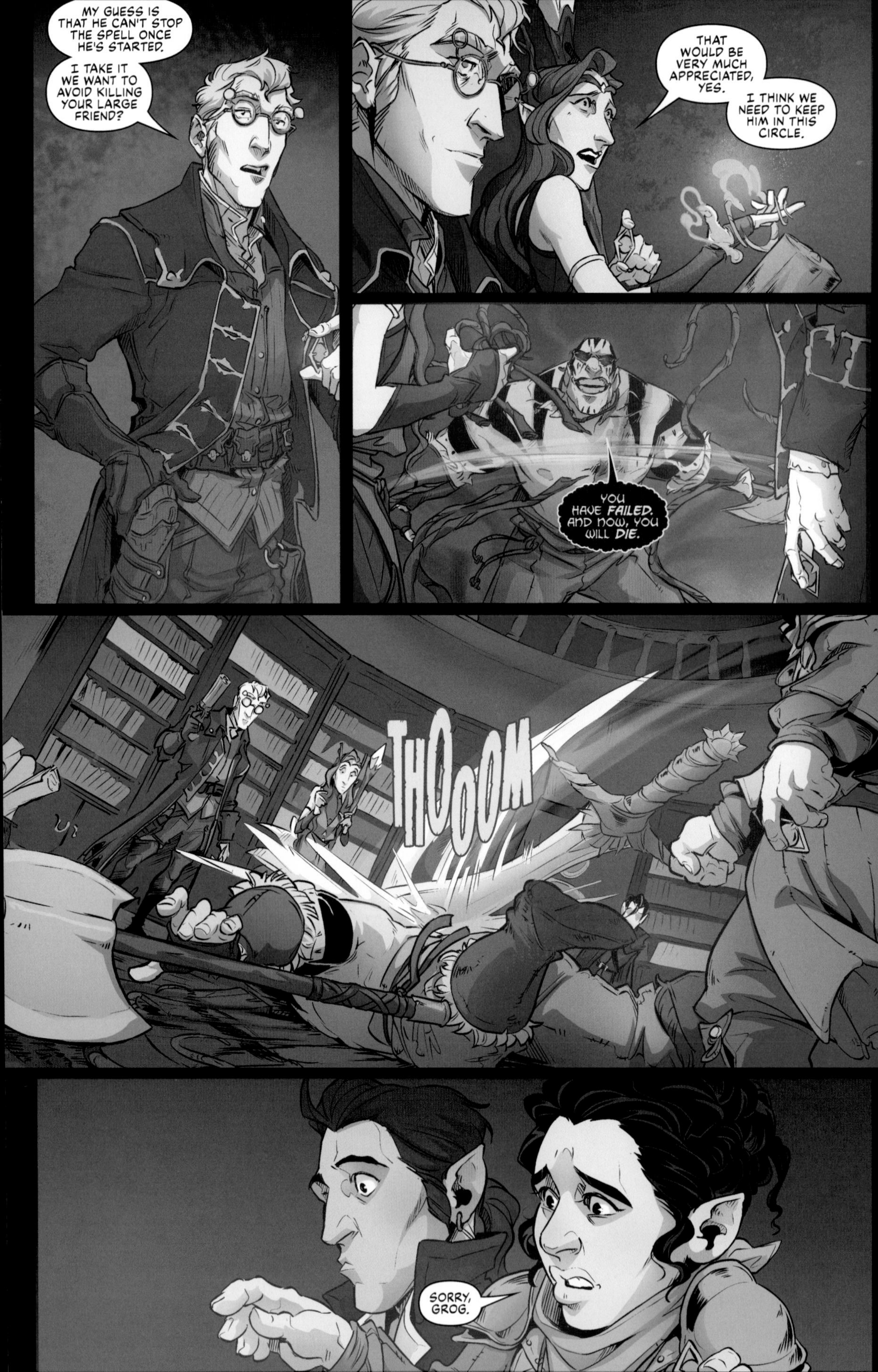
MY GUESS IS THAT HE CAN'T STOP THE SPELL ONCE HE'S STARTED.
I TAKE IT WE WANT TO AVOID KILLING YOUR LARGE FRIEND?
THAT WOULD BE VERY MUCH APPRECIATED, YES.
I THINK WE NEED TO KEEP HIM IN THIS CIRCLE.
YOU HAVE FAILED. AND NOW, YOU WILL DIE.
THOOOM
SORRY, GROG.

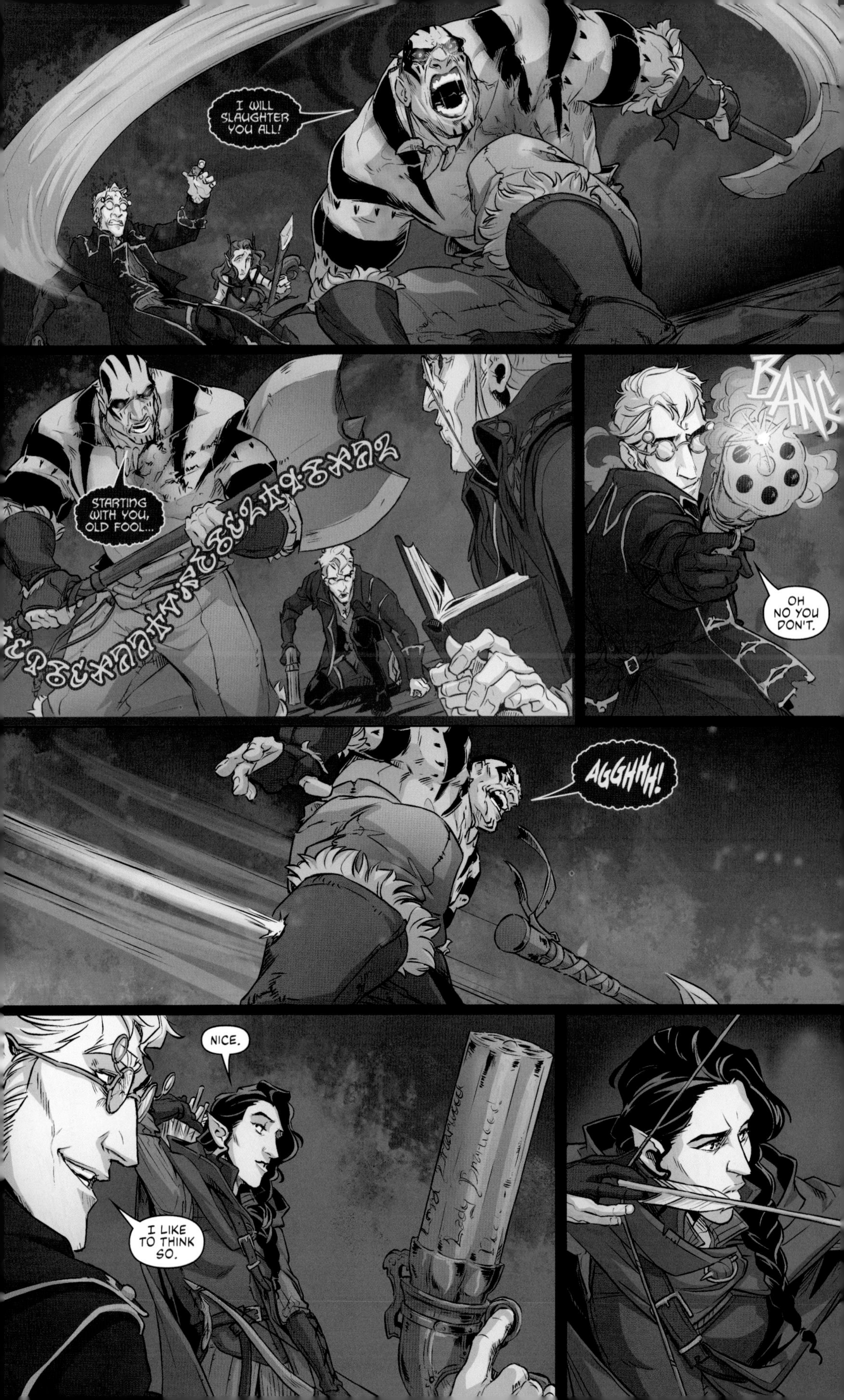
I WILL SLAUGHTER YOU ALL!
STARTING WITH YOU, OLD FOOL...
BANG
OH NO YOU DON'T.
AGGHHH!
NICE.
I LIKE TO THINK SO.

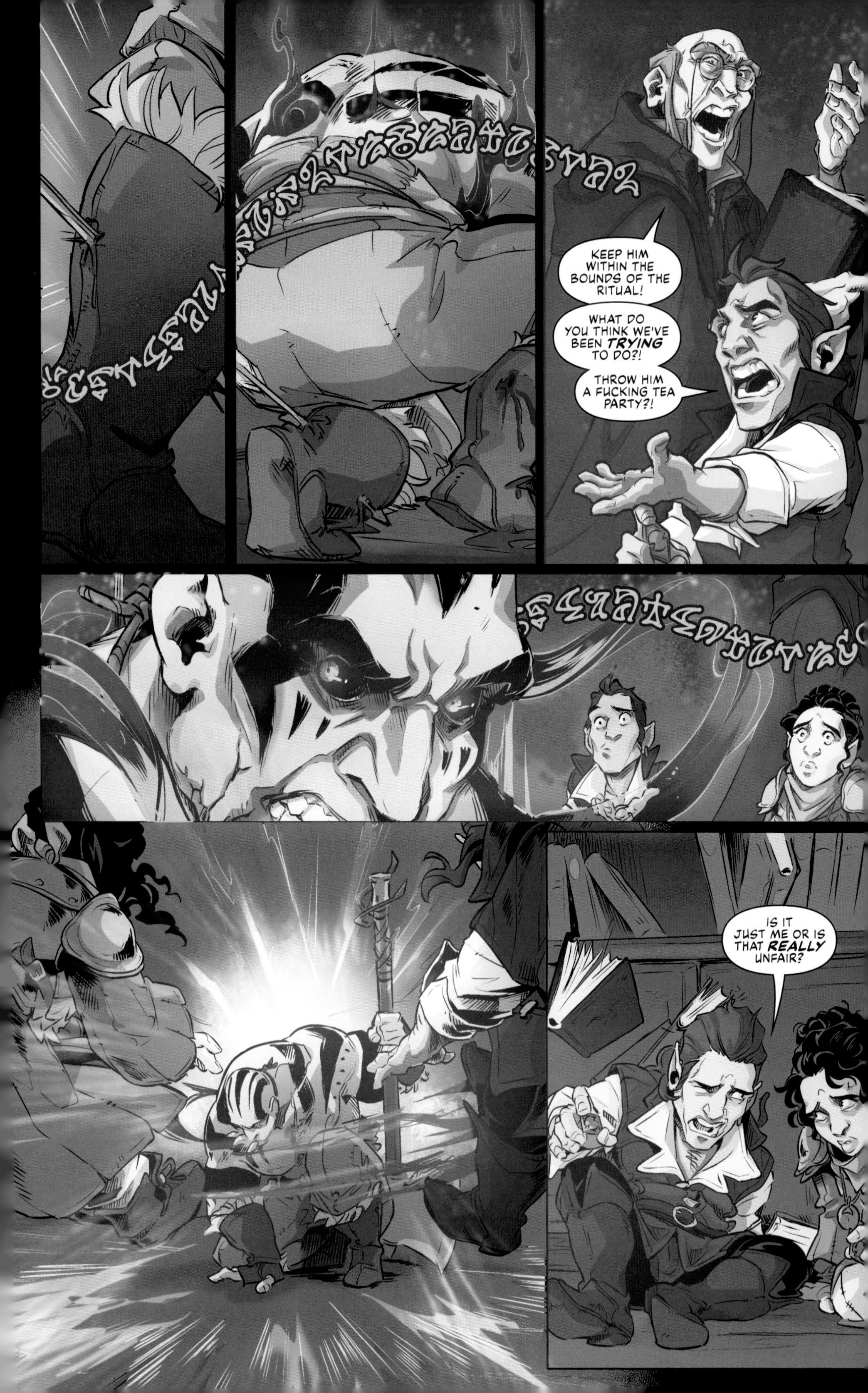
KEEP HIM WITHIN THE BOUNDS OF THE RITUAL!
WHAT DO YOU THINK WE'VE BEEN **TRYING** TO DO?!
THROW HIM A FUCKING TEA PARTY?!
IS IT JUST ME OR IS THAT **REALLY** UNFAIR?

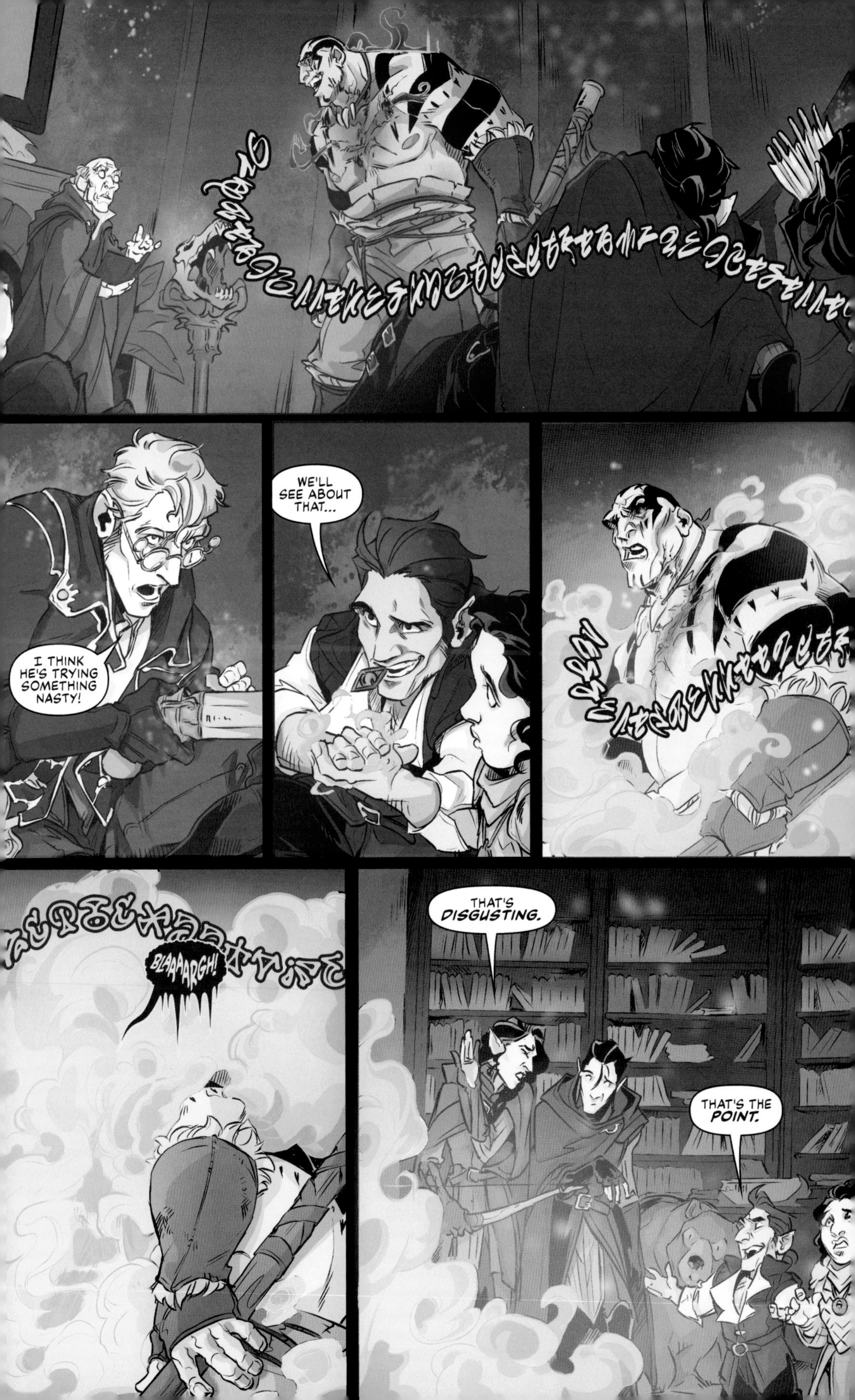
I THINK HE'S TRYING SOMETHING NASTY!
WE'LL SEE ABOUT THAT...
BLAAAARGH!
THAT'S DISGUSTING.
THAT'S THE POINT.

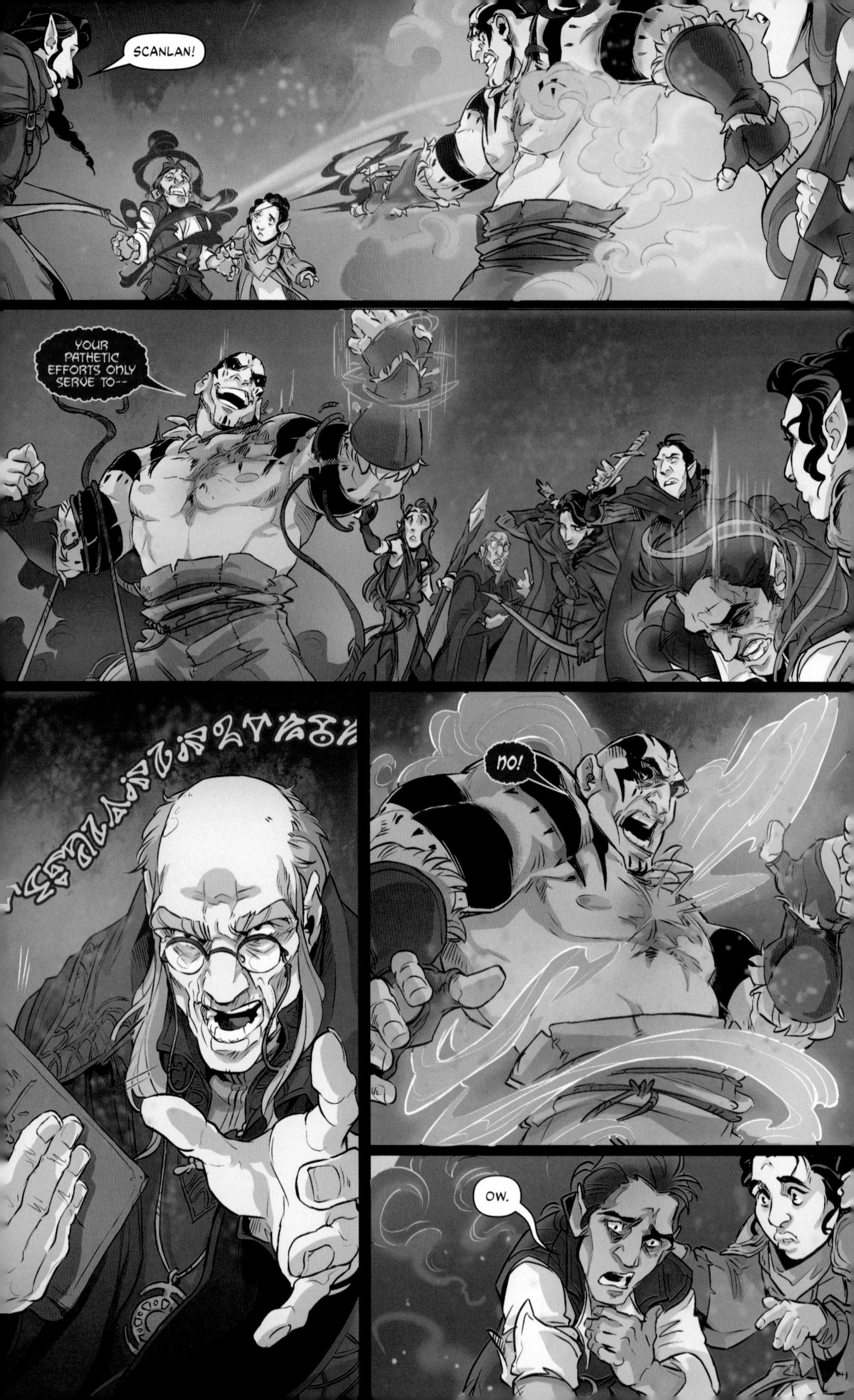
SCANLAN!
YOUR PATHETIC EFFORTS ONLY SERVE TO--
no!
OW.

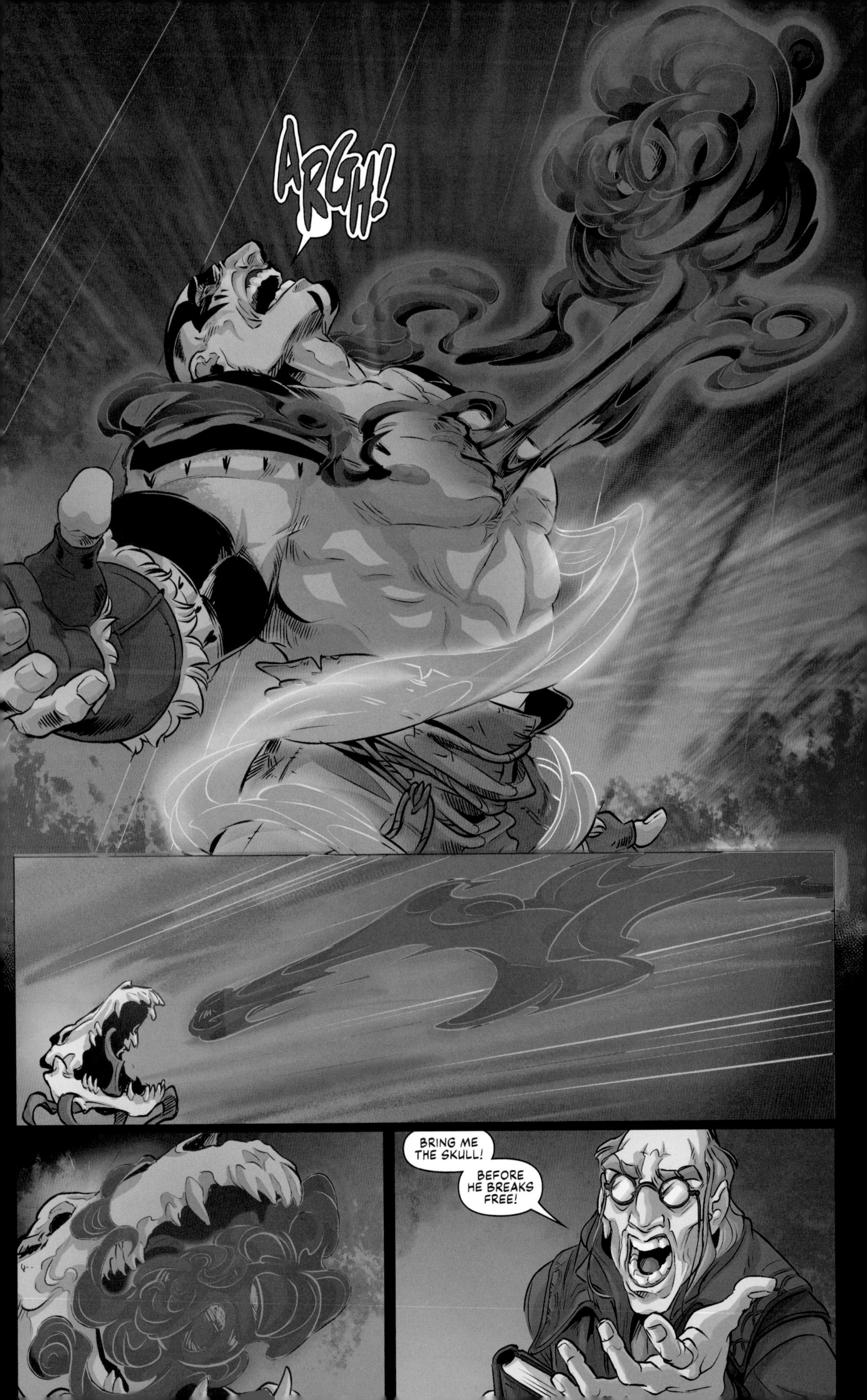
ARGH!
BRING ME THE SKULL!
BEFORE HE BREAKS FREE!

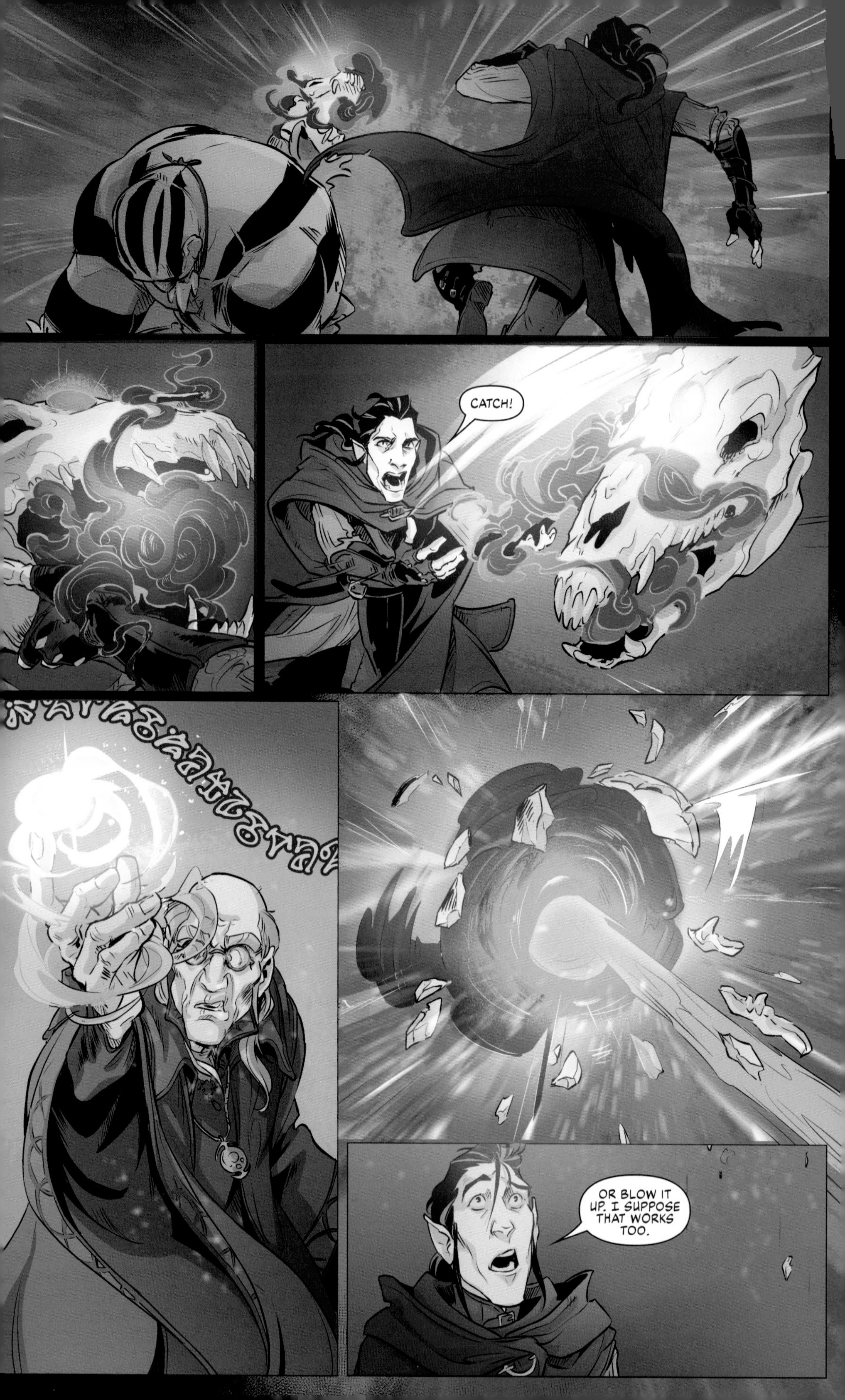
CATCH!
OR BLOW IT UP, I SUPPOSE THAT WORKS TOO.

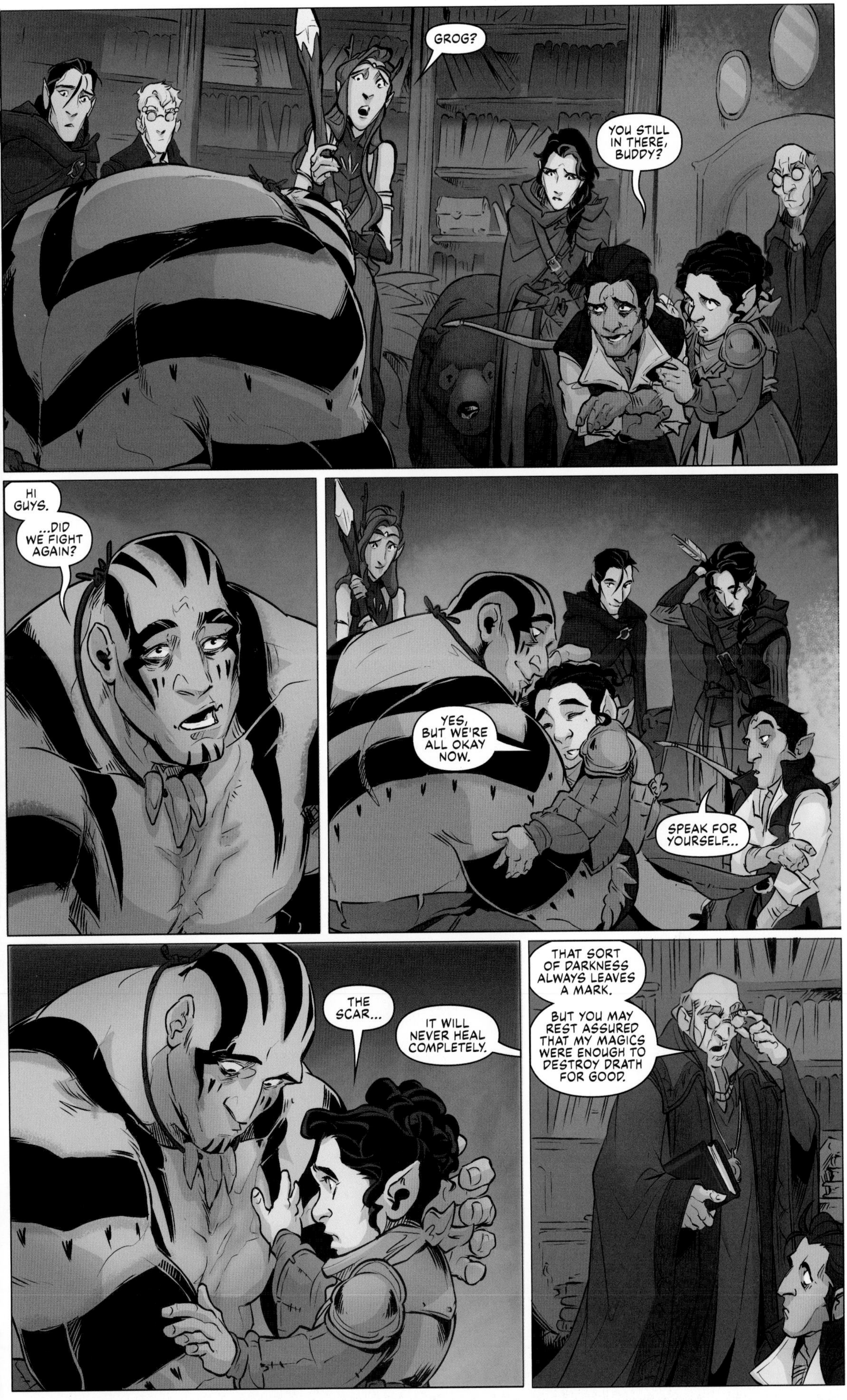
GROG?
YOU STILL IN THERE, BUDDY?
HI GUYS.
...DID WE FIGHT AGAIN?
YES, BUT WE'RE ALL OKAY NOW.
SPEAK FOR YOURSELF...
THE SCAR...
IT WILL NEVER HEAL COMPLETELY.
THAT SORT OF DARKNESS ALWAYS LEAVES A MARK.
BUT YOU MAY REST ASSURED THAT MY MAGICS WERE ENOUGH TO DESTROY DRATH FOR GOOD.

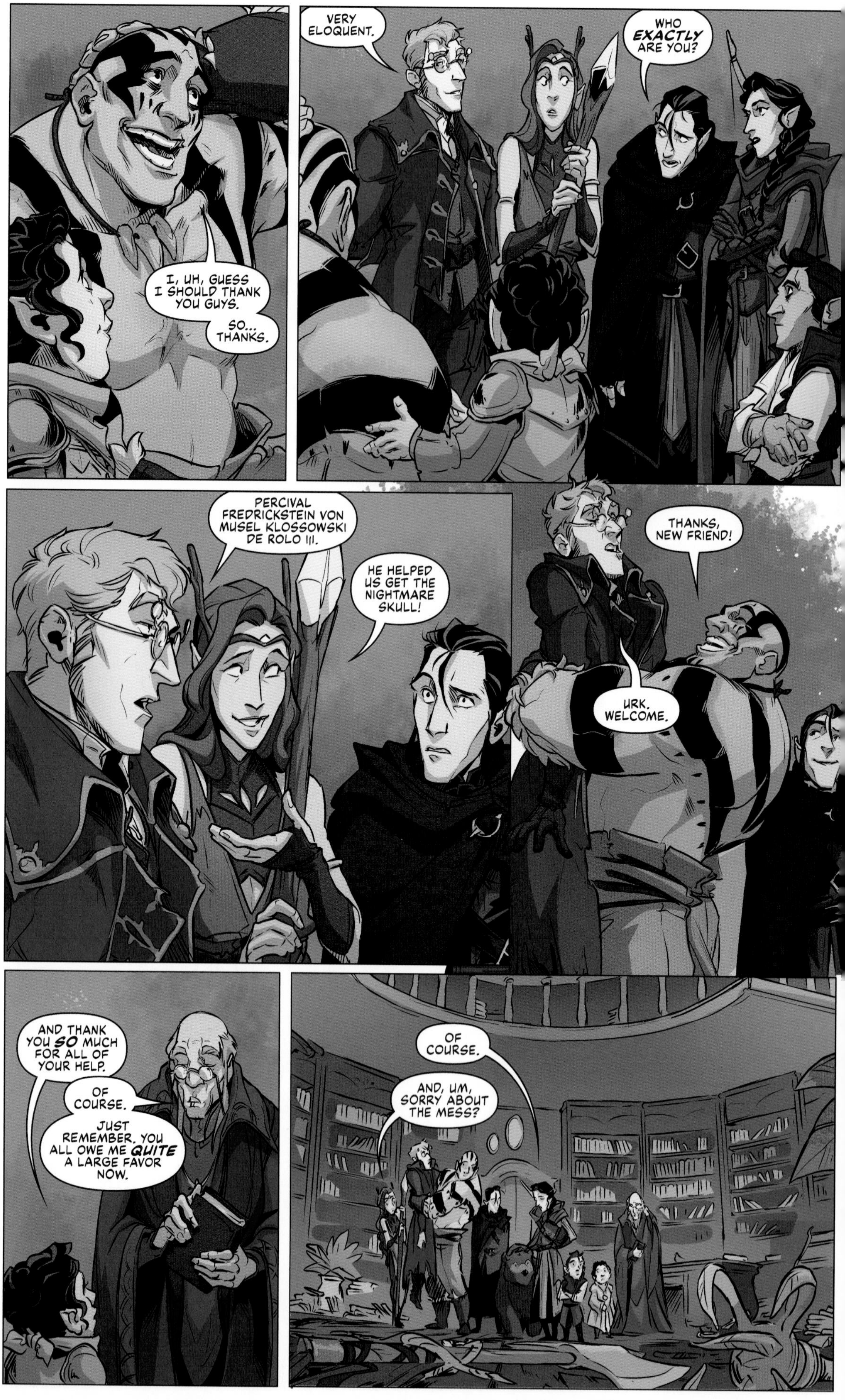
I, UH, GUESS I SHOULD THANK YOU GUYS.
SO... THANKS.
VERY ELOQUENT.
WHO EXACTLY ARE YOU?
PERCIVAL FREDRICKSTEIN VON MUSEL KLOSSOWSKI DE ROLO III.
HE HELPED US GET THE NIGHTMARE SKULL!
THANKS, NEW FRIEND!
URK. WELCOME.
AND THANK YOU SO MUCH FOR ALL OF YOUR HELP.
OF COURSE.
JUST REMEMBER. YOU ALL OWE ME QUITE A LARGE FAVOR NOW.
OF COURSE.
AND, UM, SORRY ABOUT THE MESS?

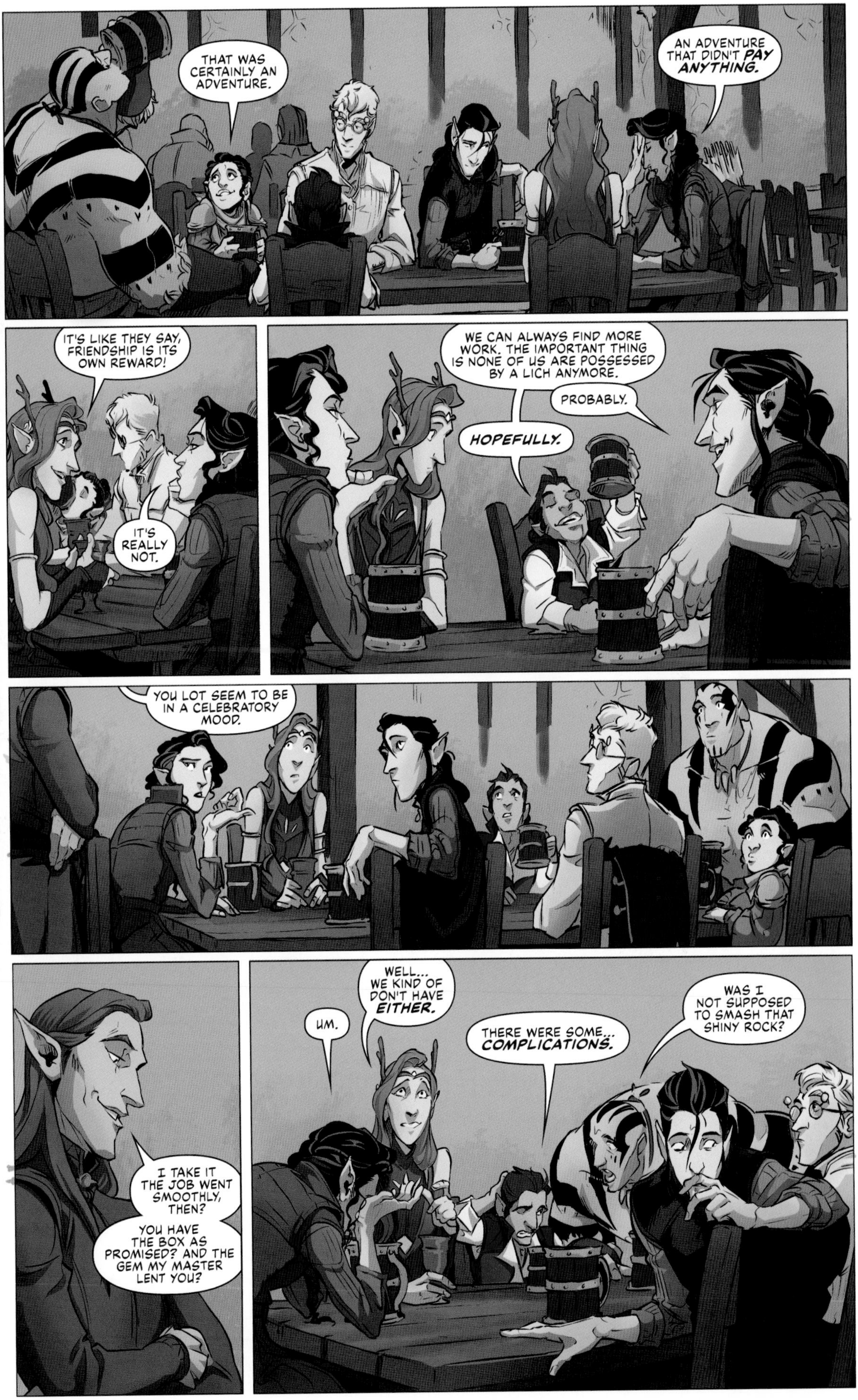
THAT WAS CERTAINLY AN ADVENTURE.
AN ADVENTURE THAT DIDN'T PAY ANYTHING.
IT'S LIKE THEY SAY, FRIENDSHIP IS ITS OWN REWARD!
IT'S REALLY NOT.
WE CAN ALWAYS FIND MORE WORK. THE IMPORTANT THING IS NONE OF US ARE POSSESSED BY A LICH ANYMORE.
PROBABLY.
HOPEFULLY.
YOU LOT SEEM TO BE IN A CELEBRATORY MOOD.
I TAKE IT THE JOB WENT SMOOTHLY, THEN?
YOU HAVE THE BOX AS PROMISED? AND THE GEM MY MASTER LENT YOU?
UM.
WELL... WE KIND OF DON'T HAVE EITHER.
THERE WERE SOME... COMPLICATIONS.
WAS I NOT SUPPOSED TO SMASH THAT SHINY ROCK?

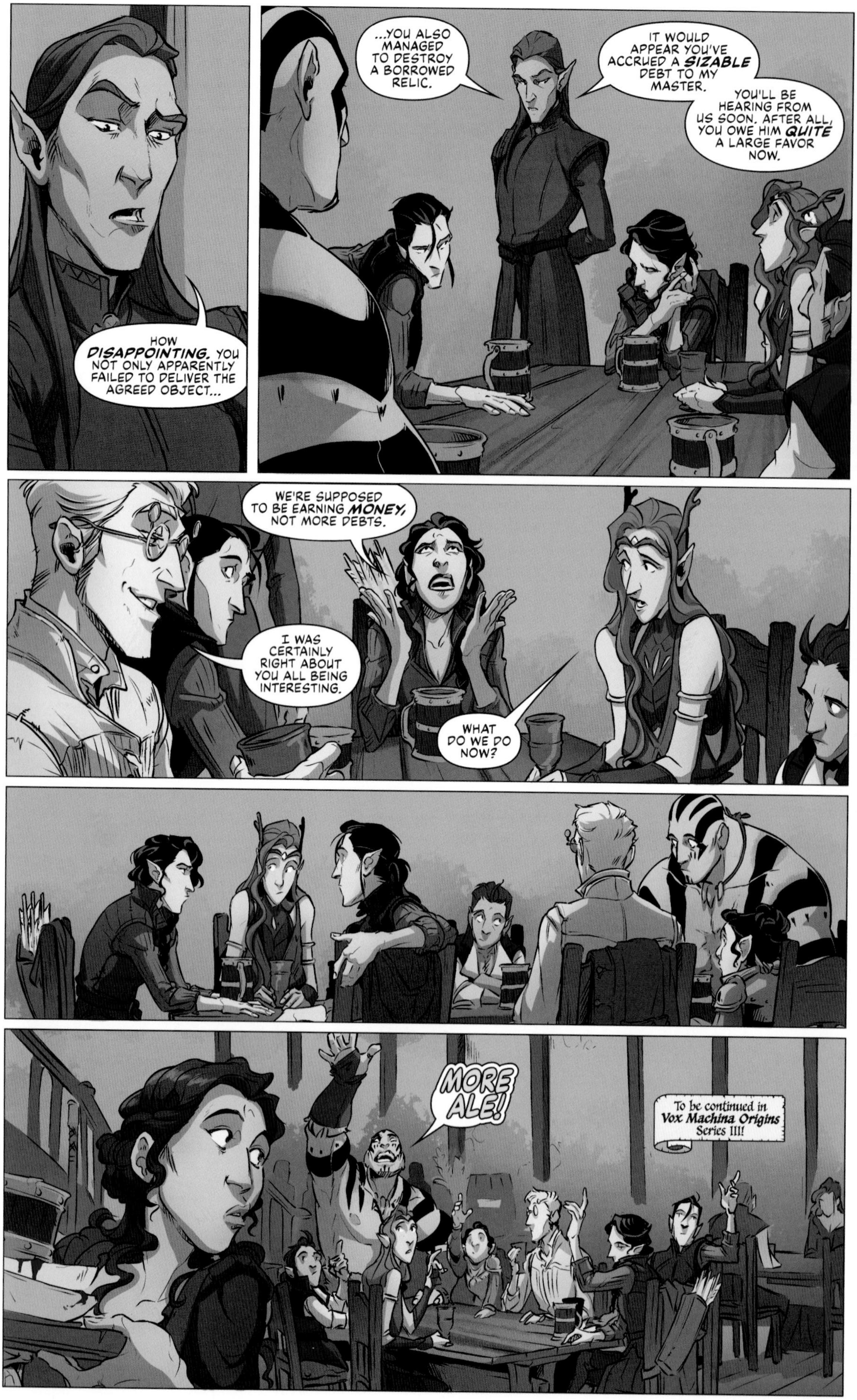
HOW DISAPPOINTING. YOU NOT ONLY APPARENTLY FAILED TO DELIVER THE AGREED OBJECT...
...YOU ALSO MANAGED TO DESTROY A BORROWED RELIC.
IT WOULD APPEAR YOU'VE ACCRUED A SIZABLE DEBT TO MY MASTER.
YOU'LL BE HEARING FROM US SOON. AFTER ALL, YOU OWE HIM QUITE A LARGE FAVOR NOW.
WE'RE SUPPOSED TO BE EARNING MONEY, NOT MORE DEBTS.
I WAS CERTAINLY RIGHT ABOUT YOU ALL BEING INTERESTING.
WHAT DO WE DO NOW?
MORE ALE!
To be continued in Vox Machina Origins Series III!

CRITICAL ROLE

VOX MACHINA ORIGINS

SKETCHBOOK

Art by Olivia Samson | Notes by Rachel Roberts

VAX'ILDAN

Vax's look didn't change too much between Series I and II, but Olivia created a remarkable update in his body language and expressions.

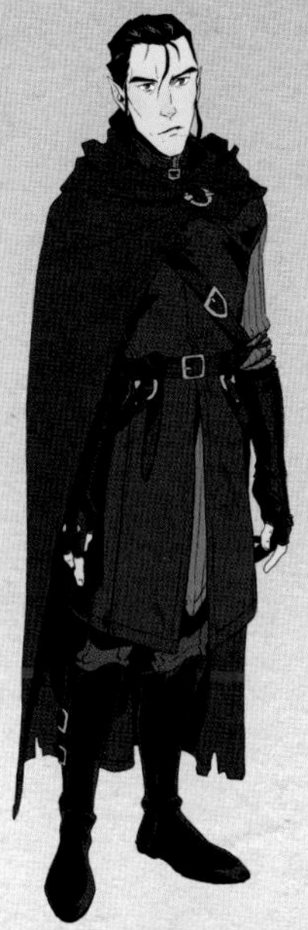

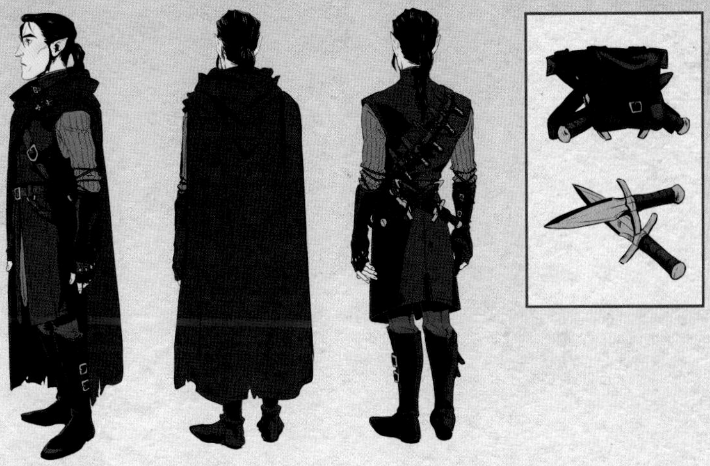

VEX'AHLIA

Vex's design became sleeker and more refined. The similarities between Vex and Vax's outfits help highlight how close-knit the twins are, while still acknowledging their different personalities.

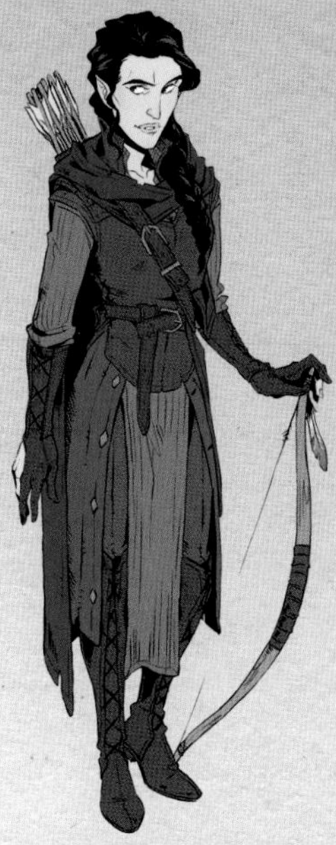

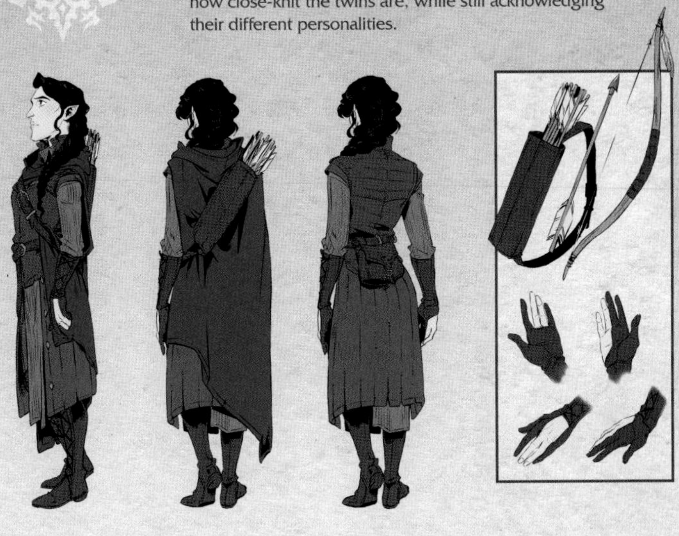

This section features all of Olivia's character reference sheets. They come in handy for a variety of reasons behind the scenes, but none more so than for MSASSYK, our colorist. Having solid reference for her to work from is instrumental in bringing the book together.

GROG

The most frequent comment we hear about Grog's appearance in the comics is "He looks strange without a beard!" Grog's baby-faced naiveté was a crucial part of his character for this arc.

SCANLAN

Scanlan is still rocking that purple, forever and always. It's part of his bardly charm.

The main cast of characters already had established looks from the first series, but Olivia polished them and gave them a few tweaks for series II, as if they had leveled up. Olivia leveled up, too, and these designs clearly show her hard work.

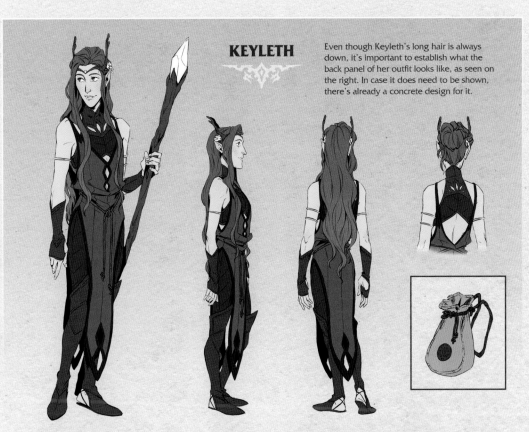

KEYLETH

Even though Keyleth's long hair is always down, it's important to establish what the back panel of her outfit looks like, as seen on the right. In case it does need to be shown, there's already a concrete design for it.

TIBERIUS

Our friendly neighborhood dragonborn's presence was short lived in this arc, but Olivia still updated his look. The blue-and-red palette somehow manages to say "stuffy scholar" and "don't mess with me" at the same time.

These reference images are also a good way for the entire creative team to share ideas, help us establish the book's aesthetic, and provide an effective way to make sure tiny details remain consistent from issue to issue.

PIKE

Both Pike's outfits needed to be designed from scratch. The cool blues in her color palette, paired with the apron and dress, give her a welcoming appearance. Her armor, on the other hand, makes her look like the competent, battle-ready badass she is.

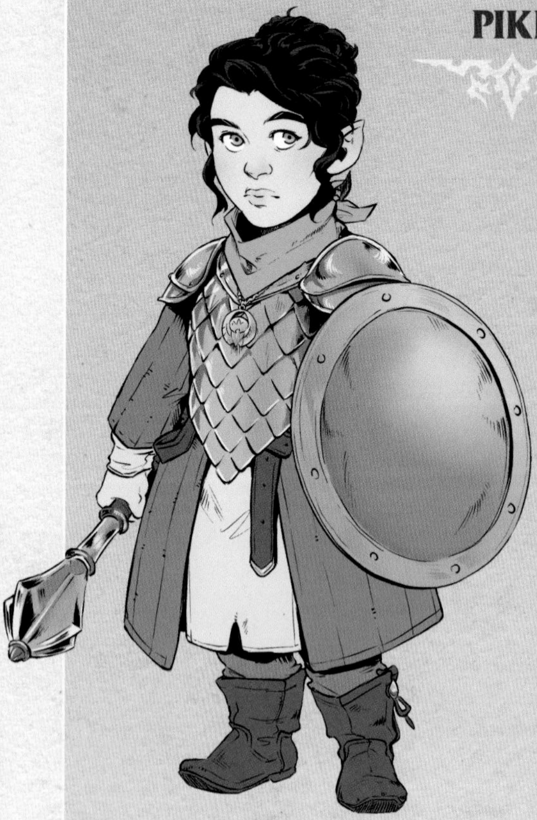

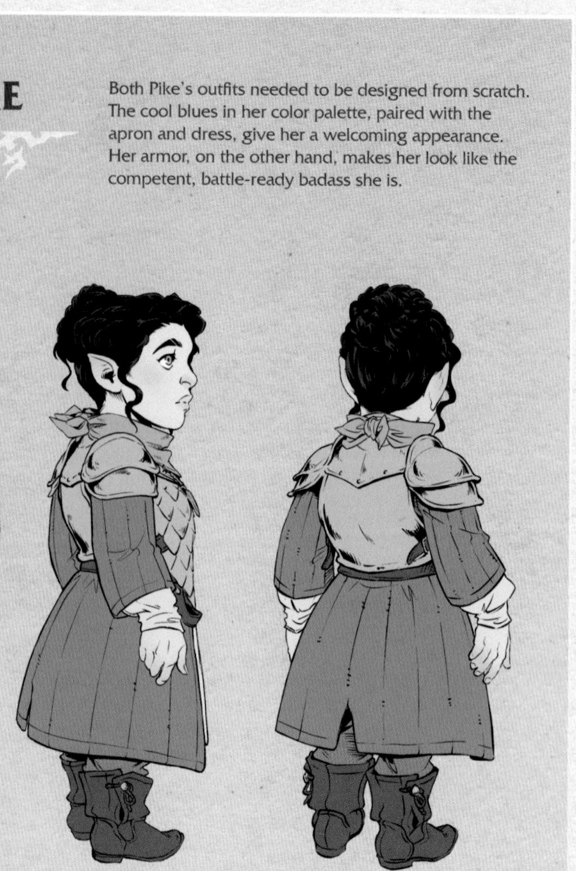

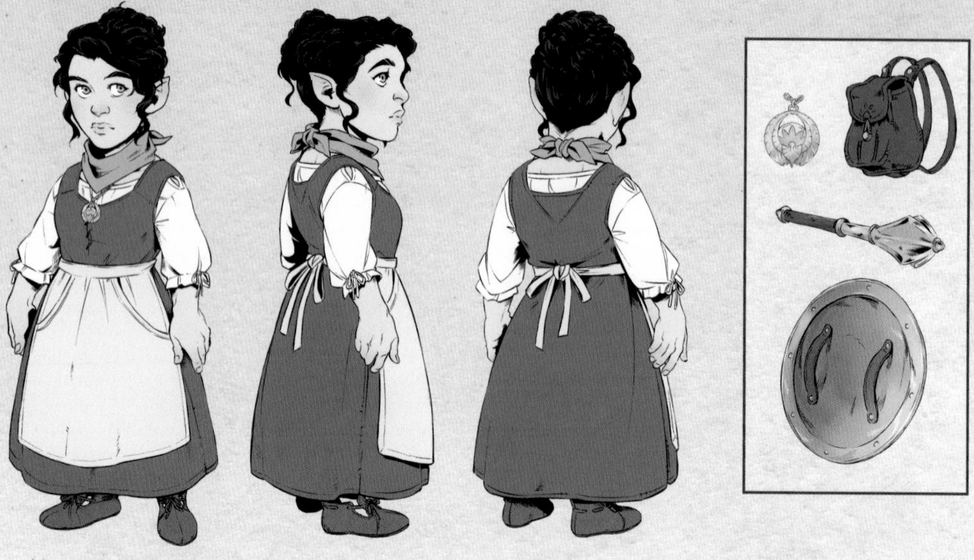

Pike and Percy make their comics debut! Because we see them in varying types of dress (and in Percy's case, almost undress), Olivia provided multiple designs for both characters.

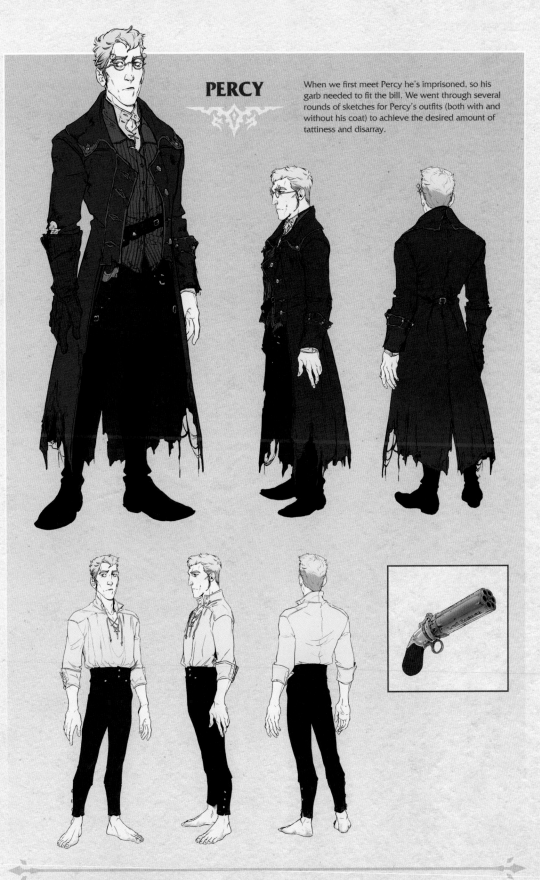

PERCY

When we first meet Percy he's imprisoned, so his garb needed to fit the bill. We went through several rounds of sketches for Percy's outfits (both with and without his coat) to achieve the desired amount of tattiness and disarray.

Having Olivia design outfits and equipment for new characters at the beginning of the art process helps us make sure she has everything she needs to begin penciling and inking the book. This also helps us ensure the characters are coming alive in keeping with the cast's wishes.

TRINKET

Even though everyone's favorite Wonder Bear didn't necessarily need a new design for series II, he got an adorable reference sheet anyway!

WILHAND

Pike's loveable Pop-pop Wilhand, described by Matthew Mercer as a "very old, very sweet . . . absent-minded but kind gnome," needed to appear aged yet respected, warm, yet a little zany. Olivia struck a perfect balance here—I certainly would drop by the Trickfoots' place for tea and talk.

DRATH MEPHRUN

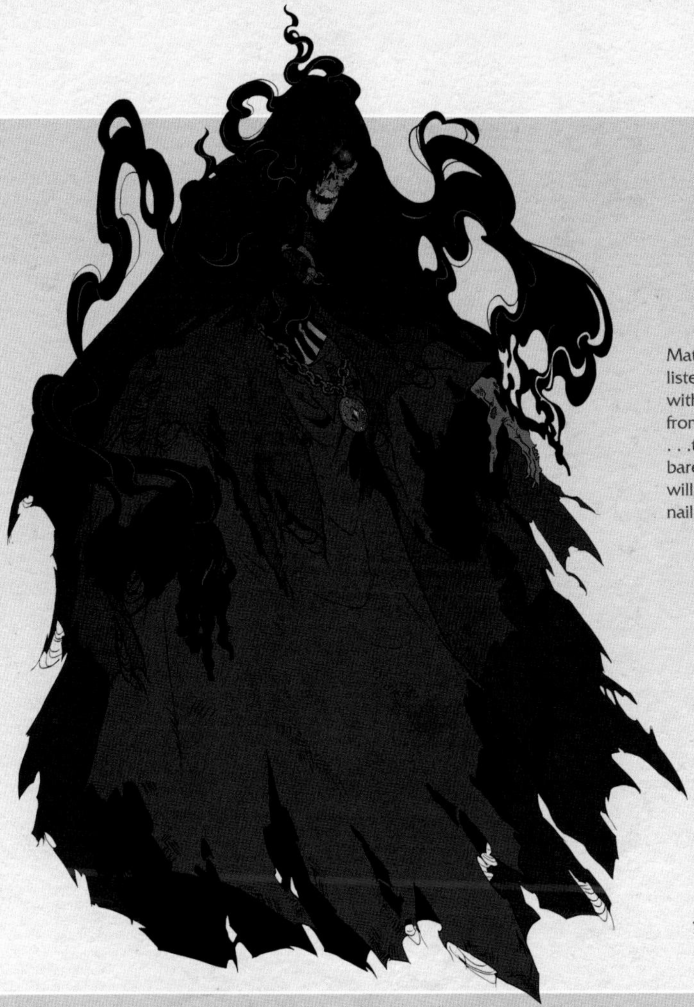

Matthew's notes about this shady fellow listed him as "a tattered shadow of a man, with vaguely skeletal features peaking from his cloak of dark smoke and umbra . . .the dregs left from a failed ritual barely clinging to unlife through sheer willpower." Yikes, my dude. Olivia hit the nail on the head with his design.

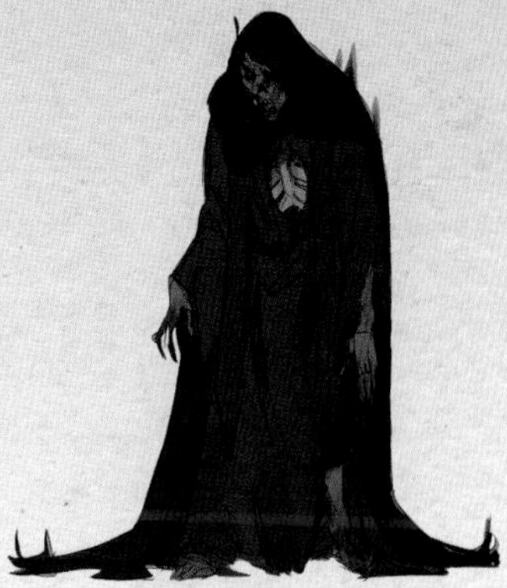

STONEJAW STRONGJAW

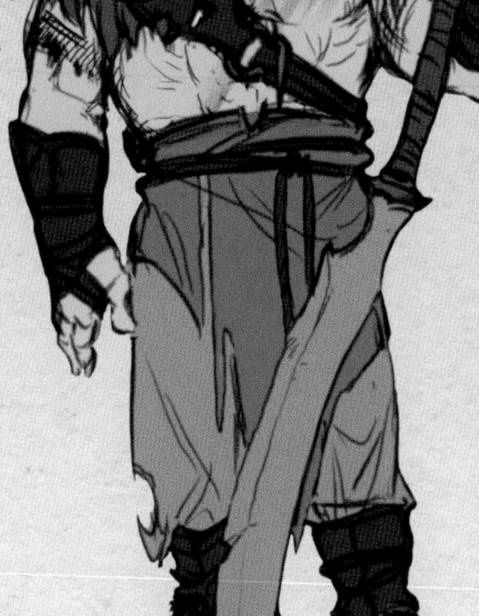

With a name like Stonejaw Strongjaw, you know this guy's look had to be as intimidating as it was *humerus*—Olivia's nicknaming him "Skelly Jaw-Jaw" got laughs out of us for weeks after she turned in this art. He received two designs: one alive for Grog's visions, and one sans flesh for everything else.

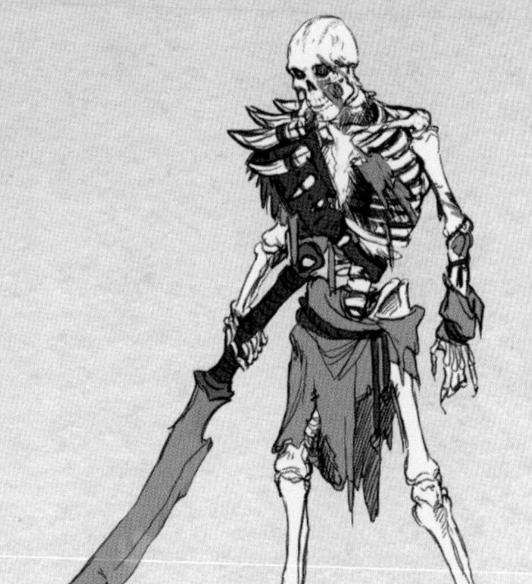
SKELLY
JAW-JAW

BOG BABY

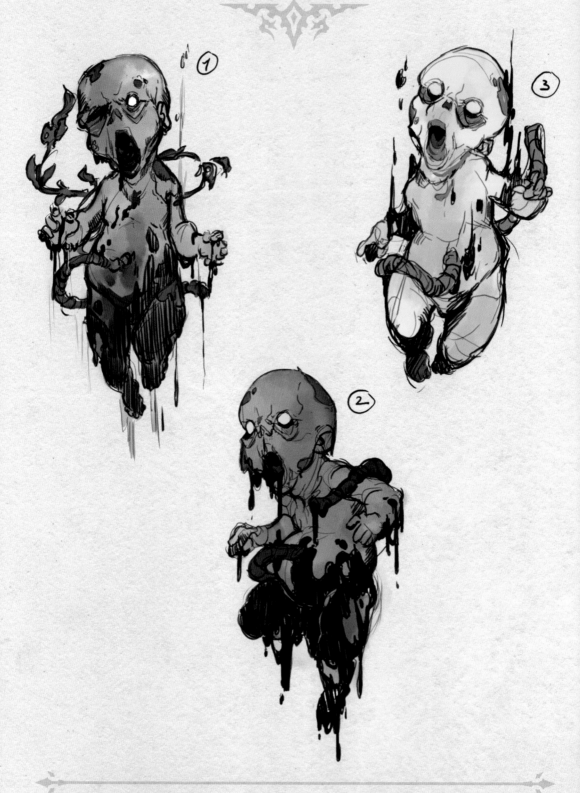

Matthew described this grotesque creature as "a bloated, mostly-rotting stillborn godling, about twelve feet tall and dissolving as [Vox Machina] battle it." Olivia provided three preliminary sketches for the overall design and color palette, so we could get the nasty factor just right.

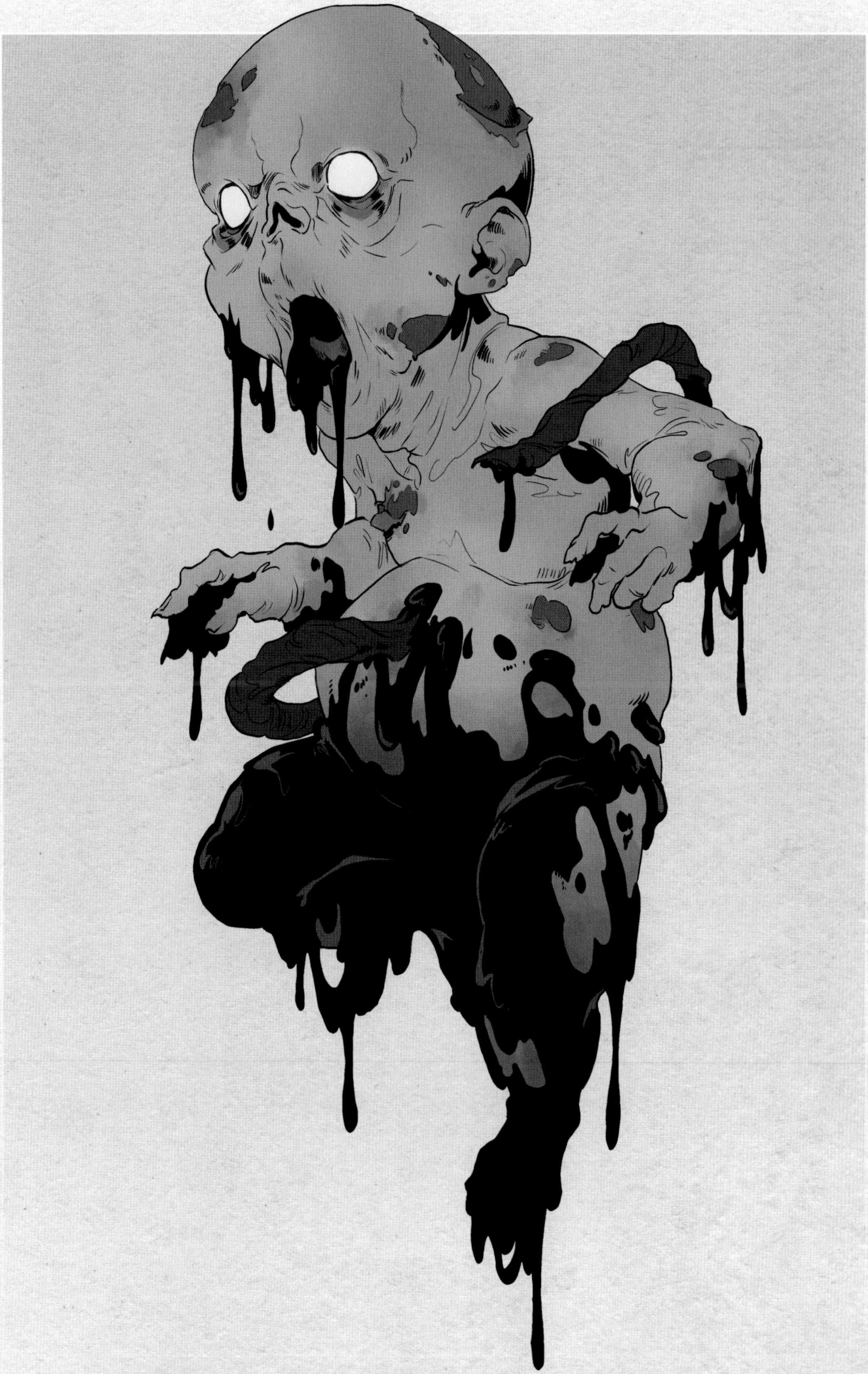

The final inked and colored design. Scanlan might not have been too put off by this thing, but we all certainly thought it was gross—what a delightfully vile way to kick off the new series!

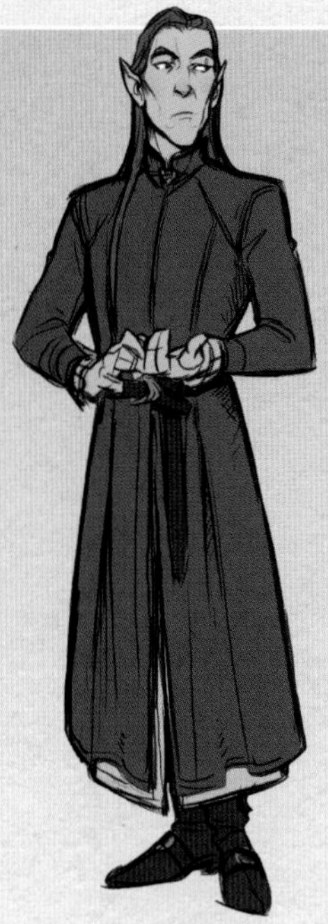

DREZ VINA

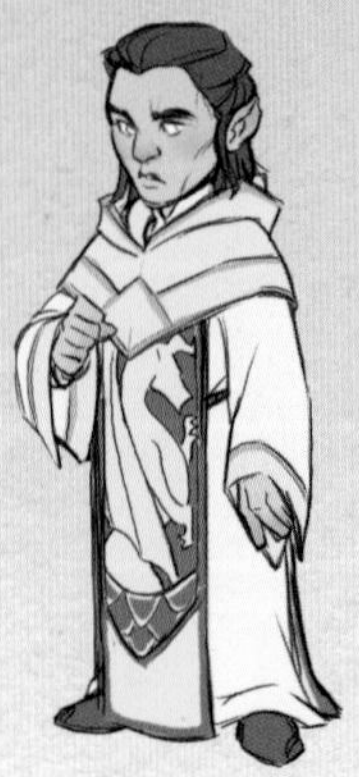

TEMPLE KEEPER

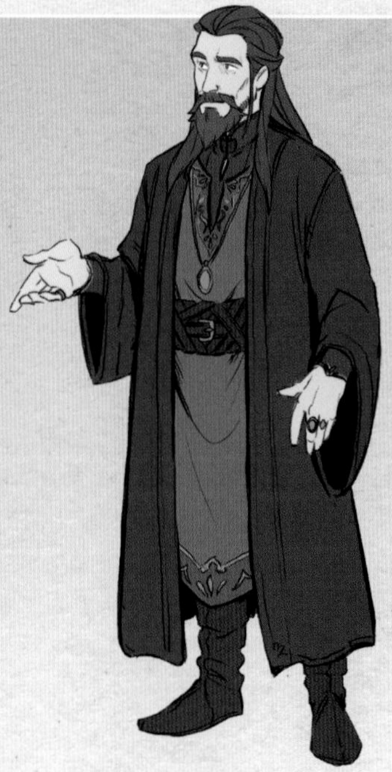

ABJURIST NOJA

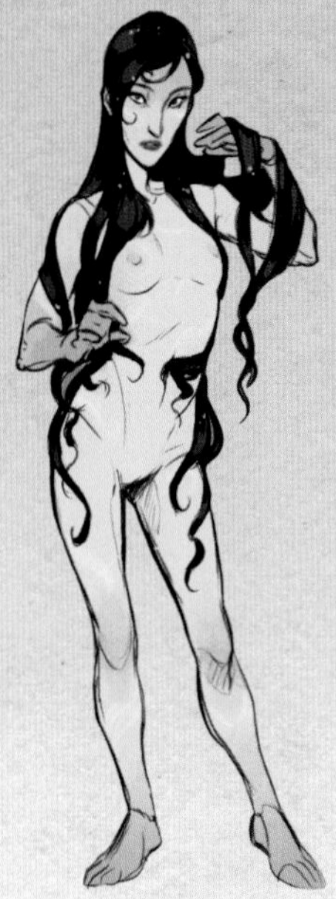

NAHLA

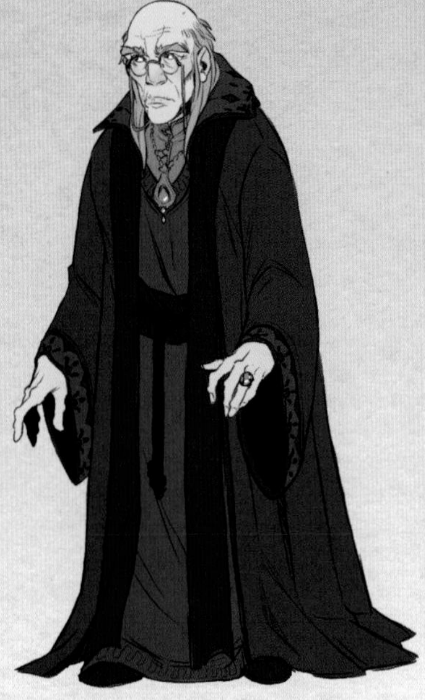

ESKIL RYNDARIAN

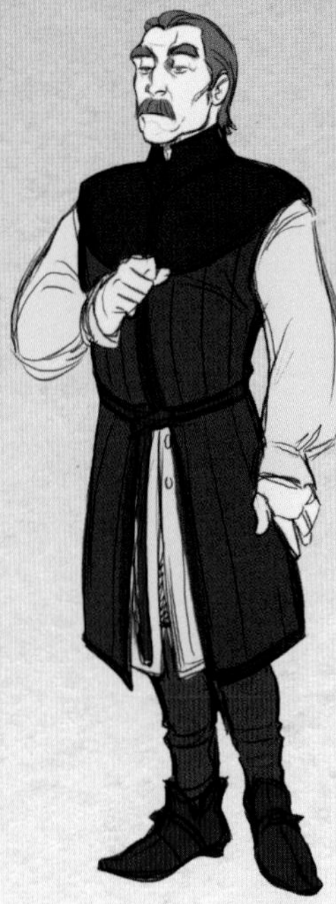

JEKT

These notable NPCs were already established in canon, but they needed fresh designs for this series. Olivia created multiple rounds for several of them, paying special attention to detail and making sure they were true to the cast's vision.

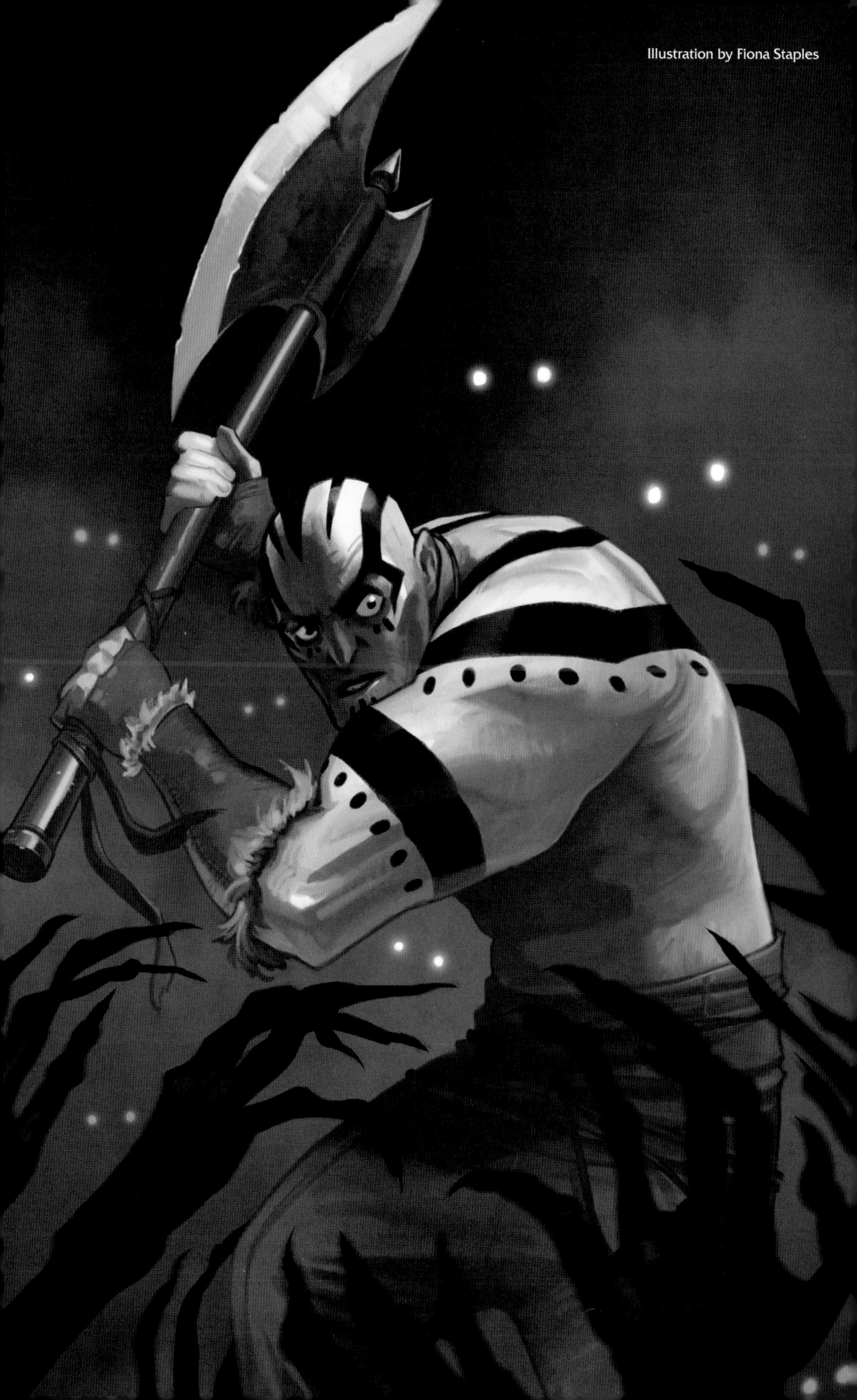

Illustration by Fiona Staples

Illustration by Benjamin Dewey

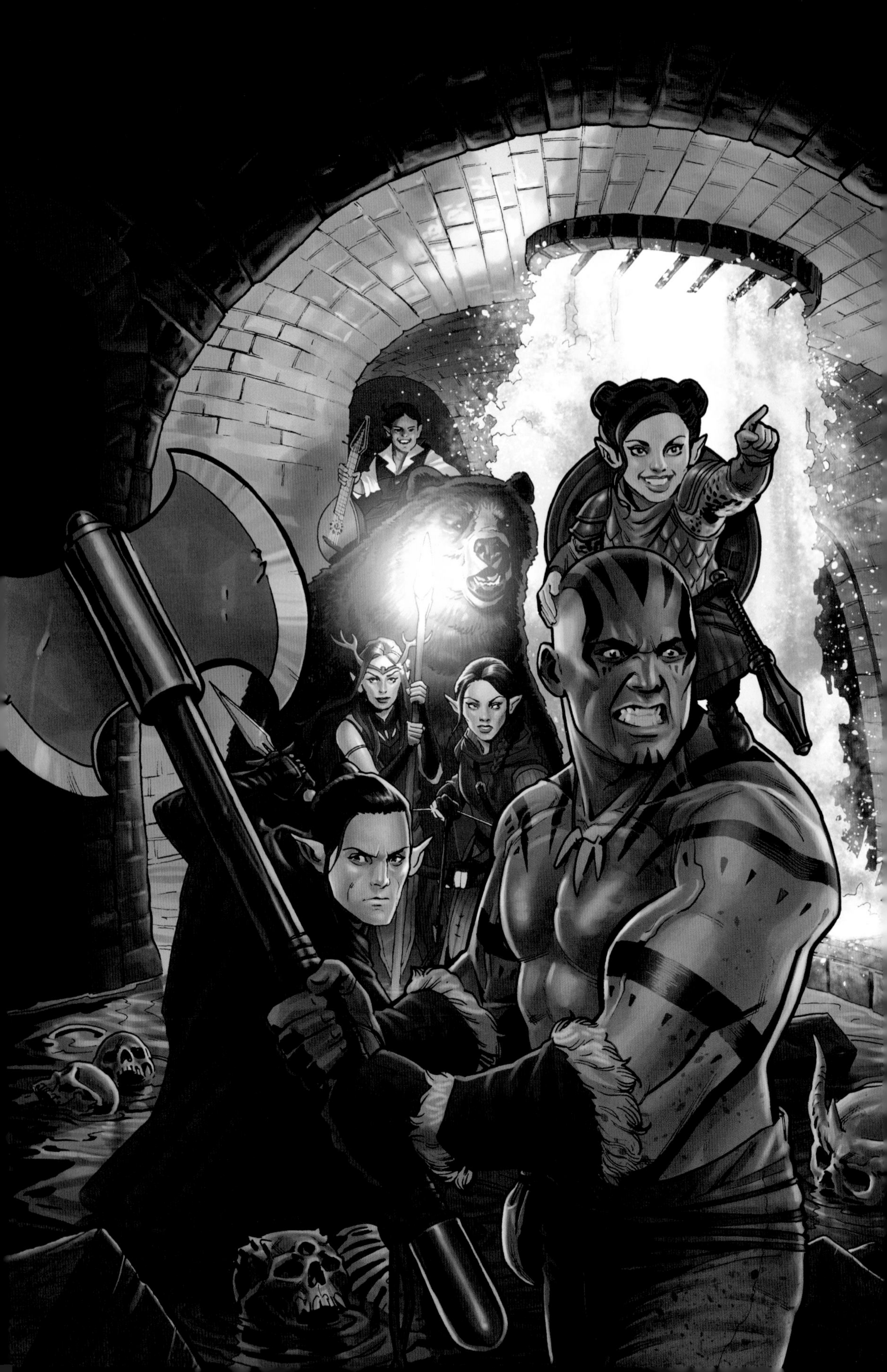

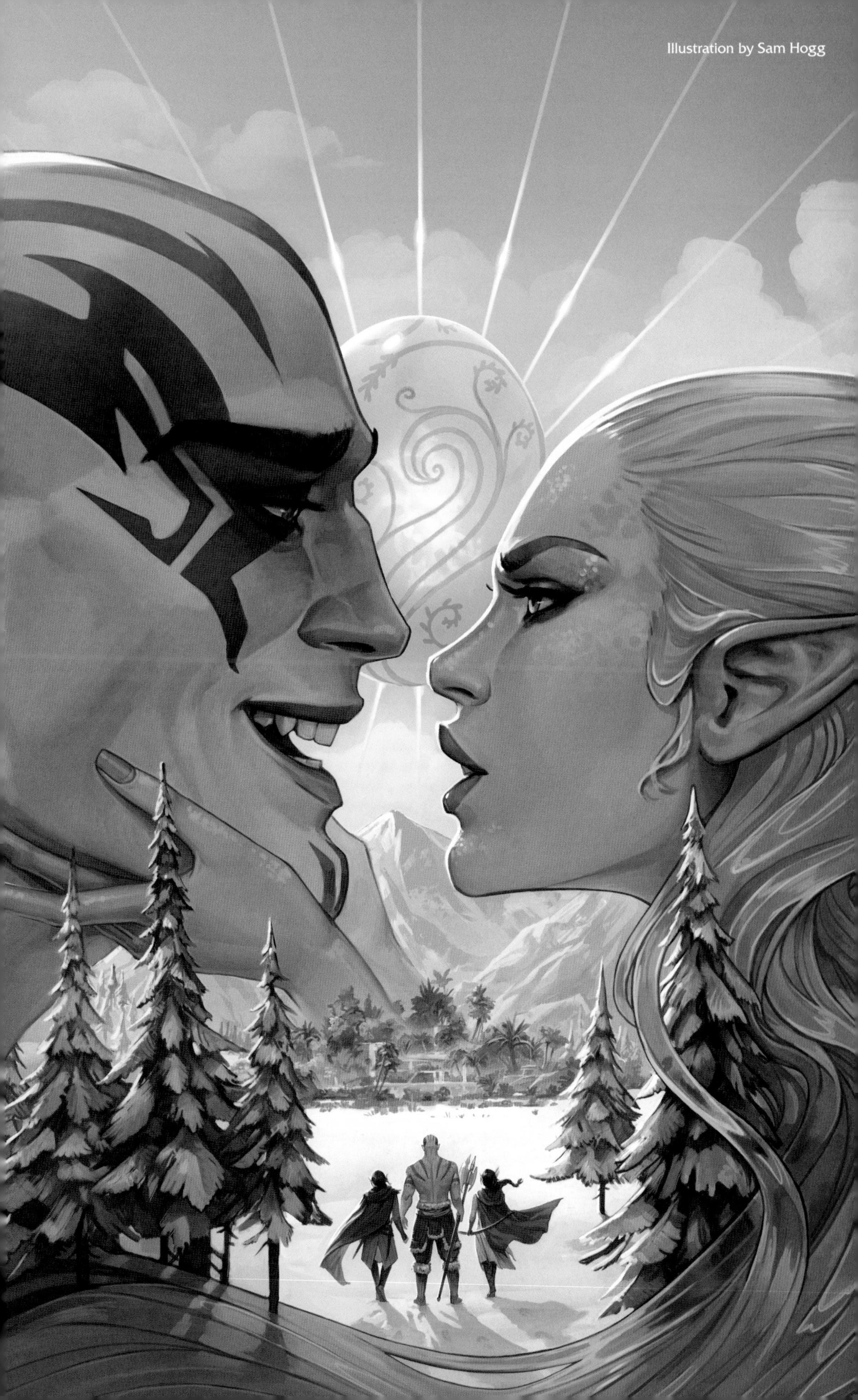

Illustration by Sam Hogg

Illustration by CoupleofKooks

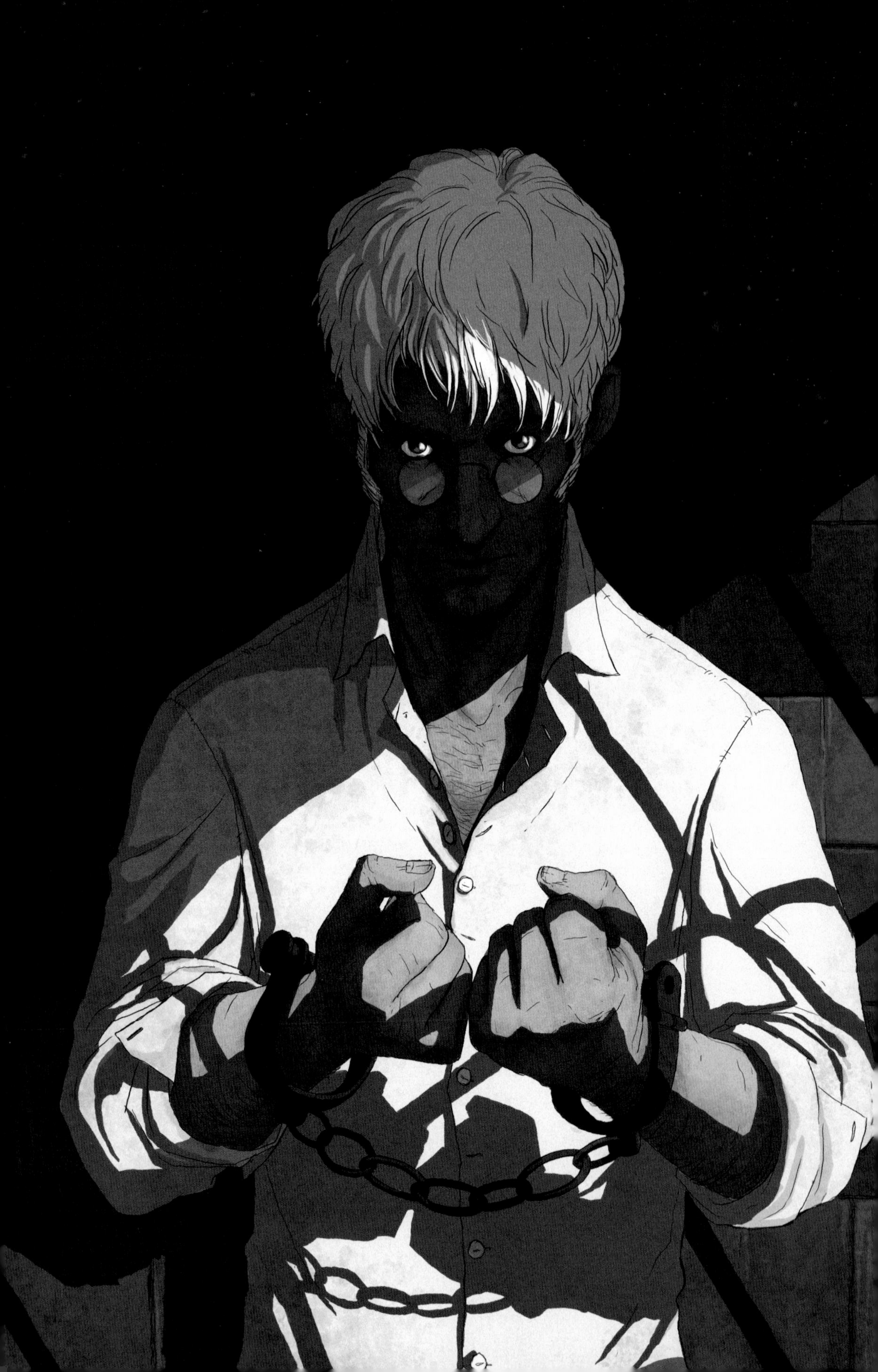

Illustration by Hunter Severn Bonyun

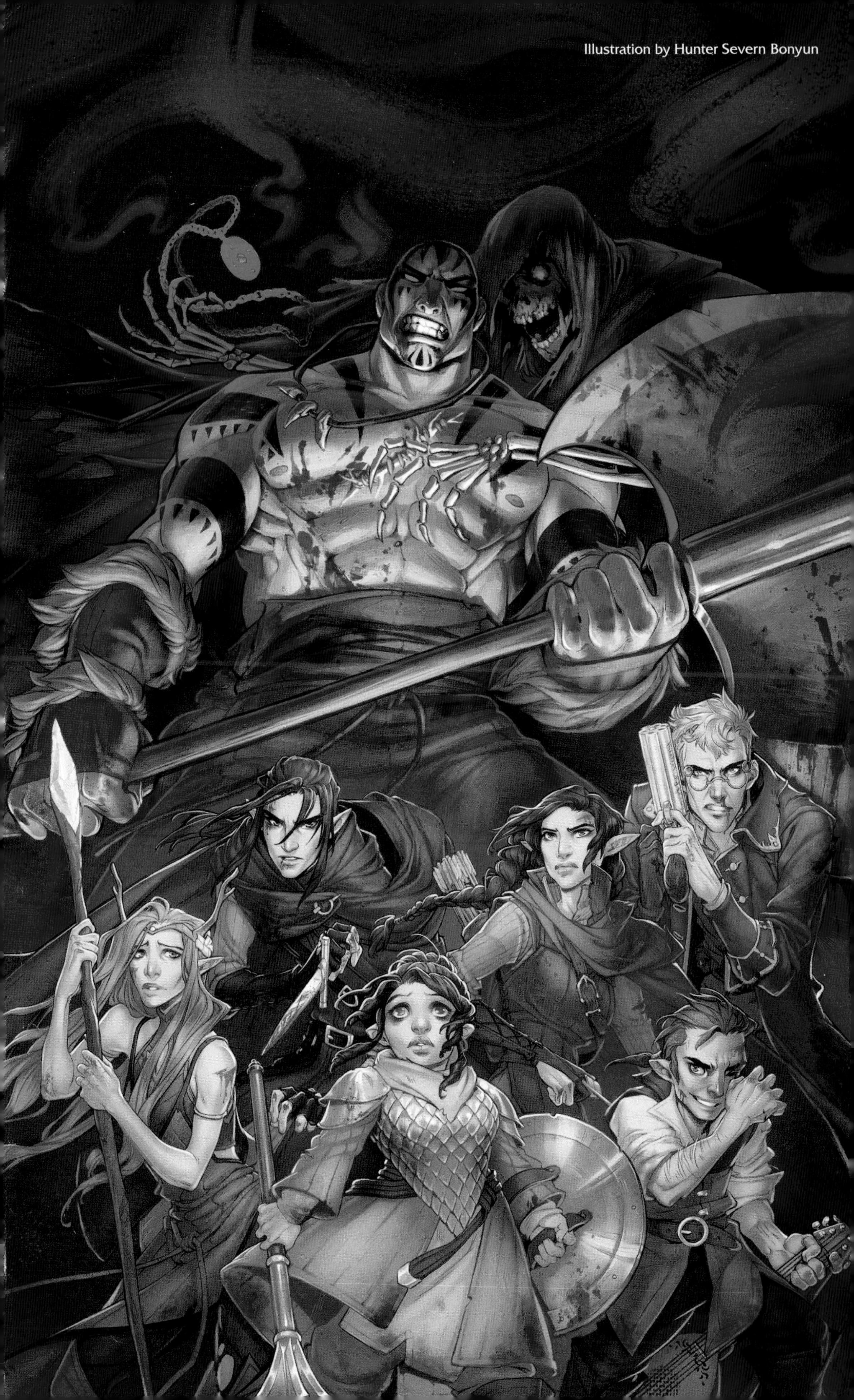